THE FOUR
ASIAN TIGERS

ECONOMIC DEVELOPMENT
—— AND THE ——
GLOBAL POLITICAL ECONOMY

THE FOUR ASIAN TIGERS

ECONOMIC DEVELOPMENT

—— AND THE ——

GLOBAL POLITICAL ECONOMY

Edited by

Eun Mee Kim

Department of Sociology
University of Southern California
Los Angeles, California and
Graduate School of International Studies
Ewha Womans University
Seoul, South Korea

ACADEMIC PRESS

San Diego   London   Boston   New York   Sydney   Tokyo   Toronto

This book is printed on acid-free paper. ∞

Academic Press
a division of Harcourt Brace & Company
525 B Street, Suite 1900, San Diego, California 92101-4495, USA
http://www.apnet.com

Academic Press
24-28 Oval Road, London NW1 7DX, UK
http://www.hbuk.co.uk/ap/

Library of Congress Card Catalog Number: 98-84346

International Standard Book Number: 0-12-407440-5

PRINTED IN THE UNITED STATES OF AMERICA
98 99 00 01 02 03 EB 9 8 7 6 5 4 3 2 1

CONTENTS

PART I
THE REGIONAL AND GLOBAL CONTEXTS FOR ECONOMIC DEVELOPMENT

CHAPTER 1
The Political Economy of Economic Growth in East Asia: South Korea and Taiwan

Kwang Yeong Shin

v

ERRATUM

The copyright footnote for Chapter 4, "Commodity Chains and Regional Divisions of Labor in East Asia," by Gary Gereffi, p. 93, is incorrect. The footnote should read: "Reprinted with permission of the Association for Asian Studies, Inc. from Gereffi, *The Journal of Asian Business* (12:1), pp. 75–112, Copyright © 1996 by The Association for Asian Studies."

The publisher apologizes for any inconvenience caused by this error.

ISBN 0-12-407440-5

PART II
THE ACTORS AND INSTITUTIONS OF ECONOMIC DEVELOPMENT

CHAPTER 4
Commodity Chains and Regional Divisions of Labor in East Asia
Gary Gereffi

CHAPTER 5
State Autonomy and Its Social Conditions for Economic Development in South Korea and Taiwan
Hee-Yeon Cho and Eun Mee Kim

CHAPTER 6

Is Small Beautiful? The Political Economy of Taiwan's Small-Scale Industry

Karl Fields

CHAPTER 7

Industrial Flexibility, Economic Restructuring, and East Asian Labor

Frederic C. Deyo

CHAPTER 8

Crisis in Korea and the IMF Control

Su-Hoon Lee

CONTRIBUTORS

Numbers in parentheses indicate the pages on which the authors' contributions begin.

Victor D. Cha (33), Department of Government and School of Foreign Service, Georgetown University, Washington, District of Columbia 20057

Hee-Yeon Cho (125), Department of Sociology, SungKongHoe University, Seoul 152-716, South Korea

Frederic C. Deyo (183), Institute for Development Studies, University of Aukland, Aukland, New Zealand

Karl Fields (159), Department of Politics and Government, University of Puget Sound, Tacoma, Washington 98416

Gary Gereffi (93), Department of Sociology, Duke University, Durham, North Carolina 27706

Eun Mee Kim (125), Department of Sociology, University of Southern California, Los Angeles, California 90089 and Graduate School of International Studies, Ewha Womans University, Seoul 120-750, South Korea

Su-Hoon Lee (209), Kyungnam University, Seoul, South Korea

Ichiro Numazaki (61), Faculty of Arts and Sciences, Tohoku University, Kawauchi, Aoba-ku, Sendai 980-77, Japan

Kwang Yeong Shin (3), Department of Sociology, Hallym University, Chunchon, Kangwon-Do 200-702, South Korea

PREFACE

FOUR ASIAN TIGERS OR KITTENS?

Will the twenty-first century be the "Century of Asia" as many had predicted? Or is the Century of Asia dead on arrival? These are questions that need to be answered in light of the financial crisis currently sweeping through Asia.[1]

Less than a year ago, there was still great optimism about the future of Asia and even a bit of fear that the Asian economies represented a new paradigm for economic development and that the rest of the world would need to adjust to the growing economic power of Asia as a whole, and not just Japan. The original goal of this book was to cast doubt on such a rosy scenario and to present a critical analysis of the four Asian tigers—Hong Kong, Singapore, South Korea, and Taiwan—by illuminating both the economic success and the sociopolitical problems associated with economic development. The intent of the book was to depart from most analyses on Asia (written before the 1997 financial crisis) and to argue that along with rapid and sustained economic development there was a high price to be paid in terms of authoritarianism, repression of labor, and a heavy dependence on the international security context of the Cold War and the global market.

However, contrary to the mainstream view that the Asian economies represented a "model" for other developing nations, the financial crisis in 1997 and the near-crisis situation felt in many Asian economies prompted us to speculate about a

[1]Prominent policy analysts have joined forces to ponder the financial crisis and its implications for Asia's long-term development. Jeffrey Sachs collaborated with Steven Radelet on a series of papers (1988a, 1998b) about Asia's crisis. They fault the international financial institutions for Asia's financial crisis and look to them for the resuscitation of the Asian economies. Their assumption is that the basic structure of the Asian economies is sound. Thus, their conclusions are rather cautiously optimistic, that with the right assistance from the international financial institutions, Asian economies will bounce back. On the other hand, Paul Krugman, who had earlier written a controversial paper titled "The Myth of Asia's Miracle" (1994), maintains that Asian economic success is based on expansion of input in terms of human and material resources and not on improvement of productivity. Krugman's (1997) take on the current financial crisis is that the major culprit is the governments' heavy intervention in their respective economies with bad and/or inefficient planning. He concludes that "Asia's growth will probably resume" (1997), especially with improvement in terms of input—i.e., education, savings, and labor force participation. Thus, Krugman's prognosis is quite different from that of Sachs. Krugman is closer to the International Monetary Fund position, while Sachs is highly critical of the IMF.

doomsday scenario for the four Asian tigers. Reports that these economies are faced with foreign currency troubles, followed by an overall crisis of financial institutions, began to decorate the front pages of major newspapers as early as spring 1997. This book also had to make adjustments to the changed status of the four Asian tigers. First, let us briefly examine what has transpired in Asia in 1997 and early 1998.[2]

- *May 1997:* Thailand's currency, the *baht* is affected by a massive attack from speculators concerned about Thailand's slowing economy and political instability.
- *July 2, 1997:* The Bank of Thailand requests technical assistance from the International Monetary Fund (IMF). This announcement effectively devalues the *baht* by about 15–20%, and triggers the East Asian crisis.
- *July 11, 1997:* The Philippines' central bank requests an extension on the Extended Fund Facility (EFF) from the IMF, and the IMF board approves the request.
- *July 14, 1997:* The IMF offers the Philippines $1.1 billion in financial support under the fast-track regulations drawn up after the 1995 Mexican crisis.
- *July 24, 1997:* Currency meltdown is reported in Malaysia.
- *July 28, 1997:* Thailand calls in the IMF.
- *August 11, 1997:* The IMF unveils a rescue package for Thailand, totaling $16 billion in loans from the IMF and other Asian economies.
- *August 15, 1997:* The Hong Kong dollar is attacked by speculators, leading to a hike on interest rates overnight, and is defended with assistance from Beijing.
- *October 8, 1997:* After the Indonesian *rupiah* hits a low of 3.845 on October 6, Indonesia says it will seek financial assistance from the IMF, following months of volatile fluctuation of the *rupiah* against the dollar.
- *October 31, 1997:* The IMF provides Indonesia with a financial support package of $23 billion.
- *November 8, 1997:* South Korea' stock market's index falls sharply, while its currency the *won* keeps losing value to reach an all-time low. (The *won* lost 14% of its value this year.) Foreign investors sell $71 million of shares in the half-day trading. Concerns rise that South Korea's financial turmoil may surpass the recent market meltdowns in Thailand, Indonesia, and the Philippines. Taiwan's stock and currency market plunges on November 7th and 8th amid concerns that the South Korean *won's* collapse will wipe out Taiwan's competitiveness against South Korea.
- *November 21, 1997:* South Korea finally decides to seek a rescue package from the IMF.

---

[2]The selective chronology is based on information gathered from various news sources, including Reuters, *Wall Street Journal, New York Times,* CNN, and *Financial Times,* as found on the website: http://www.stern.nyu.edu/~nroubini/asia/AsiaChronology1.html for chronology of 1997 and http://www.stern.nyu.edu/~nroubini/asia/AsiaChronology1998.html for chronology of 1998.

- *November 24, 1997:* Japan's fourth largest brokerage house, Yamaichi Securities, announces its decision to shut down. Concern about Japan's financial and economic conditions rises.
- *December 2, 1997:* Russia's central bank raises interest rates for the second time in less than a month, giving up efforts to shore up the country's slumping currency and bond markets with direct intervention.
- *December 3, 1997:* South Korean officials and the IMF's managing director, Michel Camdessus, sign a letter of intent covering an international accord to provide South Korea (the world's 11th largest economy) with $57 billion to rescue it from the financial crisis.
- *January 5–6, 1998:* Asian currencies plunge as investors return to the foreign currency markets. The Indonesian *rupiah,* the Thai *baht,* and the Philippines *peso* plunge to new lows each day. The volatile currencies markets in turn affect stock markets in Tokyo and Hong Kong.
- *January 6, 1998:* Thailand asks the IMF to ease the terms of its $17.2 billion bailout package. Its currency falls again and is worth less than half of its value in the summer of 1997.
- *January 15, 1998:* Indonesia signs a letter of intent with the IMF, in which Indonesian President Suharto agrees to drastically curb Indonesia's economic growth and dismantle monopolistic family-owned businesses.
- *January 21, 1998:* All Southeast Asian currencies and the South Korean *won* plunge.
- *February 13, 1998:* The IMF and major economic powers warn Indonesia not to impose a rigid currency regime, which may shake confidence in Indonesia. However, the IMF package not only has failed to stabilize Indonesia's markets, but has led to severe civil unrest, as witnessed in the riots in Jatiwangi and coastal Pamanukan and Losari.
- *February 16, 1998:* Indonesia announces its move toward a fixed exchange rate system and asks the IMF for alternative measures.
- *February 17, 1998:* The IMF releases a further $2 billion to South Korea, reaching $15 billion out of the $21 billion Seoul rescue package agreed to in December 1997. Meanwhile the National Assembly of Korea adopts legislation for labor, corporate, and government reform.
- *February 19, 1998:* The U.S. monthly trade report suggests the possibilities of the Asian financial crisis starting to affect the U.S. economy. Asian markets end mixed, with Hong Kong weak, Tokyo flat, and Singapore and South Korean stocks rallying.
- *February 21–22, 1998:* Indonesia suspends its plan to implement the controversial currency-board system, following intense pressure from the United States and other members of the Group of Seven (G-7).
- *February 24, 1998:* Following criticisms from the G-7 leading industrialized countries, Japan's market takes a nose-dive, closing at its lowest in a month amid doubts about economic reform.

- *March 2, 1998:* The Indonesian economy is on the brink of hyperinflation. Reuters calculates the year-to-year inflation to be around 31.74%. (In February alone, according to official figures, food prices rose 16.07%, housing 10.03%, textiles 15.62%, and services 9.31%. Five people died when troops opened fire during recent riots.)
- *March 4, 1998:* Malaysia's financial troubles at one of its premier banks sends shockwaves through financial markets across the region.
- *March 9–10, 1998:* The growing tension between Indonesia and the IMF radiates to other markets. The governor of Japan's central bank announces that investigations of its officials for releasing inside information for lavish entertainment.
- *March 19, 1998:* Key Asian stock markets rebound on renewed optimism that the region's economic problems might finally be easing.
- *March 21, 1998:* The IMF and the Indonesian government makes "considerable progress" toward a new deal to counter the country's economic crisis. The IMF is considering the Mexican model for solving Indonesia's debt problems.
- *March 26–27, 1998:* The news of a 16-trillion-yen economic stimulus package in Japan only temporarily cheers the market. Meanwhile, Indonesia promises cooperation with neighboring Malaysia in the repatriation of Indonesians who have fled to neighboring countries to escape the economic chaos or political repression. Eight Indonesians and a policeman are killed during the riot when Malaysian authorities begin the deportation of hundreds of immigrants detained in camps near Kuala Lumpur.

This chronology of events shows the extent to which the financial crisis has swept across Asia, with few countries unaffected. The crisis that began in Thailand quickly spread to other Southeast Asian nations, including the Philippines. Singapore, Hong Kong, Indonesia, and then to East Asian nations, including South Korea, Taiwan, and even to the once-undefeatable Japan. Taking one economy after another, the financial crisis led to capital flight, social dislocation due to rising unemployment, and overall social and political chaos.

These events have thus prompted us to take a more critical look at the Asian economies and to ask, "Is Asia's economic boom over?" This book also had to adjust to the changes. A new chapter that focuses on the financial crisis was added. Chapter 8, by Su-Hoon Lee, provides a timely analysis of the structural causes of the financial crisis, focusing on the South Korean case, which is one of the hardest hit by the crisis.

However, unlike others who had made rosy predictions for Asia, the authors in this book had already raised concerns about the Asian miracle even before the financial crisis. The chapters in Part I point to the vulnerability of the four Asian tigers to the changes in the security context as well as in the global market. These chapters highlight the implications of these broad contexts for economic systems during and after the Cold War. The shared assumption is that the economies of the four Asian tigers have benefited greatly from the regional and global security relations during the Cold War and from the favorable global market conditions. In turn, these chapters highlight the vulnerability of Asian economies to the changes in the global context. Major changes such as the end of the Cold War and the financial crisis have unduly strong effects on the region's economies.

The questions that concern the authors in Part I are how the broader contexts affect economic development, how these conditions have changed in the post-Cold War era, and how the four Asian tigers have dealt with the changing contexts in the post-Cold War era. In Chapter 1, Kwang Yeong Shin examines the broader economic context in which the four tigers developed. He focuses on the flow of capital and labor in the region as the manifestation of global capitalism

Shin develops the concept of "authoritarian capitalism" to highlight the distinct political economic system that developed in the Asian Pacific region. He argues that this system is qualitatively different from Western Europe's democratic capitalism and Eastern Europe's authoritarian socialism prior to the end of the Cold War. His discussion of authoritarian capitalism, and the pattern and role of global capitalism is imperative in our analysis of the four tigers. The fact that the four tigers are deeply rooted in the regional and global political economy sheds light on their vulnerability as well.

Victor Cha provides an in-depth discussion of how the geopolitical conditions during the Cold War and post-Cold War eras have affected the process of economic development in the four tigers. Many studies on East Asian development refer to the significance of the geopolitical situation during the Cold War. However, few examine the issues of geopolitics in-depth from a comparative or a historical perspective. Cha argues that the practice of arms purchases and long-term competition for energy are important in the selection of specific economic outlooks and resultant strategies for economic development in the four tigers.

Ichiro Numazaki examines the broader context in which export oriented industrialization (EOI) was chosen as an economic development strategy and the consequences of EOI in terms of the hierarchical relations that emerged among the nations in Asia. His chapter makes an important contribution by focusing on the post-facto impact of EOI in a region's economic development and the dynamic relations among nations in the region. This approach is distinct from earlier studies on Asia's EOI, which tend to focus only on the merits of EOI and conditions of selecting the EOI strategy. In particular, Numazaki presents the role of Japan in the region's technology transfer and foreign direct investment. Using the product cycle theory, he traces the systematic changes in the geographical location of export products. He also provides an in-depth discussion of various types of EOI relations among the nations, such as outsourcing and component subcontracting, to clearly show how these different modes led to varying hierarchical positions in the region's production and export processes. His examination of Japan's "outprocessing," in which foreign direct investment is made in firms in countries with ample cheap labor, demonstrates the systematic link created between the Pacific Rim economies and the rest of the world. Numazaki argues that the EOI in the four tigers has resulted in their "fragmented" industrialization and incomplete and partial insertion in the global market. Thus, his chapter is important in highlighting the potential weakness of the Asian Pacific economy.

In Part II the authors examine the domestic actors and institutions that have played critical roles in their respective nations' economic development. Whereas Part I explored the broader contexts of East Asian miracle economies, Part II examines the domestic actors that took advantage of the broader contexts from the perspective of relatively powerless and resource-poor small nations in the Pacific Asia.

In Chapter 4, Gary Gereffi provides a comparative analysis of how the four tigers assumed positions in the global commodity chains and how they are interconnected through a regional division of labor. Gereffi discusses the market versus the state in East Asian development, and he focuses on the *organization of production* as a "major determinant of industrial transformation in East Asia." The global commodity chains approach is used in this chapter "to highlight the role of producer-driven and buyer-driven chains in creating overlapping and at times conflicting regional divisions of labor in East Asia." Gereffi begins with a critical discussion of the World Bank 1993 study, *The East Asian Miracle*. In short, Gereffi criticizes the World Bank study for providing a rather erroneous interpretation of East Asian growth as "placeless," and he argues that the highly local and endogenous forms of economic coordination held together by various "networks" are critical for East Asian development. Gereffi examines different export roles and industrial upgrading observed in East Asia. These include: (1) primary product exports; (2) export-oriented assembly of traditional manufactured products, such as electronics and textiles; (3) components for exports in relatively advanced industries, such as computers and automobiles; (4) original equipment manufacturing (OEM), in which contractors produce goods to be sold under another company's brandname; and (5) original brandname manufacturing (OBM), in which manufacturers produce goods to be sold under their own brandname. Gereffi provides a critique of Bernard and Ravenhill's (1995) "flying geese" model, and he argues that East Asian economies are composed of overlapping and sometimes conflicting networks. These networks, Gereffi argues, are critical to understanding the tremendous economic success seen in this region, and they are the key to answering the question of why this region's success is not duplicated in other parts of the world.

Chapter 5 by Hee-Yeon Cho and Eun Mee Kim contains an in-depth discussion of the domestic social and class conditions that *enabled* institutions such as the developmental state and certain forms of business to flourish in South Korea and Taiwan. In criticizing the state-centered studies for placing unduly strong emphasis on the state, the authors argue that the social and class conditions engendered by the Cold War and by the domestic political elites have created the context in which economic development could be pursued as the states' hegemonic project.

Cho and Kim define the societies of South Korea and Taiwan during the Cold War as "conservative anticommunist." They highlight the particular class and social configurations across four development periods and argue that they *allowed* an authoritarian developmental state to pursue economic development as the sole hegemonic project for several decades without much public opposition. The four periods are: (1) the establishment of the conservative anticommunist society and the change of class conditions (1945 through the early 1960s); (2) the deepening of the conservative anticommunist society and unlimited state autonomy (1960s); (3) the rising tensions within the conservative anticommunist society and repressive state autonomy (1970s); and (4) the crisis in the conservative anticommunist society and the transformation of state–class relations (1980s). Through a careful comparative examination of South Korea and Taiwan, the authors show how the global and regional security environment of the Cold War is inexorably tied to the pursuit of industrialization in the two nations. Without the climate produced by the Cold War, it is difficult to imagine how these two nations would have pursued economic development with an iron fist and without much public opposition (at least in the beginning of economic development). Thus, like Chapter 4 by Gereffi, this chapter emphasizes the difficulty of replicating the miracle of East Asian economic development in other Third World nations.

In Chapter 6 Karl J. Fields utilizes the theoretical framework of the new institutionalism and argues that the Taiwanese industrial structure is a result of the convergence of the "regime movitations," "market opportunities," and "cultural proclivities." Fields maintains that it is not economics alone, but "flexible production" as a form of *industrial governance* facilitated by a "certain set of sociocultural and political institutions" that helps explain Taiwan's economic development. He shows that in this relatively small nation with a population of just over 21 million, there are nearly one million registered firms. The large number of these small- and medium-sized enterprises characterizes Taiwan's industrial structure, which Fields compares to the other tigers. He defines the subcontracting system in Taiwan as a form of "dependent capitalism," in which Taiwan's niche is found as a supplier of simple, labor-intensive products with readily divisible production steps. However, such a niche has also provided significant risks, as Taiwan is faced with quotas for imports, seasonal fluctuations, and mercurial shifts in consumer trends and tastes. Taiwan has responded successfully to these risks, Fields argues, "flexibly, cheaply, and efficiently." The state is described as a promoter of flexible production and, thus, of small- and medium-sized enterprises. The state does this by providing various measures to promote the technological competence of small- and medium-sized enterprises and through the "nationalization of risk." Fields also provides a comparative analysis of Taiwan's small- and medium-sized enterprises with Japan's and South Korea's big businesses, and he concludes that the former represent the reason for Taiwan's tremendous economic success as well as the exploitative nature of its firms.

In Chapter 7, Frederic C. Deyo examines organized labor in the four tigers in an era of global competition, with an emphasis on industrial flexibility and economic restructuring. Deyo also examines the economies of Thailand and Malaysia to show similarities among the four tigers and to provide an example of how different they are from other nations. Deyo questions why the tremendous economic success of the region based on EOI, which was heavily dependent on cheap labor, did not produce strong labor unions. He also examines how the post–Cold War international milieu, in which there is great pressure for fuller observation of labor and human rights and domestic movements toward political liberalization, has not resulted in the growth of unionized labor not of its political influence. He concludes that "the economic gains enjoyed by East Asian workers have generally flowed less from labor's political or organizational strengths than from labor market pressures associated with growing labor scarcities in critical skill areas." He provides alternative explanations for labor weakness by focusing on the political and economic structural causes. In addition, Deyo points out that global and regional market pressures toward "flexible production" and "new competition" are other sources of labor weakness. These can lead to the increased use of temporary, casual, or foreign labor, and extensive subcontracting to outside suppliers. These trends undercut "longer-term investment in employment skills, technological innovation, work reorganization, and supplier capacities." Deyo provides a comparative analysis of the different types of flexible production that emerged in the four tigers as well as in Thailand and Malaysia, and he discusses the resultant effects on labor. He concludes with a discussion of why East and Southeast Asian patterns of flexible production are predominantly static, and where dynamic, why they are more autocratic than their counterparts in more advanced industrialized nations. He argues that the volatile markets in which these nations competed forced them to adopt a more stable flexible production pattern and that the extensive role played by the state in many of these nations contributed to their autocratic style.

Chapter 8, in Part III, focuses on the financial crisis in South Korea in 1997–1998 and provides a skeptical view of the South Korean economy. Su-Hoon Lee argues that the combination of the changes in the world market and geopolitical context after the end of the Cold War and the inflexible reaction by key domestic institutions—i.e., state, the *chaebol,* and financial institutions—resulted in the current financial crisis. He warns that the IMF's intervention in the South Korean economy, which combines a slow growth rate and transferring of short-term loans to long-term ones, could lead to a "debt trap" similar to the one experienced in Latin America in the 1980s. Thus, he argues that the export-oriented, state-driven, and monopolistic growth strategy cannot deliver sustainable development. Deviating from the prognosis by the IMF, he posits that a domestically oriented, freer market economy and some maintenance of state regulation in the private sector are recommended for South Korea to avoid a debt-trap scenario.

Taken together, the chapters in this book provide a critical examination of the global and regional geopolitical and economic factors that had an impact on economic development and the local and indigenous institutions and actors that worked together to produce unprecedented levels of *economic development based on EOI.* It is difficult to provide "one model" for all nations in this dynamic region of the world. The economic development of the four tigers is characterized by flexibility, quick adaptation to the volatile global marketplace, the effective and efficient use of resources—material and nonmaterial—within the context of the Cold War, and the efficient use of human and social resources. There is no static formula for economic growth that prevails over time and across nations. It is precisely this dynamism that helps us to understand the dramatic and unprecedented economic transformation that we have witnessed in this part of the world. However, many analysts are concerned that the financial crisis of 1997, which continues to affect many Asian economies, may also affect the rest of the world unless there is a speedy recovery in Asia. The financial crisis is an important test of whether the four Asian tigers are truly flexible and of whether their economies are strong enough to overcome the crisis and continue on their road toward sustainable development to become the leaders of the twenty-first century. It is too soon to conclude that the Century of Asia is dead on arrival. The new millennium may indeed belong to Asia, if the Asians are able to rely on their flexibility and their institutions, as they have done so well in the recent past.

REFERENCES

- Bernard, M., and Ravenhill, J. (1995). Beyond Product Cycles and Flying Geese: Regionalization, Hierarchy, and the Industrialization of East Asia. *World Politics,* Vol. 47, No. 2.
- Krugman, P. (1997). Whatever Happened to the Asian Miracle? *Fortune,* Vol. 136, No. 4.
- Krugman, P. (1994). The Myth of Asia's Miracle. *Foreign Affairs,* Vol. 73, No. 6.
- Radelet, S., and Sachs, J. (1998a). *The Onset of the East Asian Financial Crisis.* Harvard Institute for International Development.
- Radelet, S., and Sachs, J. (1998b). *The East Asian Financial Crisis: Diagnosis, Remedies, Prospects.* Harvard Institute for International Development.
- http://www.stern.nyu.edu/~nroubini/asia/AsiaChronology1.html
- http://www.stern.nyu.edu/~nroubini/asia/AsiaChronology1998.html

PART I

The Regional and Global Contexts for Economic Development

The Political Economy of Economic Growth in East Asia: South Korea and Taiwan

Kwang Yeong Shin
Department of Sociology
Hallym University
Chunchon, Kangwon-Do 200-702
South Korea

I. INTRODUCTION

Because its economies have shown three decades of unprecedented growth rates, East Asia has become the subject of intense research since the late 1980s (see Wade, 1992, and Kang, 1995, for a review). The causes of East Asian economic growth have become one of the more competitive theoretical, and sometimes ideological, battlefields, including growth theory, developmental economics, state theory, international political economy, industrial organization, and comparative sociology (Amsden, 1989; Wade, 1992; Henderson, 1993; Lucas, 1993; Krugman, 1994; Evans, 1995). The rise of East Asia revitalizes the old issues in political economy with fresh historical experiences; why did some countries (or only four East Asian newly industrialized countries [NICs]) succeed in capitalist industrialization in the Third World? Why not the others (African and Latin American) in the Third World? Is the East Asian model applicable to other developing countries in Southeast Asia or in Eastern Europe? Some researchers even raise different, more fundamental, questions about the desirability or sustainability of authoritarian capitalism in East Asia.[1]

---

[1]The most devastating critique of the literature appraising East Asian economic growth comes not from radical scholars but from a mainstream economist, Paul Krugman (1994). Krugman argues that the rapid economic growth in East Asia is nothing but a simple reflection of large-factor input. Like the

The Four Asian Tigers: Economic Development and the Global Political Economy

In this chapter I identify some characteristics of the East Asian political economy, which I call "authoritarian capitalism," and I analyze the factors that contributed to economic growth in East Asia. Next, I discuss the nature of the East
Asian authoritarian capitalism as a political–economic system that is distinct from
democratic capitalism in Western Europe and authoritarian socialism in Eastern Europe. Then I focus on three dimensions of the operation of authoritarian capitalism
in East Asia: the developmental state, the political economy of work organization,
and geopolitics and the world system. The role of the developmental state in the
economy and the operation of the work organization are distinctive with respect to
state intervention in organizing the economy to provide financial support and guidance for private production in East Asia.[2] The core dynamic force of economic
growth in East Asia is not market demand but state command. Looking at the inside
of the production organization, I argue that soft budget-constrained firms and factory despotism have been the microfoundation of the growth machine in authoritarian capitalism. Like firms in Eastern Europe, those in East Asia faced soft budget
constraints due to state subsidies. With the help of the state's oppressive apparatus,
labor control inside firms has been despotic, denying workers' basic rights and demands. However, the growth machine has operated in the changing climate of the
Cold War and the global economy. Interactions among local, national, and international economic and political powers are continuously changing in the real world.
As far as the economy is concerned, I argue that the interaction in East Asia has been
favorable to economic growth in South Korea and Taiwan, which have been under
U.S. hegemony since 1945. The political and military alliance between the United
States and the East Asian countries gave greater advantages to those countries in
terms of aid and easy access to the U.S. market (Wood, 1986; Stubbs, 1989; Hersh,
1993). Under U.S. hegemony East Asian countries were incorporated into the international production and trade network, which was crucial for the initial stage of
export-oriented industrialization. This implies that the applicability of the East Asian
model to other Third World countries is very limited.

Understanding the causes and the process of economic growth in East Asia
requires a comprehensive comparative historical analysis as well as a subtle theoretical explanation. Focusing on the microfoundations and macrodynamics of the East
Asian economy, I discuss my own approach to East Asian economic growth, which
is inevitably synthetic and holistic. In addition, I argue that the temporal dimension

---

rapid economic growth in the Stalinist period in Russia, he argues, it cannot be sustained in the long
run without improved productivity. Raising the question about the desirability of economic growth in
East Asia, Bello and Rosenfeld (1990) shed light on the dark side of economic growth in East Asia, such
as oppression of workers, environmental pollution, and dislocation of peasants.

[2]To identify the nuts and bolts of the growth machine is to answer to the how question. Ignoring the how question, searching for an answer to the why question tends to emphasize the role of culture and mentality or values without providing the ways in which they are operating.

of the process of economic growth in East Asia is crucial to understanding economic dynamism in Taiwan and South Korea.

II. SOCIAL FORMATIONS IN THE 20TH CENTURY

In the 20th century, we observe three different types of enduring political–economic systems: democratic capitalism, authoritarian socialism, and authoritarian capitalism.[3] These are segmented geographically throughout the world. Democratic capitalism developed mainly in Western and Northern Europe and in North America, authoritarian socialism in Eastern Europe, and authoritarian capitalism in Latin Europe and in the Third World.

Democratic capitalism has existed since the beginning of the 20th century, and it now flourishes as the dominant political–economic system throughout the world, although there have been several interruptions, such as the rise of Fascism in the 1920s and 1930s and the Great Depression in the 1930s.[4] Democratic capitalism is characterized by the fact that the means of production are privately owned and political power is regularly contested and transferred through electoral competition. Economic exchange among individuals is mediated by the market through which the price mechanism maintains the transaction of goods and services.

Authoritarian or state socialism is fundamentally different from democratic capitalism.[5] Authoritarian socialism in Eastern Europe was characterized by two factors. The first is that the state owned the means of production and allocated resources and commodities (the state–owner–employer–manager–planner economy model). The second is that political power was not contested nor was it shared by the people, but has been monopolized by one party—the communist party (the party state-polity model). The state's control of the economy is possible, since the communist party monopolized political power. Thus, the mode of production and the mode of domination are not differentiated, but are coupled into one.[6]

---

[3]This typology is based on two principal modes of organizing societies: the mode of production and the mode of domination. It implies that democratic socialism theoretically can be an alternative political–economic system. For example, Bowles and Gintis (1986) and Cohen and Rogers (1980) argue that what is principally valuable about socialism is its extension of democracy into economic life.

[4]Equal and universal suffrage in the most European countries was introduced in the 1910s and 1920s. Women's right to vote was guaranteed in France after the Second World War. See Jacobs (1989).

[5]The term state socialism (Konrad and Szelenyi, 1979) is used more frequently than authoritarian socialism. However, state socialism does not show how political power operated within the formerly socialist system in Eastern Europe. It only shows who exercised political power in Eastern Europe. I would rather use "authoritarian socialism" to denote socialism in Eastern Europe to capture the ways in which political power operates.

[6]Thus the transition in East Europe can be called the "double transition," which means the transition to a market economy and to democracy (Centeno, 1994).

Authoritarian capitalism is different from democratic capitalism and authoritarian socialism. As a capitalist system, the private ownership of the means of production is the dominant form of ownership, and ownership rights exist with decentralized forms. But political power is monopolized by particular social groups, such as the military or political parties, or by individual personnels. Thus the competition for political power is severely restricted and political opposition is repressed. Civil rights are not guaranteed by the state. In fact, authoritarian capitalism is not a short-lived political–economic system. As seen by historical fact in the Third World, it has been the dominant political–economic system since the 19th century.

III. REGIME TYPES

Political regime refers to a set of rules and institutions with two aspects: the relationship between state and society and the goals the political regime tries to achieve.[7] The welfare state in Nordic countries is one type of political regime in democratic capitalism.[8] Even though the political–economic system is democratic capitalism, the welfare state in the Nordic countries intervened heavily in resource allocation and redistribution, through state social and labor market policies. By contrast, the Japanese state systematically intervened in the sphere of production and least in the sphere of redistribution. Thus, welfare provided by the state has been minimal. Instead of the state welfare system, the big private companies developed a "company welfare system," which is only beneficial to the employees of the big companies (Dore, 1973).

It is also possible to identify three different regime types in authoritarian capitalism in the 20th century with respect to mode of governance and political orientation. The first type is the populist regime, which emphasized the redistribution of income and mobilized popular support against the ruling elite (Kaufman and Stallings, 1991).[9] The best examples are the Peronist regime in Argentina in the 1970s and Alan Garcia in Peru in the 1980s. The second type is the predatory regime, in which power holders tried to maximize their own welfare by plundering private as well as public resources. The Zairian regime under Mobutu is the prototype of the predatory regime (see Evans, 1989, 1995: 43–47). The third type is the developmental regime, which emphasizes state intervention in the economy to promote economic growth by sacrificing popular sectors. In contrast to the predatory regime, the developmental regime exercises comprehensive power to

---

[7]The regime here refers to the political groups that seize the state apparatus and exercise governance power. The state refers to a set of institution and rules that allow monopoly of violence and monopoly of tax. When there is no regime change for a long period, we do not need to distinguish the regime from the state.

[8]We can identify different types of welfare state according to the comprehensiveness and the principles of welfare (for example, Esping-Anderson, 1990).

mobilize finance and even to control private investments to achieve rapid economic growth (Collier, 1979; Jonson, 1982; Evans, 1995). Even though the effectiveness of state growth policies was different, the state's mobilization of economic and social resources to promote economic growth was a common characteristic of the developmental states in East Asia and Latin America.

A. The Developmental State in East Asia

As Wallerstein (1994) correctly points out, economic development has been a common objective of almost all political regimes. Although policies to achieve economic development have not been equal, political regimes have pursued economic development regardless of ideology. In this sense, the modern political regime is a kind of developmental state.

As some scholars (Polanyi, 1943; North, 1981; Mann, 1985 and 1988) have already mentioned, state intervention in the market system has been embedded in the capitalist system. Economic activities—production, distribution, and consumption of necessary goods and services—have never been free from politics or from state intervention. With the nation–state becoming the dominant form of polity, state intervention in the economy has become more sophisticated and comprehensive than ever (Tilly, 1979). Although the degree of state intervention in the economy has not been constant across time and space, the state's role in providing basic rules and institutions for economic activities has been a prerequisite for capitalist development.

What then are the characteristics of the developmental state in East Asia? The developmental state model was originally suggested by Johnson (1982, 1987) to explain the role of the state in Japanese policy-making. The model describes the role of the government in organizing the economic activities of private firms. It is possible to identify six distinctive features of this particular entity in East Asia in terms of the mode of state intervention.[10]

First, the developmental states in East Asia exercised autocratic power, compulsion, and oppression. The military regime in South Korea and the martial law regime in Taiwan have been dictatorial regimes where power is concentrated into one man, Park Jung Hee in South Korea and Chiang Kai-shek in Taiwan. They established personalized leadership through military coup (Park Jung Hee) and military occupation (Chiang Kai-shek). They repressed political opposition to monopolize power, and they controlled each society in a fashion similar to that of military

[9]A variety of conceptions of populism have been suggested by researchers in Latin America. See Robert (1995).

[10]Johnson (1987) suggested a slightly different criterion from this. In particular, he added the autonomy of the state. I think the autonomy of the state from the society is not a typical feature of the developmental state. Rather, autonomy of the state is quite common among authoritarian states in the Third World.

generals. State terror by the developmental state, including arrest and torture of dissidents, was common.

Second, by establishing centralized economic policy-making organizations, the Economic Planning Board (EPB) in South Korea and Council for Economic Planning and Development (CEPD) in Taiwan, they launched a series of economic planning agencies and initiatives for economic growth. Thus, state intervention in the NIC economies has been more comprehensive and selective than that in any other capitalist country. "The state command" replaced "the market demand" in core economic decision making in private enterprises.[11] The series of economic plans in South Korea and Taiwan has constituted the major source of industrial transformation and economic growth (Amsden, 1989: chap. 4 and Wade, 1990: chap. 4). State intervention in East Asia is more similar to that in the Stalinist regimes in Eastern Europe than to that in Keynesian regimes in Western Europe, since the state also played a role as entrepreneur as well as planner, such that state enterprises played important strategic roles in promoting exports.[12] The state also selected several industries as strategic sectors and gave them protection from excessive competition among domestic as well as foreign enterprises. The state provided financial subsidies and supports and scrutinized their economic performance. It controlled the number of competing enterprises in the market by restricting new entry and production capacity and frequent state-led mergers of private firms.[13]

Third, the developmental state managed investment by controlling the flow of money. The most important factor for state control over the economy was the nationalization of the banks (Jones and Sagong, 1980: 103–109; Wade, 1990: 161). The state-owned banks were strategic instruments for the anticonsumption and pro-investment policy, controlling consumption levels and prohibiting the consumption of domestic and foreign luxury goods.[14] The state initiated nationwide savings campaigns to expand capital investment in strategic industries. Consequently, there has been a trend of high saving rates and high investment ratios in East Asia.[15]

[11]Gunnar Myrdal (1968: 898) used the term "strong state" to describe the state that could impose obedience of social groups to state policy.

[12]Taiwan has had one of the larger public sectors among the nonsocialist countries. Public enterprises shared one-third of gross fixed capital formation in Taiwan and one-fourth in Korea in the 1970s and 1980s. Some economists in the West described the large proportion of the public sector as a "socialist pattern" (Jones and Sagong, 1980: xxix).

[13]For example, since 1962 Korea frequently has imposed mergers of firms to control excessive production capacity in the automobile industry, and in heavy and chemical industries in the late 1970s, and to promote productivity in the construction and shipbuilding industries in 1984 (Chang, 1993: 148–150).

[14]The state-owned banks did not provide loans for consumers and importers of domestic and foreign luxury goods (Chang, 1993: 139). Luxury goods listed by the state included passenger cars, refrigerators, washing machines, and video cameras.

[15]The investment ratio to GNP was 25% in South Korea and 25.5% in Taiwan. In 1980 it was 31.7% in South Korea and 32.2% in Taiwan, while it was 17.9% in Britain and 18.9% in the United States. In 1990 the investment ratio in Taiwan decreased to 22.4%, while it increased to 36.9% in South Korea. The investment ratios in the U.S. and U.K. remained below 20% in 1990 (Korea Labor Institute, 1992, 24).

Fourth, the developmental states in East Asia initiated export-oriented industrialization as a strategy for economic growth.[16] The principal difference between the developmental state in East Asia and that in Eastern Europe is that the state in East Asia chose an outward-oriented industrialization strategy, a mercantilist strategy that stressed foreign trade. The mercantilist state made exports "a compulsion rather than a choice" for private companies (Amsden, 1989: 69–70). To promote exports, the dualist trade regime—a free trade regime for export-related production and a protectionist trade regime for import-related production with a selective tariff system—was developed in East Asia.

Fifth, the developmental states created economic agencies and big capitalists to carry out economic planning in the private sector in South Korea and Japan, and they created small capitalists in Taiwan.[17] They utilized state resources and power, financial subsidies, access to foreign capital, licenses to import scarce consumer goods, and so on, to help to make domestic capitalists internationally competitive.[18] As in the case of the *chaebol* groups in South Korea and *zaibatsu* in Japan, with the help of the state indigenous capitalists can become world-class capitalists in a short period.[19]

Finally, to maintain a "good business climate," the developmental states in East Asia pursued an oppressive labor policy either through exclusionary labor policies in prewar Japan and postwar Korea or inclusionary labor policy in postwar Taiwan (Shin, 1994: chap. 10). Mobilizing the anticommunist ideology, the developmental states did not allow the basic rights of workers, such as freedom of association and collective actions (Deyo, 1989; Shin, 1994: chap. 6). To prevent possible workers' revolts, the state tightly controlled the workplace through the use of an oppressive apparatus, such as legal, political, and physical measures that included state surveillance and violence.[20]

[16]This does not mean that import substitution policy was totally abandoned. The state continuously provided financial subsidies to the private firms for the development of domestic technology to substitute for imported intermediate goods (Green, 1989). Nevertheless, South Korea and Taiwan show high levels of export dependency in their economic growth. During the 1980s the average trade dependency ratio was almost 65% in Korea and 83% in Taiwan. It was 36% in France, 47% in Germany, and 16% in America. See IMF (1992).

[17]The most striking contrast in developmental strategy in Korea and Taiwan is that the KMT regime promoted the small employers' role in economic growth and pursued decentralized growth, while the military regime in South Korea concentrated state finances into a small number of big capitalists and limited areas. See Amsden (1989: 120–125) for the Korean case and see Ho (1980) for the Taiwanese case.

[18]Green (1992) provides an excellent example of state protection and guidance of private enterprises in South Korea's automobile industry.

[19]The combined sales of the three largest *chaebols* accounted for 9.0% of total gross production in 1974. It went up to 35.8% in 1984. The 10 largest *chaebols* accounted for 67.4% of the total gross national product in 1984 (Amsden, 1989: 116). The economic concentration in South Korea is much higher than that in Japan. The six largest *zaibatsu* in Japan accounted for 16.43% of the gross sales in 1984 (Morioka, 1989: 149).

[20]Arrests and torture of labor unionists have been ordinary events in South Korea and Taiwan. See Ogle (1990) for the South Korean case.

IV. ORGANIZATION OF PRODUCTION

Individual firms are the principal organizations for the production of goods and services. The production of commodities takes place in the individual firms, and they are "the hidden but real" microfoundations of macroeconomic performance at the national level. As Krugman (1994) argues, there is no competitiveness at the national level. Competitiveness only comes from the performance of individual firms.

The private firms face four fundamental constraints in industrial capitalism. These are financial constraints, labor constraints, and technological constraints, which are the three components of production, and market demand constraints. An individual firm can increase the volume of production increasing more than one of these three factor inputs. The degree of financial constraint of an individual firm varies according to the alternative sources of finance available to the firm. In developing countries, there has been a chronic lack of capital. Labor constraints come from labor market conditions such as the available labor force, the skills and peculiar nature of labor power as the commodity-labor force available, known as the agency problem, and the workers' commitment to work. Various labor controls in industrial capitalism have been developed to extract labor power from workers.[21] Technical constraints are also important problems for the firms in both developed and developing countries.

A. Soft Budget-Constrained Firms

What are the characteristics of the firms and work organizations in East Asia? To discern the characteristics of work organizations in East Asia, it is useful to adopt Kornai's concepts of the soft budget-constrained firm and the demand-constrained economy, which were originally developed to describe the characteristics of East European economies under socialist regimes (1983 and 1992). He suggests that firms are exposed to different constraints in socialist and capitalist economies. Under the pure capitalist economy, firms face pure hard budget constraints, in which conditions of "exogenously determined prices," "hard tax," "no free state grants," "no credit," and "no external financial investment" exist (Kornai, 1983: 36–51). The survival of firms depends on the costs of inputs and sales of outputs. The growth of firms depends on internal accumulation and technological improvement. In contrast, under the socialist economy, firms face pure soft budget constraints, in which conditions of exogenously determined prices, soft tax system,

---

[21]Marx's conceptual distinction between labor and labor power provides an excellent explanation of the labor constraints embedded in the capitalist work organization (Marx, 1967: part III). For historical explanations of the evolution of labor control in industrial capitalism, see Braverman (1974), Freedman (1877), Edwards (1979), and Burawoy (1985).

free state grants, soft credit, and external financial investment exist. Thus, survival and growth do not depend on prices in the market but on political decisions and negotiations with policy-makers.

Strategic firms supported by the state in East Asia can be categorized as soft budget-constrained firms on the basis of the soft credit, the soft tax, and the price-makers' position in the domestic market. First, Korean and Taiwanese firms are dependent more on borrowed money than on equity capital in their operation. Strategic firms receive export credit according to the previous year's export performance and their planned exports for the current year. The interest rates for export credit loans are less than the normal short-term interest rates.

Second, the firms may be given a tax exemption or lower tax rate, at the state official's discretion. The paternalistic relationship between the state and private firms has maintained a low tax level and a flexible tax burden. If firms complied with the state's policies and were not reluctant to donate money (quasi-taxes) to political elites, they evaded taxes and avoided investigation.[22] For instance, many monopoly firms keep a large number of bank accounts under pseudonyms in order to avoid taxes.[23]

Third, the monopoly firms in South Korea are not pricetakers but pricemakers in the domestic market. Even though the state regulates consumer prices, the same products in the domestic market are much more expensive than those in international markets. The state has guaranteed compensation for the low profit in the international markets with higher profits in the domestic market through price distortions.

However, unlike in the socialist economy, profit is the key factor that motivates production for private firms. Whereas production of goods in the socialist economy was controlled and commanded by the state plan, those under authoritarian capitalism in East Asia have been motivated by the market mechanism through which surplus profits are legitimized and guaranteed. Even though the state intervened in the economy by guidance and command, benefits from compliance to state policy lead to guaranteed profits from the market.

B. Factory Despotism

Because of the state's oppression of the labor movement, manufacturing firms in South Korea and Taiwan did not experience serious disruption of production until 1987. Although there were several worker-organized strikes in the 1970s and

---

[22]Due to the paternalistic relations between state officers and private firms, there has been a chronic corruption problem with government officers. The government used the tax investigation as a threat to private firms when they did not obey government directions (Jones and Sagong, 1980: 114–115).

[23]When Kim Young Sam's government declared that all the bank accounts should be under real names in 1993 to eradicate tax evasion, the most seriously damaged groups were the major chabols in South Korea.

the 1980s, their impact on the national economy was trivial. The strikes did not address the problems of labor relations within firms. The state managers played the same role as managers in the private firms in dealing with labor unrest. Thus, the managerial manpower used by the firms in South Korea and Taiwan was less than that used in the advanced industrial countries.[24]

In addition, individual firms did not experience any labor shortages, because the labor force was unlimited until the mid-1980s. The large population of the rural areas was transformed into urban workers in South Korea. In 1961, 61% of the economically active population in South Korea was engaged in agriculture or in fishing. This dropped to only 18.3% in 1991, and has decreased by more than 40% in three decades. Almost one-third of rural family members became industrial workers, while another one-third of the rural population became urban petty bourgeoisie (Cho, Kang, and Shin, 1994). Because the military regime pursued spatially concentrated development in major cities, social mobility accompanied a massive spatial mobility, that is, rural–urban migration.

Taiwanese firms also enjoyed an abundant labor supply from rural areas. Because the KMT state emphasized decentralized industrial development, firms are scattered throughout the Taiwanese island (Ho, 1979). The rapid growth of rural nonagricultural employment reveals a sharp contrast between Korea and Taiwan. As in Mao's China, Chiang Kai-shek's Taiwan emphasized development of the rural areas. Thus, Taiwanese firms could fully utilize the underemployed rural labor forces at low wages.[25] Taiwanese workers who stayed in rural areas had lower living costs than did the Koreans who moved to large cities.

The first generation of Korean workers was the proletariat, separated from the countryside and forced to survive in the urban areas. Because of their weak position, they could not escape working long hours under poor conditions and low wages. Although large enterprises provided relatively higher wages than did small enterprises to induce skilled workers, these enterprises wished to maintain the lowest possible labor costs. To provide monetary incentives, the large enterprises in Korea introduced seniority wages into a system that was based on the piece-rate. However, they did not introduce the Japanese concept of lifetime employment and company welfare.

[24]The ratio of managers or supervisors to workers was 1:4.41 in South Korea (Cho et al., 1992: 35), 1:2.92 in Sweden (Wright, 1985: 195), 1:2.23 in Britain (Marshall et al., 1988) and 1:1.76 in the United States (Wright, 1985: 195). Those calculations were done by me.

[25]Firms established in the rural areas of Taiwan have been more labor intensive and smaller than those in urban areas (Ho, 1979: 86). The firms in the rural areas contributed to lowering the wage of rural workers who had an alternative source of income, agriculture. Although per capita GNP in Taiwan has been higher than that in South Korea, the hourly wage has been lower in Taiwan than in South Korea (BLS, 1990).

[26]Chung Ju Young, chairman of the Hyundai group, worked extremely hard, 14 hours a day, 6 or 7 days a week, and he expected all his employees to follow his work habit. Chung's view on work is

Under the repressive labor policy, management complained of the lack of workers' commitment to work.[26] Although working hours in South Korea and Taiwan were very long compared to those in other countries, large capitalists demanded even longer working hours. In the 1980s the average working hours per week in the manufacturing sector was 53.4 hours in South Korea and 48.4 hours in Taiwan. The long working hours were common in all East Asian countries, including Japan. Furthermore, because of short paid vacations, the working hours per year differ significantly in Western European and East Asian countries.[27] Because of long working hours and a bad working environment, there have also been high rates of fatal injuries in the manufacturing sectors in South Korea and Taiwan.[28]

Labor–management relations in the workplace have been characterized as despotic in the sense that managerial authority was considered sacred and any disobedience by the workers was penalized by managers. Because workers had no voice or channel through which to express grievances, the turnover was extremely high in South Korea and Taiwan. Management reports to police those suspected of speaking out by trying to organize unions or collective actions. State agents and enterprise managers in private firms cooperated with each other to prevent workers' collective actions.[29] Even in cases of collective action, which have been frequent since 1987, big enterprises organized "enterprise rescue teams (*kusadae*)" with white collar employees to break strikes, and they sometimes hired gangsters to attack and kidnap union leaders.[30] With the help of the KCIA, the police, and hired gangsters, the big enterprises repressed workers' resistance and they maintained managers' despotic power in the factory.

---

well represented in his remark: "Other industrial countries have lost their advantages to Japan mainly because their workers don't have the proper attitude to work" (cited from Ogle, 1995: 25).

[27]The paid vacation was 10.3 days in South Korea (1989), 15.3 days in Japan (1988), and 10.3 days in Taiwan (1987). Working 5 days a week is uncommon in East Asia. Only 1% of Korean workers and 29.5% of Japanese workers regularly worked 5 days a week (Park *et al.*, 1991: 44). Thus, the working hours per year were 2590 in Korea, 2124 in Japan, 2522 in Singapore, and 2423 in Taiwan. They were 1683 in France, 1598 in Germany, and 1948 in the U.S.

[28]In 1965 the rate of fatal injury was 0.32% in South Korea and 0.36% in Taiwan. In 1986 it was 0.18% in South Korea and 0.13% in Taiwan. These rates were still seven to nine times higher than rates in the U.S. and Sweden.

[29]In Taiwan, retired military personnel took key positions in the state-controlled labor unions and cooperated with the security agencies; see Arrigo (1985). In the South Korea labor department, the prosecutor's office, the KCIA, and the police were involved in the surveillance of workers; see Ogle (1990: 53–64).

[30]In addition to help from the state agency, Hyundai Motor Company, for instance, hired local gangsters who stormed the meetings of union leaders in 1990. Almost 30 union leaders were seriously injured and hospitalized. Terror and violence against union leaders have been common tactics adopted by chabols in Korea. See Lee (1994) for an excellent description of the Hyundai's anti-union terror and violence as well as the state's oppression of union movements in Hyundai groups.

Because of the strong repression of the labor movement and the lack of protection of worker's rights by the state, the despotic control of workers by managers was a common phenomenon in East Asia. It could be called "factory despotism," in contrast with "market despotism" in early capitalist Britain.[31] The mobilization of highly disciplined workers being paid low wages and working long hours was made possible by factory despotism guaranteed by the oppressive state apparatus. The powerless workers in South Korea and Taiwan were not controlled by market dynamics or rules made by labor and capital but by state repression and managerial despotism. The state also provided guidelines to control wage increases and inflation. The low wages of workers were not a product of market mechanisms but were a product of state intervention in wage determination.

V. EAST ASIAN PRODUCTION AND THE SEGMENTED AMERICAN MARKET

One of the more distinctive features of the East Asian NICs is the formation of "asymmetric economic networks": technological dependency with Japan and a trade dependency with the United States. The core element of asymmetric economic networks is the combination of foreign technology, cheap domestic labor, and American consumption. Japan was the major source of the production technology for South Korea and Taiwan. Because of the low level of production technology, Taiwan and South Korea attempted to develop domestic technology that could promote import-substitution industrialization. However, it was almost impossible to catch up to the advanced technology of Japan and the United States in a few years. After South Korea and Taiwan switched to export-oriented industrialization, they commonly tried to overcome the technological bottleneck by importing capital goods from Japan. Japan has been the largest exporting country to South Korea and Taiwan since the mid 1960s, when both countries began export-oriented industrialization. Imports from Japan accounted for more than 35% of all imports during the 1960s and 1970s in both countries. More than 80% of the imports were composed of the capital goods to produce consumer and intermediate goods for export. This technological dependency led to a chronic trade deficit with Japan in both countries.

However, this process of technology transfer did not indicate a homogeneous level of production technology. As Bernard and Ravenhill (1995) correctly point out, South Korean and Taiwanese manufacturers lacked the capacity to indigenize foreign technology because their R & D expenditures were low. Original equip-

---

[31]According to Buraway (1985), market despotism in early capitalist development was possible because of the real subordination of workers to capital, high unemployment, and a lack of state protection for workers.

ment manufacturing (OEM) has been a dominant form of production for export in major industries such as consumer electronics, apparel, and steel, in which more than 80% of total exports were OEM products (Bernard and Ravenhill, 1995: 191). The hierarchy of production technology contributed to the maintenance of economic dependency based on technology and marketing.[32]

Another element of the triad, the trade dependency with the United States, was beneficial to East Asian economies until the late 1980s. The rise of the East Asian economy cannot be explained without considering trade with the United States. The articulation of East Asian production and the American market reveals how East Asian countries succeeded in export-oriented industrialization. Exploitation of the American market has been possible because of its relatively unique characteristics.

The developmental states played roles in conforming and governing the market. The market, in fact, is an illusive concept because it comprises a variety of different systems of transaction, from potatoes and labor power to money itself (see Swedberg, 1994). As Amsden (1989: 11) correctly points out, the market is different from the market mechanism. Whereas the market refers to a locus of exchange, market mechanism refers to the dynamics of processing exchange. When we talk about the role of the market as an alternative to the state, we refer to the market as a mechanism that is supposed to allocate economic resources according to the impersonal logic of supply and demand. When the states could not govern the market, more correctly, when they could not intervene in the market mechanism, they chose the market-conforming strategy. The developmental states in East Asia did not have enough power or leverage to control international markets; they simply tried to follow their logic and utilized their comparative advantages. However, in the domestic market they intervened in the market mechanism by price setting and import/export policies. "Getting the price wrong" in the financial market as well as in the product market, they intervened in the market mechanism (Amsden, 1989: chap. 6; Wade, 1990: chap. 10).

Domestic and international market conditions were differentiated across countries in terms of consumer preferences and price structures. We can call the differentiation of markets the "product market segmentation."[33] As with the segmented labor market, the global product market is highly segmented because of the variation in consumer preference according to class and culture and because of the differential prices of commodities according to the different tariff and tax systems. As a result, the product markets are as heterogeneous and fragmented as the labor markets.

Two types of commodity market can be distinguished, according to the operating principle. The first type of market is the price competition market, in which the preference of consumers is not sophisticated or well articulated. Price

[32]Hyundai motor company, which exported almost one million cars, barely succeeded in making its own engine by reverse technology in 1990.

[33]Market niches refer to the part of the segmented product market in which comparative advantages of the goods can be guaranteed.

elasticity is so steep that the effective demand as an aggregated volume of individual consumption changes drastically according to changes in the price of products. The cost of entry into the price competition market is low, because there are many ways to reduce production costs, such as low wages, mass production, and the use of more efficient technology. Consequently, to use Vernon's term (1971), "product life cycle" in the price competition market is very short because less-developed countries can produce the same kind of product while taking advantage of their lower wages. As wages in South Korea and Taiwan rise, products of these countries are gradually losing their competitiveness in the price competition market. The second type of market is the quality competition market, in which preferences of consumers are sophisticated and price elasticity is not so steep. The barrier to entry into the quality competition market is very high because it requires high levels of production technology and quality control. Thus, economy of scale or low price based on low wages does not necessarily guarantee strong competitive advantages in the quality competition market. Advanced technology and skills are more crucial factors for increasing the share in this market. Successful entry into and survival in this market require incessant innovation of products and manufacturing processes with massive R & D spending and organizational flexibility.

The East Asian NICs have been highly dependent on the U.S. market. The NICs in East Asia successfully penetrated the price competition market in the United States by relying mainly on low wages, borrowed standardized technology, and economy of scale. As a result, compared with that of the industrialized countries, the level of productivity in East Asia has been very low. Good performance of East Asian countries comes not from high productivity but from economy of scale (Kwon, 1986; Chen and Tang, 1990; Krugman, 1994). Nevertheless, products from East Asia found market niches in the United States because the price competition market in the United States has been well developed. Because American society is highly stratified according to class, gender, and race, the large number of poor and underclass people mainly concerned with the price of a commodity have been major consumers in the price competition market. Japan explored the price competition market in the United States in the 1960s and 1970s and then moved into the quality competition market with the help of high technology and innovation. South Korea and Taiwan rushed into the price competition market in the United States with the help of transferred technology and capital goods from Japan and the United States in the 1970s and 1980s. Throughout the 1980s some enterprises in Taiwan and South Korea moved into the quality competition market.[34] In replacing South Korea and Taiwan, China and the Southeast Asian NICs entered the price competition market utilizing massive low-wage labor in the late 1980s.

[34]One good example is the Taiwanese bicycle industry upgrading product quality rather than lowering prices to increase competitiveness in the U.S. market. To solve the rising export price of Taiwanese bicycles due to the devaluation of the U.S. dollar, Taiwanese bicycle manufacturers moved to a quality production system by developing new materials and components. The price of a bicycle rose

The success of economic growth in South Korea and Taiwan lies partly in their taking advantage of the price competition market in the United States. In poor countries whose domestic markets were small, economic growth was possible only by exporting goods to the large markets. However, exports to the large markets do not necessarily guarantee the success of the export-oriented strategy. Capital accumulation based on export is possible only when the exported goods are matched with sufficient market demand. Export-oriented industrialization was possible in South Korea and Taiwan because they could exploit the U.S. market with low wages and low-priced goods. As with Japan, South Korea and Taiwan partly succeeded in moving up to the quality competition market in the United States, replacing American goods as well as European goods. A heavy dependence on exports to the American market for more than three decades became a source of trade conflict between East Asian NICs and the United States after the end of the Cold War in the late 1980s.

VI. GEOPOLITICS AND THE DYNAMICS OF THE GLOBAL ECONOMIC SYSTEM

The rise of East Asia reveals the distinctive interconnection of economic dynamism and geopolitics, and the Cold War (Hersh, 1993; Stubbs, 1989 and 1994). Beginning in 1945, the United States rebuilt South Korea and Taiwan, as well as Japan, to contain the socialist bloc. During the early period of industrialization in South Korea and Taiwan, U.S. aid based on the mutual security alliance was crucial to consolidating unpopular regimes and creating the foundations of economic growth. Economic and military aid compensated for the low rate of private savings in Korea and Taiwan.[35] In addition, two Asian wars following the Second World War—the Korean War and the Vietnam War—boosted the economy in that region in two ways: direct transaction of remittance and indirectly expanding exports due to the war boom. The greatest and longest lasting effect of the Cold War was to lower the entry barrier to the U.S. market to consumer goods from South Korea and Taiwan.

---

from $47.10 in 1986 to $119 in 1993 in the U.S. market. Competitiveness in the price competition market was no longer guaranteed because products from China and other Southeast Asian countries were much cheaper than those from Taiwan.

[35]Contrary to the conventional argument that the major source of the rapid economic growth in East Asia was the high rate of private saving, it was low until the mid 1970s. During the 1960s it was 14.5% in South Korea and 14.2% in Taiwan, slightly higher than that in the U.K. and almost half of that in Japan. South Korea and Taiwan were among the countries with the lowest level of gross domestic savings in the Third World. In 1970 the gross domestic savings rate in Korea (15%) was much lower than that in other Third World countries such as Bolivia (31%), Tunisia (22%), Algeria (36%), Thailand (21%), Malaysia (27%), and Argentina (23%).

A. U.S. AID

After the Second World War, the United States launched massive aid programs to Europe (the Marshall Plan), to revive the capitalist economy, and to the Third World, to support anticommunist and counterrevolutionary movements. South Korea and Taiwan became nation states with Western institutions under the sole influence of the United States due to the geopolitics of the Cold War. South Korea and Taiwan were the capitalist bulwarks against the continental socialist bloc in Asia. There has been consistent system competition as well as military confrontations between the two blocs.

To contain socialist expansion, the United States provided both economic and military aid to the anticommunist regimes in East Asia.[36] Because East Asia was considered strategically important to containing socialist power and maintaining American hegemony in the world (Cumings, 1987: 65–66), the United States provided huge amounts of economic aid to South Korea and Taiwan, which were impoverished in the 1950s and early 1960s.[37] For example, 64% of the total U.S. foreign aid to underdeveloped countries went to the countries that resisted communism in Asia—South Korea, Taiwan, and the Philippines (Wood, 1986: 40–41). U.S. economic aid constituted about 75% of total imports during the period from 1953 to 1960 in South Korea (Krueger, 1979: 67). Because of the low domestic savings rate, foreign aid contributed significantly to the capital accumulation necessary for investment. According to one econometric estimation, foreign aid contributed to about 4% of South Korea's growth rate from 1960 until 1970 (Krueger, 1979: 211). Access to U.S. aid also has influenced the possibility of alliance with foreign capital and production technology. South Korea received the largest World Bank loan given between 1978 and 1981.[38]

After the defeat of the KMT regime in mainland China, the U.S. government considered Taiwan more important than ever for containing communist power. The United States assisted the KMT regime by providing massive economic and military aid to strengthen the refugee regime (Haggard and Pang, 1994: 62–65). The U.S. government agency and the KMT regime jointly formulated economic reform to demonstrate the superiority of the market economy over the communist system. U.S. economic and military aid to Taiwan, which was almost 80% of Taiwan's import surplus at about $1.7 billion and $2.4 billion, respectively, contributed to vitalizing Taiwan's economic growth in the 1950s and early 1960s

---

[36]In fact, the distinction between economic and military aid is not clear-cut since the donor's decision does not necessarily correspond to the receiver's usages. See Wood (1986: 10–15) for conceptual problems associated with aid.

[37]According to the U.S. Agency of Economic Development (1983), more than $27 billion has been spent on economic assistance in East Asia since 1945.

[38]The amount of the loans to South Korea was $605 million, which was almost twice that provided to Mexico and almost 10 times that given to Brazil. For details, see Wood (1986: 166–176).

(Stubbs, 1994: 367). The military alliance with the United States also made it easy for Taiwan to get international funds. During the 1960s Taiwan received massive foreign direct investment with the help of the United States (Gold, 1986: 76–78). While U.S. political support of Chiang Kai-shek's KMT regime stabilized the shaky political power in the island of Taiwan, economic aid financed the industrial basis for export in Taiwan during the 1950s and 1960s. In sum, "South Korea received some $813 billion in American military and economic aid or $600 per capita. Taiwan, $5.6 billion, or $425 per capita" (Aseniero, 1994: 289).

The transition in developmental strategies was directly associated with the termination of U.S. aid. Although the KMT regime launched a series of Four Year Economic Plans as early as 1953 (1953–1956, 1957–1960, 1961–1964), it was in the late 1950s and early 1960s that the KMT regime emphasized an export-oriented industrialization strategy. As U.S. economic and military aid had been gradually decreasing during the latter half of the 1950s, the KMT regime adopted an export-oriented industrialization strategy to solve the balance of payment problem. Total U.S. aid to Taiwan peaked at $442.6 million in 1955. It decreased almost 60% to $160.4 million in 1962, and it was finally supposed to end in 1965 (Chang, 1965: 154–156). To respond to the balance of payment, the KMT regime adopted the mercantilist way of accumulating foreign exchange—that is, the EOI—as a long-term strategy.

B. TWO WARS AND THE EAST ASIAN ECONOMY

Two wars have contributed to the rise of the East Asian economy since 1945. The Korean War began in 1950, and continued for 3 years, and the Vietnam War lasted for more than 10 years. The outbreak of the Korean War contributed to the growth of the Taiwanese economy as well as to the revival of Japanese economy (Cumings, 1984). The American military's purchase of goods from Japan increased "from zero in 1949 to nearly $600 million in 1951 and $825 million in 1952," and the war economy allowed Japan to expand exports from $510 million in 1949 to $1.36 billion in 1951 (Stubbs, 1994: 367). Furthermore, the impact of the Korean War extended to Southeast Asia, with demand for strategic materials such as rubber and tin. The 3-year war destroyed almost everything in Korea, but it completely revitalized Japanese industrial production to the prewar level.

The Vietnam war contributed to South Korean and Taiwanese economic growth. As a result of its participation in the Vietnam War, South Korea "received about $50 million per year in remittances in the late 1960s" (Stubbs, 1994: 369). In exchange for South Korean participation in the Vietnam War, the U.S. permitted South Korean enterprises to participate in the construction of ports and roads and in arsenal transportation in South Vietnam. Major enterprise groups such as Hyundai, which were then rather medium-sized enterprises, succeeded in contracting with the U.S. military and got the opportunity to expand their enter-prises.[39] In the 1970s the total amount of overseas work contracts reached nearly 20% of South Korean exports (Aseniero, 1994: 240). Thus, the South Korean government and enterprises received the hard currency necessary for new invest-ment in industry (Cole and Lyman, 1971).

South Korea was not the only beneficiary of the Vietnam War during the 1960s and the early to mid-1970s. During the 1960s U.S. economic aid to Taiwan was gradually decreased. It was suspended in 1965, but Taiwan utilized the oppor-tunity of exports to Vietnam to get hard currency (Cumings, 1984: 33 and Stubbs, 1995: 369). As Stubbs shows, "Taiwan's exports to Vietnam tripled from $34 mil-lion in 1964 to over $90 million in 1968" (1994: 369). Although Taiwan did not send military forces to Vietnam, with other countries in Southeast Asia it rapidly expanded its export industries, supplying goods for the Vietnam War.[40] The eco-nomic impact of the Vietnam War on Taiwan was an expansion of markets for chemicals, textiles, and transportation equipment.

During the 1960s and 1970s South Korea and Taiwan pursued import-substitution industrialization first and export-oriented industrialization later. When they anticipated difficulty in getting hard currency because of decreases in - economic aid from the United States, they pursued import substitution industri-alization (ISI) to reduce trade deficits. They also moved to export-oriented industrialization, which was a more aggressive strategy than ISI strategy. The Viet-nam War occurred during the 60s and 70s, a period that was vital to the early stage of economic growth in East Asia. The American commitment in East Asia and dur-ing two international wars in Asia after the Second World War significantly con-tributed to the foundation of the East Asian economy. The Vietnam War provided "a breathing space" for the anticommunist bloc in East Asia to launch their economies (Hersh, 1995: 8).

C. ACCESSIBILITY OF THE U.S. MARKET

The linkage of economic and diplomatic alliance was the core element of the United States foreign policy during the Cold War (Verdier, 1994: 207–217). The trade–security linkage aimed at keeping foreign countries in the American security framework was established just after the Second World War. One of the more im-portant effects on the East Asian economy has been the accessibility of the Ameri-can market to the newly industrialized countries in East Asia. The mode of incorporation of the Third World into the international economy has been deter-

[39]Hyundai in Vietnam operated as a subcontractor of the RMK-BRJ, the big U.S. conglomer-ate responsible for the U.S. military construction work, naval base construction, and waterway dredg-ing (Kirk, 1994: 77).

[40]Singapore, Thailand, and Malaysia also benefited from the Vietnam War by providing and transporting war-related materials. See Stubbs (1989).

mined according to geopolitics and locations within the global production system. Under U.S. hegemony, South Korea and Taiwan have been allowed to export industrial products to the American market with preferential tariff treatment under the General System of Preferences (GSP). As the military tension escalated in Asia, the United States was in greater need of political and economic cooperation with Asian countries. Because of the political and military alliance between the United States and the East Asian countries, Korea and Taiwan were able to penetrate the American market under the favorable climate guaranteed by the United States.

South Korea and Taiwan exported labor-intensive goods such as clothes, textiles, footwear, and travel goods to the United States. The competitiveness of the exporting countries in this market came mainly from the low wages. South Korean and Taiwanese firms utilized low-wage labor to expand their share of the price competition market. The United States has been South Korea's largest trading partner since 1945. South Korea was the seventh largest trading partner of the United States in the late 1980s. The United States sponsored South Korea and Taiwan in their export of industrial goods, as it did for Japan in the 1950s and 1960s. One of the consequences is that South Korea and Taiwan followed the trade pattern of Japan with the United States (Yoo, 1985).

As we discussed before, the peculiarity of the U.S. market contributed to the successful placing of the low-price and low-quality goods from East Asian countries on the U.S. market during the 1960s and 1970s. The U.S. market has been crucial to the Asian NICs in increasing their trade surplus. South Korea and Taiwan enjoyed trade surpluses with the United States, and these surpluses compensated for the trade deficit with Japan. The U.S. trade deficit now comes mainly from the trade with East Asia, including Japan, South Korea, and Taiwan. The U.S. trade deficit with the NICs was about $31 billion in 1988, which invoked aggressive unilateralism to manage the trade deficit problem.[41] South Korean and Taiwanese firms effectively utilized market niches in the large but segmented U.S. market. The choice of the U.S. market was an economic choice to maximize profit, but the constraints placed on firms in South Korea and Taiwan were rather political due to the Cold War.

D. Global Capitalism: Flow of Capital and Labor

During the 1970s the advanced industrialized countries experienced a serious economic crisis due to labor shortages, high wages, environmental pollution, and a sharp increase in production costs due mainly to oil shocks. One way to escape these problems was to move more capital to Third World countries. For the last

---

[41]In 1988 the Reagan administration announced that South Korea and Taiwan had graduated from preferential tariff system under the General System of Preferences in 1988. With the end of the Cold War, economic interest became more salient than diplomatic relations in U.S. policy-making. A shift to aggressive unilateralism in the U.S. reveals the change in environment that shapes foreign economic policy (Bhagwati and Patrick, 1990).

three decades, foreign direct investment has increased more than 12 times from $9 billion in 1960 to $103 billion in 1988. The annual growth rate of foreign direct investment has been almost 40%, which is greater than the growth rate of world trade (13%) and GDP (12%) (UN, 1992: 1). The absolute majority of capital export, 87% of the total foreign direct investment, has been given by the major industrial countries: the United States, Great Britain, Germany, Japan, France, the Netherlands, and Canada.

Direct foreign investment in South Korea and Taiwan was dominated by Japanese firms in the 1960s and 1970s. Small- and medium-sized capital with labor-intensive industry and low productivity moved to South Korea and Taiwan (Ozawa, 1979: 26–28). The multinational firms moved to South Korea and Taiwan; these had been declining because they were labor intensive and they generated heavy industrial pollution (UN, 1992: 346). Japanese manufacturers competed with American manufacturers to utilize low-waged, disciplined, and well-educated workers in Taiwan (Gold, 1986: 79). American firms that lost competitiveness against Japanese manufacturers with lower prices invested in Taiwan to recover market share in the United States. Japanese firms also invested in Taiwan to compete with offshore production by American firms. This consequence was a product of the KMT policy to solicit foreign capital investment. Although the proportion of direct foreign capital investment to the total capital formation is small, its contribution to trade is significant. Direct foreign investment constituted 24.6% of exports in Korea in 1978 and 25.6% in Taiwan in 1981 (Shin, 1995).

Dictatorial regimes in East Asia provided "the best business climate" for Japanese and American capital through their repressive labor policies and their cheap and abundant labor. Manufacturers in Japan and in the United States, which competed mainly on price, transferred their capital to South Korea and Japan. Direct foreign investment in South Korea and Taiwan increased dramatically. As labor movement intensified and wages increased, South Korean as well as foreign capital began to move to Southeast Asia, particularly to Indonesia, Malaysia, Thailand, the Philippines, and Vietnam.[42]

The crisis in the Western economy took place in the context of the rise of the Third World in the 1970s. With the defeat of the United States in Vietnam, the coalition of oil-exporting countries in the Middle East was at the peak of Third World political ascendancy, in the name of resource nationalism. The Middle Eastern countries undertook big construction projects with surplus oil dollars beginning in 1975. The South Korean government sent several private construction

---

[42]The total amount of investment in Southeast Asia from South Korea increased by 109 times from $10.3 million in 1984 to $1.092.0 billion in 1994 (Korean Bureau of Statistics, 1995: 362). Taiwan's foreign investment in Southeast Asia also increased rapidly. Taiwan's foreign investment was concentrated on Malaysia, Indonesia, and Thailand. During the period of 1987–1994 the total amount of Taiwan's investment in Southeast Asia was almost $15 billion (Schive, 1995: 76).

firms, including Hyundai and Daewoo, to take advantage of the projects, as soon as the South Vietnam construction market was closed. It orchestrated the labor export policy as a part of the strategy to promote industrial export, controlling the process of labor migration through government organization and assisting companies in winning contracts with Middle Eastern countries. South Korean construction firms employed temporary contract workers with limited terms for work in the Middle East. Workers from South Korea, with other workers from Southeast Asian countries such as the Philippines, Thailand, Bangladesh, Pakistan, and India, accounted for 5.1 million, or almost 70% of the total workers, with 7.1 million in the Middle East in 1985 (Birks, Seccombe and Sinclair, 1988: 267).

The outflow of workers was a significant source of release from the pressure of high unemployment, and a large inflow of remittance contributed to improving the balance of payment. In 1974 there were only 395 South Korean workers in the Middle East. This number rose to 172,968 in 1982, which was 1.17% of the economically active population and almost 4% of all employees in 1982. As construction projects in the Middle East came to an end in 1983, the number of South Korean workers in that area also declined. Furthermore, South Korea became a country that imported labor from the other Southeast Asian countries (Fong, 1992).

Remittances from migrant workers had been a substantial resource for the balance of payments and total national income. Before 1973 most of the remittances came from the workers in Vietnam and a small number of miners and nurses in West Germany (UN, 1987: 64). They peaked in 1967 at $114.7 million, which was 35.8% of total exports and almost 87% of the total exported to the United States. Following the Vietnam War, the Middle East became the major source of remittances. The South Korean government imposed a mandatory remittance rule by which at least 80% of the workers' earnings had to be remitted through the South Korean banks (Athukorala, 1993: 105). It was an effective remittance mobilization policy to maximize the workers' deposits in South Korean banks. Remittances from the Middle East also contributed substantially to GDP growth. They amounted to 2.7% of the GDP in 1979, 2.3% in 1980, 2.5% in 1981, and 2.7% in 1982 in South Korea (see Table 1). One UN study reported that the effect of remittances on GDP growth was an increase between 1.3% and 7.1% from 1976 to 1981 (UN, 1987: 91).[43] Considering the fact that South Korean economic growth rates were 6.8% in 1979, −3.9% in 1980, 5.5% in 1981, and 7.5% in 1982, the economic impact of remittances was substantial. As the outflow of workers decreased, the impact of remittances on the South Korean economy has decreased since 1983. Nevertheless, remittances from workers contributed substantially to rapid economic growth in South Korea.

---

[43]The estimate of contributions of remittances to GNP growth was done by dividing the net increase in remittances in constant prices by the net increase in GNP in constant prices.

Table 1

Remittances from Labor Migrations in South Korea (Millions of U.S. Dollars)

	Remittances (1)	Export (2)	(1)/(2) percent	% of GNP
1965	18.4	175.1	10.5	—
1966	57.3	250.3	22.9	—
1967	114.7	320.2	35.8	—
1968	86.5	455.4	19.0	—
1969	69.2	622.5	11.1	—
1970	48.4	835.2	5.8	—
1971	46.4	1,067.6	4.3	—
1972	56.8	1,624.1	3.5	—
1973	113.3	3,225.0	3.5	—
1974	114.4	4,460.4	3.2	—
1975	158.2	5,081.0	3.1	—
1976	303.4	7,715.1	3.9	1.1
1977	584.2	10,046.5	3.4	1.7
1978	769.8	12,710.6	5.1	1.6
1979	1,158.3	15,055.5	7.7	1.8
1980	1,292.4	17,505.9	7.4	2.3
1981	1,673.4	20,670.8	8.1	2.5
1982	1,939.4	20,879.2	9.3	2.7
1983	1,663.0	23,203.9	7.2	2.2
1984	1,490.0	26,334.6	5.6	1.8

Source: Bank of Korea, *Economic Statistical Yearbook,* various years.

From the 1950s through the 1970s, sequential changes in economic factors have contributed to economic growth in South Korea and Taiwan. Economic and military aid in the 1950s was crucial to the economies of South Korea and Taiwan. As the amount of aid gradually decreased, each country tried to solve the balance of payment problem by import substitution industrialization in the 1960s. As this was less effective in protecting the hard currency, both countries began the active economic policy of export-oriented industrialization. The Vietnam War contributed significantly to capital formation in each country. They were able to expand industrial infrastructure with remittances (the case of South Korea) and through a trade surplus (the case of Taiwan). The economic effect of the Vietnam War on the East Asian economy was substantial beginning in the mid-1960s, when South Korea and Taiwan suffered from a lack of investment capital. In addition, the South Korean state and chabols have taken advantage of the resource nationalism in the Middle East since 1975. Under the control of the state, South Korean construction firms recruited temporary workers and labor exports to the Middle East contributed significantly to the balance of payment and the growth of GDP in the 1970s.

VII. SUMMARY AND DISCUSSION

A. Interaction of Multiple Factors and the Applicability of East Asian Economic Model to Other Third World Countries

It is misleading to try to find one key factor to explain economic growth in East Asia, because many factors can contribute to economic growth. In a closed economic system and a system with no state intervention, an increase in more than one of the three factors of production—capital, labor, and technology—results in an increase in productivity. However, the increase in productivity does not necessarily generate economic growth because the profitability of goods is not solely dependent on productivity. Rather, the profitability of goods relies on market demand, which is an aggregated outcome of individual consumer preferences.

Growth theory focuses on the supply side, the growth of human capital, technological improvement, an increase in capital investment, and so on, but it cannot explain why export-oriented industrialization has been more successful in East Asia than in Latin America (for example, Lucas, 1993). This approach totally neglects international political economy and the role of the state. It also downplays the fact that the effect of human capital on economic growth depends on the context within which it operates.

The state or neostate approach (Johnson, 1987; Amsden, 1989; Wade, 1990; Weise and Hobson, 1995) ignores the fact that the state does not produce commodities in capitalist societies. The state produces only economic policies and it sets rules to regulate, govern, and promote the economic activity of private enterprises. The role of the state is crucial in the formation and maintenance of economic rules and institutions. Nevertheless, it does not produce commodities, except for public services or public goods.

The production of commodities takes place within the organization of production, of firms or of the workplace where management and labor are major actors. The extraction of labor power from workers has shown distinctive patterns according to the relationship between labor and capital. Furthermore, unless the quality and price of the goods produced in private enterprises are attractive enough to increase demand, state policies are of no use in promoting economic growth through the activities of private enterprises.

By contrast, the market approach or neoclassical approach (Krueger, 1981 and 1990; Hughes, 1988) neglects the role of state intervention in the economy and the nature of the soft budget-constrained firms in East Asia. The state command rather than market demand initiated the dynamic growth of the East Asian economy. The state has oppressed market competition as well as political competition while providing protection from foreign competition and allowing monopolies.

Although the state never totally replaced the function of the market and never denied private ownership of the means of production, the state initiated and implemented the operation of the economy through planning, investment management, and controlling trade and market in South Korea and Taiwan.

The effectiveness of state intervention in the economy depended on the state's capacity to mobilize finance and foreign loans, and to gain preferential treatment from the importing countries. The Cold War provided a friendly environment for South Korean and Taiwanese firms during the 1960s and 1970s. By taking advantage of the military and economic alliance with the United States, South Korea and Taiwan received massive amounts of economic and military aid, which contributed to the formation of capital. Moreover, industrial products from South Korea and Taiwan penetrated the price competition market in the United States as a result of the economic alliance with the United States.

In this chapter I have argued that a more holistic and historical explanatory approach is necessary to comprehend economic growth in East Asia. The three explanations that I have provided are based on the state level in the sense that only the internal dynamics of the economy have been taken into account. We should also consider the international politics and economy that provide the environment for the East Asian economy. Systemic competition, including wars between authoritarian capitalism and authoritarian socialism, accelerated economic growth under American hegemony in East Asia.[44]

Moreover, I argue that we should identify the microfoundation of economic growth to fully understand the economic dynamism in East Asia. Factory despotism as a characteristic of work organization in East Asia contributed to the accumulation of capital as did market despotism during early capitalist development in the West. Despotic control under the state's oppression of labor made it possible to exploit workers through extremely long working hours with a high rate of industrial injuries.

I will briefly summarize my arguments as follows. First, despotic control of workers by management took place in the workplace. Under factory despotism, the input of the labor factor could be increased by simple measures such as an extension of working hours and days. As in the case of South Korea, the economy of scale in big enterprises substantively enhanced the productivity and profitability during the economic upswing.

Second, the major characteristic of strategic enterprises in East Asia is the soft budget constraint, which is quite similar to that in Eastern Europe. However, the soft budget-constrained firms in East Asia generated growth dynamics through the scaled economy and state disciplines. More importantly, private appropriation of profits with the help of the state accelerated the competition for profit. Because for-

---

[44]It is interesting to note that the Cold War factor is considered important by many researchers but it is totally ignored in major analyses of economic growth in East Asia (Krueger, 1990: 244; Wade, 1990: 346).

eign direct investment in East Asia was much less than it was in Latin America, disjunction of production and consumption did not generate economic dependency.

Third, the developmental state in East Asia paved the way for rapid economic growth at the expense of civil rights. This is also a by-product of the operation of the developmental state. The military regime in South Korea and the martial law regime in Taiwan managed the economy as they controlled the army brigade, oppressing workers' rights and demands.

Fourth, the Cold War and U.S. hegemony provided a safe and favorable economic climate for South Korea and Taiwan to develop authoritarian capitalism through export-oriented industrialization. Two wars in Asia since 1945 reinforced the authoritarian regime and promoted East Asian growth. Moreover South Korean and Taiwanese enterprises took advantage of the price competition market in the United States under the political and military alliance. The United States allowed market access with favorable conditions. Until the early 1980s the competitiveness of South Korean and Taiwanese goods came mainly from low wages and the scale of economy.

It is obvious that in the real world the state, politics, the economy, and class conflicts are in continuous interaction at various levels. Sometimes it is arbitrary to delineate and accentuate one part of the whole process. Thus, we need a holistic approach to capture the core dynamics of social change. How to do this is also a matter of debate. The assertion of a holistic approach does not itself guarantee the explanatory power of the argument. The more important imperative is to find a more comprehensive and at the same time parsimonious holistic model.

The approach presented in this chapter gives us a good reference for the discussion about the applicability of the East Asian economic model to other Third World countries following the Cold War. As do explanations for East Asian economic growth differ, policy implications or lessons from East Asia suggested by scholars also differ. For instance, Hughes (1990) and the World Bank (1993), among others, argue that the East Asian model can be replicated in other developing countries. They totally ignore the difference in the international situation between the 1960s and the 1990s. Due to the end of the Cold War and U.S. hegemony, the United States became more defensive in its economic policies. And all the prosperous countries are not fully recovered from an economic recession, and thus the cost of entry in to their market is much higher than before. In other words, it is very difficult for developing countries in the Third World to imitate the South Korean or Taiwanese export-oriented industrialization strategy.

Wade (1990: chap. 11) provides prescriptions different from those of Hughes and the World Bank, emphasizing the major characteristics in South Korea and Taiwan. His prescription is very specific, with an economic and political recipe. But he makes a mistake by ignoring the role of work organization and technology, that is, the microfoundation for economic growth. If all developing countries imitate the policies of the South Korean and Taiwanese governments, will they see steady and rapid economic growth as is the case in East Asia? This depends on other conditions such as repressive labor control and a quasi-command economy, which inevitably implies state as well as managerial dictatorship. More importantly, he underestimates the economic effect of the Cold War on the rise of East Asia.

We cannot easily infer a recipe for economic growth from the experience of the East Asian countries because many temporal or historical elements contributed to this growth. To fully explain the operation of the economy in East Asia, we need a new holistic approach within a comparative historical framework. The East Asian experience provides a theoretical challenge to the compartmentalized social science that hinders rather than promotes a proper understanding of the interconnectedness of politics and economy and local production and a global world system.

REFERENCES

Amsden, A. (1981). "Asia's Next Giant." Oxford: Oxford University Press.

Arrigo, L. C. (1985). Economic and political control of women workers in multinational electronics factories in Taiwan: Martial law coercion and world market uncertainty. *Contemporary Marxism* 11, 77–95.

Aseniero, G. (1994). South Korea and Taiwanese development: The transhistorical context. *Review* XVII, (3), 275–336.

Athukorala, P. (1993). Improving the contribution of migrant remittances to development: The experience of Asian labour-exporting countries. *International Migration,* 31, (1), 103–123.

Bayard, T. and Elliott, K. A. (1994). "Reciprocity and retaliation in U.S. trade policy for international economy." Washington: Institute for International Economy.

Bello, W., and Rosenfeld, S. (1990). "Dragons in Distress." San Francisco: The Institute for Food and Development Policy.

Berger, P. (1986). "The capitalist revolution: Fifty propositions about prosperity, equality and liberty." New York: Basic Books.

Bhagwati, J., and Patrick, H. T. (eds). (1990). "Aggressive unilateralism: America 301 trade policy and the world trading system." Ann Arbor: University of Michigan Press.

Birks, J. S., Seccombe, I. J., and Sinclair, C. A. (1988). Labour migration in the Arab Gulf states: Patterns, trends and prospects. *International Migration,* 26 (3), 269–285.

U.S. Bureau of Labor. (1990). "Hourly Compensation Costs for Production Workers in Manufacturing, 34 Countries: 1975 and 1979–1989."

Bowles, S., and Gintis, H. (1987). "Democracy and Capitalism." New York: Basic Books.

Braverman, H. (1974). "Labor and Monopoly Capital." New York: Monthly Review Press.

Buroway, M. (1985). "Politics of Production." London: Verso.

Chang, D. W. (1965). U.S. aid and economic progress in Taiwan. *Asian Survey,* V, (3), 152–160.

Centeno, M. A. (1994). Between rocky democracies and hard markets: Dilemmas of the double transition. *Annual Review of Sociology* 20, 123–147.

Chen, T. J., and Tang, D. (1990). Export performance and productivity growth: The case of Taiwan. *Economic Development and Cultural Change* 38 (3), 577–586.

Cho, E., Kang, J. K., and Shin, K. Y. (1992). Class structure in Korea. *Journal of Korean Sociology* (25), 27–52 [in Korean].

Cohen, J., and Rogers, J. (1980). "On Democracy." New York: Basic Books.

Cole, C. D., and Lyman, P. N. (1971). "Korean Development: The Interplay of Politics and Economics." Cambridge, MA: Harvard University Press.

Collier, D. (ed). (1979). "The New Authoritarianism in Latin America." Princeton, NJ: Princeton University Press.

Deyo, F. C. (ed.). (1987). "The Political Economy of the New Asian Industrialism." Ithaca, NY: Cornell University Press.

Deyo, F. C. (1989). "Beneath The Miracle." Berkeley: University of California Press.

Doner, R. F. (1992). Limits of state strength. *World Politics* 44 (3).

Doner, R. F. (1988). The Japanese political economy: A crisis in theory. *Ethics and International Affairs* 2, 79–97.

Dore, R. (1973). "British Factory, Japanese Factory." Berkeley: University of California Press.

Edwards, R. (1979). "Contested Terrain." New York: Basic Books.

Ellison, C., and Gareffi, G. (1990). Explaining strategies and patterns of industrial development, *in* "Manufacturing Miracles," (Gareffi, G., and D. Wynam, Eds.), pp. 368–403. Princeton, NJ: Princeton University Press.

Fong, P. E. (1992). Labor migration to the newly-industrialising economies of South Korea, Taiwan, Hong Kong and Singapore. *International Migration* 31, (2/3), 300–313.

Evans, P. (1989). Predatory, developmental, and other apparatus: A comparative political economy perspective on the Third World state. *Sociological Forum* 4, 561–587.

Evans, P. (1995). "Embedded Autonomy: States & Industrial Transformation." Princeton, NJ: Princeton University Press.

Freedman, R. (1977). "Industry and Labour." London: McMillan.

Gardezi, H. N. (1995). "The Political Economy of International Labour Migration." New York: Black Rose Books.

Gareffi, G., and Wyman, D. (1990). "Manufacturing Miracles." Princeton, NJ: Princeton University Press.

Gareffi. G. (1992). The international political economy and economic development, *in* "The Handbook of Economy Sociology" (N. Smelser and R. Swedberg, Eds.). Princeton, NJ: Princeton University Press.

Gold, T. (1986). "State and Society in the Taiwan Miracle." New York: M. E. Sharpe.

Green, A. (1992). South Korea's automobile industry. *Asian Survey* 32, (5), 411–428.

Haggard, S., and Pang, C.-K. (1994). The transition to export-led growth in Taiwan, *in* "The Role of the State in Taiwan's Development" (J. D. Aberbach *et al.,* Eds.). Armont: M. E. Sharpe.

Henderson, J. (1993). The role of the state in the economic transformation of East Asia, *in* "Economic and Societal Development," (C. Dixon and D. Drakakis-Smith, Eds.). London: Routledge.

Hersh, J. (1995). "The Impact of US Strategy: Making Southeast Asia Safe for Capitalism," unpublished paper.

Hersh, J. (1993). "The USA and the Rise of East Asia since 1945." London: St. Martin's Press.

Hirono, R. (1988). Japan: Model for East Asian industrialization? *in* "Achieving Industrialization in East Asia," (H. Hughes, Ed.). Cambridge: Cambridge University Press.

Ho, S. P. S. (1979). Decentralized Industrialization and Rural Development: Evidence from Taiwan," *Economic Development and Cultural Change* 28 (1), 77–96.

Ho, Y. (1980). The production structure of the manufacturing sector and its distribution implications: The case of Taiwan. *Economic Development and Cultural Change* 28 (2), 321–344.

Horthorn, R. E., and Wells, J. R. (1987). "De-Industrialization and Foreign Trade." Cambridge: Cambridge University Press.

Hughes, H. (Ed.) (1988). "Achieving Industrialization in East Asia." Cambridge: Cambridge University Press.

IMF. (1992). "International Financial Statistics: Yearbook." New York: IMF.

Jacob, F. (1989). "Western European Political Parties." London: Longman.

Johnson, C. (1982). "MITI and the Japanese Miracle." Stanford: Stanford University Press.

Johnson, C. (1987). Political institutions and economic performance: the government-business relationship in Japan, South Korea and Taiwan, in "The Political Economy of the New Asian Industrialism" (F. C. Devo, Ed.). Ithaca: Cornell University Press.

Jones, L. P., and Il, S. (1980). "Government, Business, and Entrepreneurship in Economic Development: The Korean Case." Cambridge, MA: Harvard University Press.

Kaufman, R. R., and Stallings, B. (1991). The political economy of Latin American populism, in "The Macroeconomic of Populism in Latin America" (R. Dornbush and S. Edwards, Eds.). New York: Johns Hopkins University Press.

Kirk, D. (1994). "Korean Dynasty, Hyundai and Chung Ju Yung." Armonk, NY: M. E. Sharpe.

Kornai, J. (1979). "Contradictions and Dilemmas: The Study of Socialist Economy and Society." Budapest: Corvina.

Kornai, J. (1986). The soft budget constrained. *Kyklos* 36.

Kornai, J. (1992). "Socialist System: Political Economy of Communism." Princeton, NJ: Princeton University Press.

Krueger, A. O., Lary, H. B., Monson, T., and Akrasanee, N. (Eds). (1981). "Trade and Employment in Developing Countries," Vol. 1, "Individual Studies." Chicago: University of Chicago Press.

Krueger, A. O. (1979). "The Developmental Role of the Foreign Sector and Aid." Council of East Asian Studies, Harvard University.

Krueger, A. O. (1990). "Perspectives on Trade and Development." New York: Harvester Wheatsheaf.

Krugman, P. (1994). The myth of Asia's miracle. *Foreign Affairs* 73 (6), 62–78.

Kwon, G. (1986). Capital utilization, economies of scale and technical change in the growth of total factor productivity. *Journal of Developmental Statistics* 24, 75–89.

Lee, S. (1994). "A History of Labor Movement in Hyundai Group." Seoul: Daeryuk [in Korean].

Lee, K. (1993). "New East Asian Economic Development." New York: M. E. Sharpe.

Lucas, R. E., Jr. (1993). Making a miracle. *Econometrica* 61 (2), 251–272.

Maddison, A. (1991). "Dynamic Forces in Capitalist Development: A Long-run Comparative View." Oxford: Oxford University Press.

Mann, M. (1986). "The Sources of Social Power," Vol. 1. Cambridge: Cambridge University Press.

Mann, M. (1988). "States, War and Capitalism." London: Blackwell.

Marshall, G., Rose, D., Newby, H., and Vogler, C. (1988). "Social Classes in Modern Britain." London: Unwin Hyman.

Marx, K. (1867) [1954]. "Capital," Vol. I. London: Lawrence and Wishart.

Morioka, K. (1989). "Japan," in "The Capitalist Class: An International Study." New York: Harvester Wheatsheaf.

Myrdal, G. (1968). "Asian Drama: An Inquiry into the Poverty of Nations." New York: Basic Books.

North, D. (1981). "The Structure and Change in Economic History." London: Norton and Co.

Ogle, G. E. (1990). "South Korea: Dissent within The Economic Miracle." London: Zed.

Ogle, G. (1995). Employee rights and industrial justice: Religious dimensions. *Bulletin of Comparative Labour Relations* 28, 19–27.

Ozawa, T. (1979). "Multinationalism, Japanese Style: The Political Economy of Outward Dependency." Princeton, NJ: Princeton University Press.

Przeworski, A. (1991). "Democracy and the Market: Political and Economic Reforms in Eastern Europe and Latin America." Cambridge: Cambridge University Press.

Roberts, K. M. (1995). "Neoliberalism and The Transformation of Populism in Latin America: The Peruvian Case." *World Politics*, Vol. 48, 82–116.

Shin, K.-Y. (1994). "Class and Politics of Production." Seoul: Nanam [in Korean].

Shin, K.-Y. (1995). The restructuring of East Asian system: The trade and foreign direct investment. *Currents and Prospects,* 179–205 [in Korean].

Stubbs, R. (1989). Geopolitics and the political economy of Southeast Asia. *International Journal* 44.

Stubbs, R. (1995). The political economy of the Asia-Pacific region, *in* "Political Economy and The Changing Global Order" (Stubbs, R. and Geoffrey, R. D., Eds.). Underhill, Toronto: McClelland & Stewart Inc.

Swedberg, R. (1994). "Market as Social Structures," *in* "Handbook of Economic Sociology" (Smelser, N. and Swedberg, R., Eds.). Princeton, NJ: Princeton University Press, 255–282.

United Nations. (1987). "International Labour Migration and Remittances between the Developing ESCAP Countries and the Middle East: Trends, Issues and Policies." Development Papers, No. 6.

United Nations. (1992). "World Investment Report." New York: UN.

Verdier, D. (1994). "Democracy and International Trade: Britain, France and the United States, 1860–1990." Princeton, NJ: Princeton University Press.

Vernon, R. (1971). "Sovereignty at Bay: The Multinational Spread of U.S. Enterprises." New York: Basic Books.

Wade, R. (1990). "Governing the Market: Economic Theory and the Role of Government in East Asian Industrialization." Princeton, NJ: Princeton University Press.

Wade, R. (1992). East Asia's economic success: Conflicting perspectives, partial insights, shaky evidence. *World Politics* 44, 270–320.

Wade, R. (1993). Managing the trade: Taiwan and South Korea as challenges to economics and political science. *Comparative Politics* 25 (2), 147–167.

Weiss, L., and Hobson, R. (1995). "States and Economic Developments: A Comparative Historical Analysis." London: Polity Press.

Wood, R. (1986). "Foreign Aid and Developmental Choice in the World Economy." Berkeley: University of California Press.

Wright, E. O. (1985). "Classes." London: Verso.

Yoo, J. H. (1985). Does Korea trade Japan's footsteps? A macroeconomic appraisal. *Kyklos* 38.

CHAPTER 2

Defining Security in East Asia:
History, Hotspots, and Horizon-Gazing

Victor D. Cha

Department of Government and School of Foreign Service
Georgetown University
Washington, District of Columbia 20057

I. INTRODUCTION

Economies operate within an overarching security environment, and in many ways their success is contingent on this environment. While the postwar economic growth of the four Asian Tigers was a function of successful export-oriented development strategies, strong state controls, and vibrant societal forces, one cannot discount the role played by the Cold War, and in particular, the West's underwriting of security costs such that prosperous economies could grow in Japan, South Korea, and Taiwan. In the future as well, the region's continued economic successes in part will be dependent on the degree to which regional powers can still concentrate resources on economic needs rather than on security threats. In a similar vein, future success will also be dependent on the degree to which past growth has created forces for interdependence that mitigate against interstate conflict. Any discussion of East Asian economic development therefore cannot ignore security factors.

As a result, this chapter provides an introduction to the question of security in Asia. It begins with a discussion of the security identity of East Asia from a historical perspective. It then examines the evolution and modification of Cold War bipolarity as the dominant security framework for the region in the post-1945 era. The second half of the chapter focuses on the impact of the post-Cold War era on East Asian security. It first explores how the demise of the Soviet threat eliminated,

The Four Asian Tigers: Economic Development and the Global Political Economy

changed, or left untouched certain traditional "hotspots" or security contingencies in the region. It also investigates the degree to which new issues of potential danger have arisen. The final section peers into the horizon of East Asian security and tries to lay out some of the crucial factors that will determine the likelihood of continued peace or new-found conflict in the region.

II. HISTORY: THE ORIGINS OF SECURITY IN EAST ASIA

When one thinks about Asian security from a historical perspective, a set of overarching themes or questions comes to mind: From when do we define Asia as a region of security? How have larger global security concerns impacted the region, or to what extent has the region been isolated from such forces? And finally, what factors indigenous to the region helped shape the security landscape?

An answer to the first of these questions requires a general definition of security. Security in international relations, in essence, is the protection and preservation of core values and sovereign rights. If one accepts this definition, then the origins of security might be traced to the start of the modern nation–state system with the Treaty of Westphalia in 1648. In this European context, states interacted with one another as relatively equal sovereign entities and security derived from balance of power dynamics among these states. In Asia, however, the identification of a security order predates the creation of the modern nation–state system in Europe; instead, it dates back to the Chinese regional empire. For more than 2000 years from 206 B.C. to 1911, the region's organization was based on a group of relatively autonomous states (Japan, Korea, Annam) that paid tribute to the Chinese authority. The ordering principle was Confucian, emphasizing harmony and hierarchy, and the region was "secure" in the sense that it remained insular and rejected foreign influences. Moreover, unlike Europe the predominant security dynamic in Asia was not balancing among relative equal states, but "bandwagoning" by groups of smaller states with the dominant Chinese power. This "clustering" of subjects around the core power reinforced Confucian notions of hierarchy and the empire system of international relations in Asia. By the mid-nineteenth century, however, this empire system began to break down not of its own accord but due to outside intervention. The Opium war (1839–1842) was particularly significant in this regard. Defeated in its attempt to fend off British pressures, the Chinese thereafter fell prey to a series of unequal treaties and the carving up of its domain by hungry Western imperialist powers. Piece by piece, the Chinese lost the building blocks of its empire, culminating in the defeat by Japan in 1894–1895 and the loss of Korea and Taiwan in the Treaty of Shimonoseki.

The developments of the nineteenth century highlight three dynamics that still remain relevant to Asian security today. The first is the issue of unsettled historical scores. Trepidations expressed today about China's post-Cold War hegemonic rise and its opaque intentions are implicitly or explicitly grounded in China's past victimization. As a Chinese official put it, "We've had a bad 150 years . . . but now we're back." This history, not only in China's case but also that of other powers in the region, is an important determinant of the relative contentment or discontentment with the status quo, and therefore an important determinant of stability in the region. A collection of historically exploited, discontented powers bode greater ill for peace than not. The second identifying security dynamic to emerge from this period is the notion of "Asia through the West." The definition of the Pacific Rim as a security region was largely a function of Western imperialism. The initial motive for Western penetration was largely commercial and cultural, the latter particularly in the form of missionary activity.[1] However, as economic stakes grew, competition for influence also grew, and the region became an arena for transplanted Western power rivalries. In this regard, policies such as the open door to China, and Western interventions in the Boxer rebellion (1900) and in Siberia (1918) were as much about checking rival powers' influence as they were about securing commercial and cultural interests. Finally, the developments of the nineteenth century raise the question of whether balancing or bandwagoning is the primary security dynamic in Asia. The European experience has shown that states have traditionally balanced against external threats, forming temporary alliance coalitions with the adversaries of the perceived threatening power. This "enemy-of-my-enemy is my friend" strategy thus led to the "checkerboard" pattern of relatively equal and autonomous powers that characterized Europe.[2] In addition, because of the Western experience, the belief has been that balancing leads to stability because non-status quo and revisionist powers are inherently prevented from dominating the system.[3] The experience of the Chinese empire, however, raises the question of whether bandwagoning, not balancing is the norm among states in East Asia; moreover, given the relative peace of the Chinese empire compared with Europe, it also raises the broader question of whether bandwagoning leads to greater stability than balancing. Assessments today about post-Cold War East Asian stability implicitly hinge on this yet-unanswered question of whether powers in Asia will oppose or join with states that seek to change the regional distribution of power.[4]

[1]For example, in the eighteenth and nineteenth centuries, U.S. trade with Asia constituted only a small percentage of its total external trade. At the same time, there was tremendous missionary zeal to bring Western civilization to Asia (Robert Sutter, "Peaceful Cooperation Between Asian Countries and the United States," in Young Jeh Kim, ed., *The New Pacific Community in the 1990s* [Armonk, NY: M.E. Sharpe, 1996], 52).

[2]Among the many works in this vein, see Kenneth Waltz, *Theory of International Politics* (NY: Addison-Wesley, 1979), chapters 6, 8.

[3]For the logic of this argument, see Stephen Walt, *The Origins of Alliances* (Ithaca: Cornell University Press, 1987), chapter 2, especially, pp. 27–28.

[4]This is an avenue of research in East Asian international relations that has yet to be explored. For initial suggestions in this vein, see Samuel Huntington, *The Clash of Civilizations and the Remaking of World Order* (NY: Simon and Schuster, 1996), 229–238. Huntington argues that historically Asia has

In the first half of the twentieth century, the Japanese drive for regional hegemony gave East Asian security a much sharper focus. Victories over China (1894–1895) and Russia (1904–1905), in conjunction with the destruction of the German, Italian, and French navies during World War I paved the path for Japan's arrival as a Great Power.[5] Yet as a latecomer to the imperialist game, its endeavors met with a Western opposition now enamored with Wilsonian principles of self-determination. The West's ambivalent acceptance of Japan's new status was manifest in the Washington conference treaties (1921–1922) that conceded to Japan a degree of naval primacy and influence in the region, albeit at ratios that maintained Western superiority.[6] Dissatisfaction with this arrangement, in conjunction with a number of domestic factors, propelled ultranationalist military leaders in Japan to expand the nation's domain into Manchuria (1931), and China (1937), ultimately leading to the Pacific War.

Japanese wartime actions and its drive for regional hegemony remain the primary source of continued suspicions and historical animosity among Japan's neighbors today. At the same time, these actions did play a significant role in the security identity of the region. While Japanese actions were undoubtedly aggressive, they also represented the first modern effort to define the region in non-Western colonial terms. The Greater East Asian Co-Prosperity Sphere sought to form an indigenously based, autarkic region that excluded Western influence. Japan's legitimation of this vision was of course self-serving, and motivated by its perceived unequal treatment by the West as a major power commensurate with its capabilities; nevertheless, it was with Japan's actions that East Asia's security was defined exclusive from, rather than derivative of, Western interests. In addition, regardless of the way one feels about Japanese wartime actions, these did impact Asian conceptions of nationalism and self-identity. While Western imperialism in Asia imparted notions of superiority, Japan's defeat of Russia in 1904, its supplanting of European colonists in Hong Kong, Singapore, Malaysia, Burma, Vietnam, Indonesia, and the Philippines, all couched in the rhetoric of racial equality, effectively shattered colonial myths of Occidental superiority. This did not mean that Asian

---

sought peace through hegemony and deference to the dominant power (p. 238). Moreover, this bandwagoning dynamic is fundamentally different from Europe: "A functioning balance of power that was typical of Europe historically was foreign to Asia. Until the arrival of the Western powers in the mid-nineteenth century, East Asian international relations were Sinocentric with other societies arranged in varying degrees of subordination to, cooperation with, or autonomy from Beijing. The Confucian ideal of world order was, of course, never fully realized in practice. Nonetheless, the Asian hierarchy of power model of international politics contrasts dramatically with the European balance of power model" (pp. 234–235).

[5]In terms of military capabilities, the destruction wrought on Europe by World War I effectively left Japan with the third largest navy behind Great Britain and the United States.

[6]The 5:5:3 ratios on ships and carriers set out in the 1922 Five-Power Treaty, and later 10:10:7 ratios at the London Naval Conference (1930) reflected Britain and America's continued maintenance of superior capabilities.

states embraced their new Japanese rulers, but it did mean that these nations were less willing to accept the return of the European powers after Japan's defeat in 1945.

A. The Cold War, Decolonization, and Containment

With the end of the Pacific War, Japan's drive for hegemony as the key dynamic of East Asian security was replaced by two new dynamics: the Cold War and decolonization. The former was again derivative of Western security concerns. In Europe, the origins of the Cold War were clearly marked by events such as the Truman doctrine, and the U.S. decision to aid Greece and Turkey. In Asia, however, things were not initially as clear-cut. For example, while the United States was proclaiming the Truman doctrine and Marshall Plan for Europe, it was relinquishing its occupation of Korea, and it lacked direction in the Chinese civil war. However, the 1949 Chinese Communist victory, the 1950 Sino-Soviet alliance, and the Korean war (1950–1953), brought the Cold War into clearer focus.

The Korean War was an especially significant watershed as many of the characteristics later associated with the Cold War in Asia followed directly from it. For example, it was as a result of Korea that the United States abandoned its ambiguous China policy and committed itself to the defense of Taiwan. The conflict reinforced Western perceptions of an expansionist communist monolith; in addition, China's decision to fight the Americans also allayed Stalin's suspicions about Mao's commitment, thereby solidifying Sino-Soviet ties (at least initially). The war also prompted SCAP authorities to reverse the course of the U.S. occupation in Japan, seeking to rebuild rather than emasculate the former enemy as a bulwark against communism in the region. Perhaps most important, the war led to the full extension of the policy of containment to Asia. It validated the views laid out in NSC-68 that the emerging conflict with the Soviet Union was one over ideology and a basic way of life that was not resolvable through compromise. And this prompted the massive increases in U.S. defense spending and the construction of a network of alliances in the region that one associates so closely with the Cold War in Asia.

East Asia was therefore fully integrated into the global Cold War dynamic; at the same time, however, indigenous forces also impacted the security landscape of the region. In particular, forces for nationalism and decolonization in the Southeast Asian subregion were both embedded in and clashed with the larger imperatives of the Cold War. This became evident in the immediate aftermath of the Japanese defeat. The abrupt liberation of the Southeast Asian states after the Allied victory over Japan posed a problem for postwar planners. On the one hand, recolonization under the European powers was the best way to retain control and shore up stability of the West in the budding competition with the Soviets. On the other, recolonization ran counter to indigenous nationalist sentiments that were no longer awed by the myth of European colonial superiority; moreover, it was hypocritical to the very core values of self-determination fought for in the war. And on a third hand, *de*colonization, in many cases, meant handing power to communist-inspired nationalist groups, a thought anathema to the Cold War mentality. This dilemma was managed in cases such as the Dutch East Indies and the Philippines.[7] However, it was in French Indochina that the countervailing forces of colonization, self-determination, and the Cold War directly clashed. French attempts at recolonization met with the fierce and broad-based resistance from the Vietminh, who eventually succeeded in ousting their former colonizers at Dien Bien Phu (1954).[8] The dilemma for the West at this point was clear. An independent and united Vietnam was desired; however, the French and American-supported regime in the South lacked the legitimacy of its northern counterparts (Eisenhower privately admitted that communist leader Ho Chi Minh was Vietnam's only true nationalist). As a result, the West supported the South's reneging on the 1956 national elections, the breakdown of the Geneva Agreement, and the renewal of hostilities that eventually led to America's deep and unsuccessful involvement in the conflict.

Vietnam was important in many different respects. It illustrated the limitations of a state's capacity to exert influence over others despite superior capabilities; it revealed American insecurities about having "lost China"; it also tore so fiercely at the social fabric of the United States that it would affect the basic way America viewed future ground troop commitments to contingencies around the world. In terms of East Asian security, however, a couple of additional points deserve mention. First, the debacle of Vietnam was symptomatic of the larger contradictions of containment in Asia. Again, the issue here is "Asia through the West." Containment was a strategy designed for Europe that was then superimposed on Asia. What fit the former also fit the latter, albeit much more imperfectly. In Europe, containment was at its most fundamental level, a battle between the forces of good and evil, a moral crusade for the ideals of self-determination, liberalism, and capitalism. There was a clear dividing line in Europe (both ideologically and geographically)

---

[7]In the Dutch East Indies case, the Japanese defeat left a well-trained Indonesian army and vigorous youth movement both strongly desirous of independence. As a result, when British and Dutch forces returned in October 1945 to reclaim the colony, they met with fierce resistance. Western powers soon came to the realization that suppressing this resistance might push nationalist sentiment to associate independence with being anti-West, thereby elevating the not insignificant communist forces to power (i.e., Tan Malaka). For this reason, the United States persuaded the Dutch to abandon their colonial ambitions and support Indonesian independence under non-communist nationalists (i.e., Sukarno and Hatta) in 1948. Similarly, in the Philippine case, the United States managed the Cold War/recolonization dilemma by backing independence under former collaborators with the Japanese while suppressing the procommunist and nationalist Hukbalahap.

[8]Following the battle of Dien Bien Phu, the ensuing Geneva Agreement provisionally partitioned Vietnam at the 17th parallel with nationwide elections scheduled for 1956 to unify the country.

between right and wrong. The problem in Asia was that things were not as clearly delineated. Rather than dichotomies of black and white, there were numerous shades of gray. This was evident, for example, in the decolonization dilemmas faced in Southeast Asia where forces for self-determination and independence often intermingled with forces for communism. Similar contradictions existed in Northeast Asia. As alluded to above, containment was not solely about guarding against communist expansionism, it was also about the preservation and promotion of liberal-democratic ideals. In Northeast Asia however, the latter objective was often sacrificed for the former in states like South Korea, Taiwan, Philippines, and to some extent, Japan. It is of course easy to criticize with hindsight. The security imperatives and perceptions of the moment did not allow for anything but stark black and white distinctions. Nevertheless, the point still remains that because East Asian security was seen through the West, European-based containment was a doctrine that did not allow for greater subtleties and discrimination of Asian conditions.

Second, Vietnam was a watershed in East Asian security in that it revealed Western security motives in the area. East Asia in these early Cold War years was an arena of security competition valued for *strategic* rather than *intrinsic* reasons. Regarding the latter, states protect or value something intrinsically because of its substantive worth to one's well-being (e.g., in terms of land, resources, power accretion, etc.). When states value something strategically, they are less interested in its intrinsic worth (i.e., what it offers in terms of power accretion), and more interested in the value gained from keeping it out of the adversary's hands. The primary manifestation of this type of strategic thinking in Asia was the domino theory. The U.S. decision to fight in remote and intrinsically not valuable places like Vietnam (and Korea) was because these were considered strategically valuable to keep out of the communist camp.[9] If one fell to communism, the belief was that the others would do so as well. Dominoes and the strategic motivations for security competition in the region were therefore inextricably intertwined.

B. LOOSE BIPOLARITY AND THE SINO-SOVIET SPLIT

Another manifestation of the imperfect fit of European containment in East Asia was the different security architectures that emerged in the two regions. In Western Europe, security revolved around the collective organization of NATO; in Asia, however, containment took the form of a series of bilateral alliances centered around the United States. The original intention was to construct something similar to NATO,[10] and while this met with some short-lived success in the Southeast

[9]By contrast, the French valued Vietnam for much more intrinsic reasons as a colony (in terms of rice, rubber, etc.), while Cold War imperatives heightened the strategic value for the United States.
[10]In fact, such aspirations were made clear in the preambles of U.S. defense treaties with a number of powers in the region (e.g., ROK, Philippines).

Asian subregion (i.e., SEATO in 1955), the vision of a collective security body in Asia was never fulfilled, especially in the Northeast Asian subregion. As a result, although the Cold War bipolar conflict dominated both Asia and Europe, in the former it was a much "looser" form of bipolarity. The region's security was not organized into a tight, coherent NATO versus Warsaw Pact-type configuration, but was based on what James Baker once described as a more nebulous "hub and spokes" arrangement of bilateral defense commitments radiating out from the United States, with only vague connections between them. Several factors accounted for this difference. Geographically, Europe was a contiguous land theater with a clear line of demarcation between the two sides. This lent itself more easily to tighter bipolarity than did Asia, a predominantly maritime theater with more nebulous geographical lines of distinction. Economically, Asia on the whole was less developed than its European counterparts. This lessened the need among states for multilaterally organizing (e.g., for intraregional trade purposes), and instead focused attention on aid and trade solely with the U.S. benefactor. As noted above, the newly liberated states in postwar Asia were also not enamored with the idea of subjecting this new-found sovereignty to the constraints and obligations imposed by a regional organization; instead, many of the newly liberated colonies chose not to side with either pole and opted instead for neutrality. Although this existed in Europe as well (e.g., Sweden, Switzerland, and Austria), the Non-Aligned Movement (NAM) in Asia was more widespread, naturally clouding the region's bipolarity. In addition, cultural factors were important. An equivalent to a common "European" identity that underlay NATO and the European Community was conspicuously absent in Asia. As one scholar noted, the extent of Asian diversity is best appreciated when one considers that Europe would have to be stretched to the Middle East and down to Northern Africa to replicate the religions, races, and cultures found in Asia.[11] However, perhaps the most proximate causes of loose bipolarity have to do with the diffuseness of threats and the power distribution in the region. Regarding the former, in Europe there was a single identifiable threat that all agreed on. In Asia, however, threat perceptions were more varied and a consensus was much less evident. In good part, this stemmed from suspicions and animosities toward Japan. For example, while the South Koreans may have seen North Korea and the Soviet Union as the Cold War threat, they also remained averse to cooperation with Japan. Second, and perhaps most important, the power distribution in Asia was complicated by the existence of a third major power not evident in Europe, namely China. Here was a state that did not fall neatly into one of the two blocs, and in fact, shifted its alignments on a number of occasions, the most significant being Beijing's breakoff from the communist monolith in the 1960s.

---

[11] Aaron Friedberg, "Ripe for Rivalry: Prospects for Peace in a Multipolar Asia," *International Security* 18.3 (Winter 1993/94), 24.

The Sino-Soviet split was essentially a breakup over power and interests couched in terms of ideology. Until the border clashes at Damansky Island and on the Sinkiang border in 1969, dissension within the monolith was largely expressed in ideological terms, as this was the primary means by which legitimacy was claimed in the communist cause. Khrushchev's de-Stalinization campaign (introduced in the 1956 Twentieth Party Congress), his calls for peaceful coexistence with the West, and his emphasis on achievement of socialist goals through gradualist means drew criticisms from Mao as antithetical to Marxist-Leninism and as "social imperialism." The Soviets, on the other hand, denounced Beijing's continued advocacy of violent revolution and wars of liberation as "fanatic dogmatism." This rhetorical war reached a climax at the 1960 World Communist conference in Moscow.[12] But behind this rhetoric was a basic dispute over power and interests. For the Soviets, concerns mounted that China was attempting to consolidate its leadership of an Asian and African communist front. For this reason, Moscow harshly condemned programs like the Great Leap Forward, and celebrated its failure as proof that the Chinese brand of communism was not viable.[13] From the Chinese perspective, the split stemmed from Moscow's efforts at preventing China from attaining great power status. Soviet reneging on the promise of nuclear technology in 1960 and its support of the 1963 Test Ban treaty all signaled to Beijing tacit collusion between the superpowers to prevent China from entering the elite nuclear circle. The Brezhnev doctrine and the invasion of Czechoslovakia in 1968 drove home Chinese concerns about the extent to which Moscow would go to punish dissenting regimes.

C. Détente

A key effect of the end of the communist monolith on East Asian security was that it transformed the loose bipolarity of the Cold War years into a tripolar arrangement. The product of this new triangular dynamic was détente. It is important to remember that détente was not the result of some new-found affinity among the United States, China and Soviet Union; instead, it was the product of basic balance of power calculations arising out of new geostrategic conditions. In particular, Nixon and Kissinger saw a unique opportunity for the United States to occupy the pivot position between the two feuding communist powers. They accomplished this in rather dramatic form with the PRC with Nixon's surprise July

---

[12]Key events preceding the 1960 conference that made the dispute more public were Moscow's reneging on the promise of nuclear technology to Beijing in 1959, and the withdrawal of thousands of technical advisors in 1960.

[13]The Soviets also sought to distance themselves from China's revolutionary rhetoric to avoid entrapment into a confrontation with the United States.

1971 announcement of his intention to visit Beijing, followed by the February 1972 Shanghai communique.[14] The latter ended decades of nondialogue and animosity since the Korean war, and pledged both sides to peaceful coexistence. A few months after the China announcement, Nixon disclosed his intention to visit Moscow. The ensuing May 1972 Nixon–Brezhnev summit was the first of an unprecedented four summits over the next 2 years, in which the two leaders also established principles of peaceful coexistence, agreements on MFN and grain credits, as well as the first major arms limitation accords (SALT I). From the American perspective, then, détente was a calculated balancing exercise that enhanced U.S. security by making it the object of courting by two Cold War adversaries.

Calculations in Moscow and Beijing were also based on balance of power criteria but with slightly different twists. Both were certainly motivated by desires to avoid a great power condominium directed against it involving the United States, but China's most immediate incentive for American rapprochement was Soviet aggression in Czechoslovakia (1968) and on the Sino-Soviet border (1969). These events made Moscow the most proximate threat to Chinese security interests. Enjoying strategic parity with the United States, the Soviets were less worried that China would replace the Soviets as the power the United States took most seriously. As Brezhnev once said about the Shanghai communique, Nixon may go to Beijing for banquets but he comes to Moscow to do business.[15] Instead, the appeal to the United States was as a fellow superpower to help contain China and its revolutionary rhetoric.

To what extent did détente stabilize regional security? On the one hand, Sino-American rapprochement and Soviet-American détente bridged Cold War divides (albeit temporarily) previously believed unbridgeable, and committed the major powers to the status quo. In addition, as Assistant Secretary for Asia and Pacific Affairs Marshall Green once stated, détente resulted in a "discernible escalation toward peace in Asia" as it set off a series of unprecedented diplomatic initiatives in the region.[16] In particular, following the U.S. lead, Japan sought to fulfill long-held desires to improve relations with China, resulting in the Tanaka-Zhou September 1972 summit and the normalization of Beijing–Tokyo relations. During the period, Japan also held talks with the Soviet Union on issues such as Siberian investment, the Northern territories dispute, and a peace treaty, marking the most substantive

[14]Nixon's announcement was preceded by a number of secret overtures and communications between Kissinger and Zhou Enlai. These culminated in Kissinger's trip to Pakistan in July 1971, during which he secretly met with Zhou in Beijing to finalize the agreement on Nixon's visit (see Henry Kissinger, *White House Years* [NY: Little, Brown and Co., 1979], 723, 781–782).

[15]Cited in Michael Yahuda, *The International Relations and Politics of the Asia-Pacific, 1945–1994* (London: Routledge, 1996), 78.

[16]Testimony of Marshall Green in House of Representatives, Committee on Foreign Affairs, *The New China Policy: Its Impact on the United States and Asia: Hearings Before the Subcommittee on Asian and Pacific Affairs* 92nd Cong., 2nd sess. (Washington: GPO, 1972), 27.

dialogue between Tokyo and Moscow since the mid-1960s. Major power détente also spurred a relaxation of tensions on the Korean peninsula. Emulating Kissinger, representatives of the two Koreas announced a surprise joint communique in 1972 pledging both sides to peaceful unification and tension-reduction measures. Détente also enhanced regional stability by effectively localizing the conflict in Vietnam. At one end of the escalation spectrum, it reduced U.S. concerns that the conflict would spiral into a direct major power confrontation (especially with regard to U.S. bombing near the Chinese border). At the other end, it also mollified concerns that a U.S. withdrawal from the region would leave a destabilizing power vacuum. Finally, détente enhanced stability by providing benefits to the most dissatisfied power in the region, China. In dramatic fashion, the combination of détente and the Sino-Soviet split transformed China from a nemesis of the Western world to a partner. Beijing opened relations with a number of powers in the region (the United States, Japan, Malaysia, Philippines, Thailand); moreover, in the zero-sum game of politics with Taiwan, it scored major victories in getting many of these new partners to abrogate relations with Taipei, admit that Taiwan was a part of China (at least in rhetoric), and support Beijing's successful bid to replace its nemesis in the UN.

While détente engendered a number of positive trends for East Asian stability, it also set off some dynamics that were not in the best interests of stability. First, détente raised a great deal of suspicion and concern among Western alliance partners in Northeast Asia about great power condominiums. U.S. initiatives for détente also coincided with professed American desires to reduce defense commitments to the region. Nixon's 1969 "Asia for Asians" doctrine, for example, stated that the United States would no longer bear the primary burden of defense for its Asian allies. Policy manifestations of this doctrine were the massive drawdown of U.S. ground troops in Vietnam from 1969 through 1971, and the withdrawal of one division from Korea (1970–1971). Coupled with this, the manner in which the United States carried out the China opening, without prior consultation of its allies, undercut trust in the United States as a reliable patron. These actions raised deep anxieties among U.S. allies that Sino-American rapprochement symbolized China's emergence as the new U.S. partner in Asia.[16a] Second, détente had the unintended consequence of intensifying Sino-Soviet antagonism. For example, some scholars argue that Sino-Japanese normalization in conjunction with the American rapprochement raised encirclement fears in Moscow and compelled them to take actions such as building up forces on the Sino-Soviet border; encouraging Vietnam to invade Cambodia; and invading Afghanistan. Similarly, while détente offered benefits that pacified China, the argument could be made that détente was also destabilizing in the sense that it effectively gave security assurances to a non-status

[16a]See Victor Cha, *Alignment Despite Antagonism: The United States-Korea-Japan Security Triangle* (Stanford: Stanford University Press, forthcoming), Chaps. 3 & 4.

quo power to act on its ambitions. Normalization with Japan and rapprochement with the United States enabled Beijing to direct all of its attention to the Soviet and Vietnamese threats. For this reason, China took the Paracel Islands in 1974; attacked Vietnam in 1979; and built up forces on the Sino-Soviet border. In sum, détente was not engendered by altruism but by power politics; and contrary to the conventional wisdom, it had both stabilizing and destabilizing effects on East Asian security.

D. Bipolarity's Return: The New Cold War

Toward the end of the 1970s and through the 1980s, the key security dynamic in the region was a renewal of Cold War tensions. The demise of détente was reflected in several developments. After the initial euphoria of Sino-American rapprochement faded, growing disillusionment and realization of the limits of this new relationship set in. Despite the Shanghai communique, normalization of U.S.–China relations came in 1979, a whole 7 years later. This was largely a function of friction over Taiwan, and in particular U.S. refusal to abandon its Cold War ally completely, particularly after the demoralizing outcome in Vietnam in 1975. Disillusionment with détente was also evident on the Korean peninsula. Despite the breakthrough communique in 1972, meetings of the NSCC (North-South Coordinating Committee) quickly deteriorated into Cold War recrimination sessions; moreover, a series of North Korean provocations during the period (including an assassination attempt on the ROK president and the discovery of northern infiltration tunnels under the DMZ) made clear that peaceful coexistence was far from workable. The demise of détente was also a function of a perceived decline in U.S. power in the latter half of the 1970s. The fall of Saigon in 1975, Carter's plan for the complete withdrawal of U.S. forces from the Korean peninsula, economic difficulties as a result of the two oil shocks, and general post-Vietnam disdain at American overextension signaled to Soviet planners a significant trend toward U.S. disengagement from defense commitments abroad. Soviet attempts to capitalize on this relative decline in U.S. power took the form of Cuban-backed actions in Angola (1975), support of anti-West forces in the Middle East (Yom Kippur War, 1973) and Nicaragua, and the invasion of Afghanistan in 1979. Furthermore, in East Asia, by the late-1970s, Moscow had deployed its most advanced weaponry in the Russian Far East and on the Sea of Japan (e.g., SS-20s and backfire bombers), substantially expanded the Pacific Fleet, obtained long-sought warm water ports from Vietnam at Cam Ranh and Da Nang, and introduced forces in the Northern Kuriles proximate to Japan. Any aspirations for continued superpower détente were deflated by these developments and replaced by a renewal of the Cold War standoff in Asia.

The election of Ronald Reagan in 1981 ushered in a sea change in U.S. foreign policy, and with it, a change in regional security dynamics. For Reagan, the pursuit of cooperative resolutions to superpower disputes was still the objective; however, the means of achieving this required change.[17] The Soviet Union was no longer a misunderstood adversary that could be coaxed into mutual accommodation, but an inherently "evil" empire best deterred by an overwhelming and unchallengeable deportment of U.S. power.[18] These "peace though strength" policies sought to reclaim American leadership and confidence through a massive arms buildup and the reaffirmation of security commitments to traditional allies.[19] Containment and deterrence were still the cornerstones of defense doctrine; however, these were based not on notions of parity but on superiority. The Reagan braintrust pressed for weapons programs such as the MX and Trident II missiles and the Strategic Defense Initiative, and held off on arms control dialogue like INF and START. These policies reflected the belief that a strategic counterforce doctrine and offensive conventional force capabilities would provide the United States with the escalation dominance at all levels of warfare necessary to deter the Soviets.[20]

Reagan's policies impacted the East Asian security landscape in two ways. First, it took the region from tripolarity of the 1970s back firmly to bipolarity. The primary difference between the bipolar structure of the early Cold War years and that of the "new" Cold War was that in the former case, the Soviet threat had been refracted through China or Vietnam. Under the "new" Cold War conditions, threat perceptions now squarely focused on the Soviet Union. Second, the means by which the United States met the Soviet challenge had implications for the strategic importance of China. In general, states can deal with threats through one of two means. They can internally balance against the threat (i.e., through the buildup of defense capabilities), or they can externally balance (i.e., seek out new allies or reinforce existing alignments as a means of power accretion). While Reagan did reaffirm and strengthen security relationships with East Asian allies, the primary means by which he met the Soviet challenge was through internal balancing (i.e., arms buildups) that preserved across-the-board superiority at every level of escalation.

---

[17]This reversal in U.S. policy actually began in the latter years of the Carter presidency, in particular after the overthrow of the Shah in Iran (January 1979) and the Soviet invasion of Afghanistan (December 1979). However, it was with the Reagan presidency that this new policy thrust was sustained, expanded, and explicitly stated.

[18]For the speech in which Reagan introduced this often-cited vision of the Soviets, see *Weekly Compilation of Presidential Documents* (March 14, 1983), also Raymond L. Garthoff, *Détente and Confrontation: American-Soviet Relations from Nixon to Reagan* (Washington, DC: Brookings Institution, 1985), 1015.

[19]For example, during Reagan's first term, defense spending increased in real terms by 32% from $199 billion to $264 billion. This constituted an unprecedented peacetime increase from 5.2% to 6.6% of total GNP.

[20]For analysis and critique of this doctrine, see Barry Posen and Stephen Van Evera, "Reagan Administration Defense Policy: Departure from Containment," in Kenneth Oye, Robert Lieber, Donald Rothchild, Eds. *Eagle Resurgent? The Reagan Era in American Foreign Policy* (Boston: Little, Brown & Company, 1987), 75-115; and Michael Smith, "The Reagan Presidency and Foreign Policy," in Joseph Hogan, Ed., *The Reagan Years: The Record in Presidential Leadership* (Manchester: Manchester University Press, 1990), 259–285.

What this meant was that the strategic importance of China to the East Asian balance decreased markedly. By comparison, Nixon and Kissinger's policies valued China to a much greater degree because they sought both to decrease the U.S. presence in the region and maintain security through new external alignments. Thus, while Kissinger sought to do "more with less," Reagan sought to do "more with more." The emphasis on internal power accretion to balance the Soviets in Asia therefore reduced the need for China.

The bipolar security structure of the new Cold War in Asia remained intact through the 1980s until the Soviet demise. One minor variation that would have consequences for the post-Cold War was Gorbachev's initiation of a reconciliation with its long-feuding Chinese neighbor in 1989. This was largely the result of Gorbachev's economic reform programs and in particular, the desire to reduce the financial strains that security tensions with Beijing were placing on the Soviet economy. In the 1986 Vladivostok speech, the Soviet leader announced his acceptance of China's three preconditions for a resumption of dialogue.[21] Although overshadowed by the events in Tiananmen Square, Gorbachev's Beijing summit marked the end of the long-standing estrangement. The years immediately preceding the Soviet collapse also saw the start of gradual transformation in Soviet perceptions of East Asian security. Again motivated by pressing economic reform needs, Gorbachev viewed the region less in traditional Cold War ideological terms and more in terms of economic opportunities. Soviet reformers sought to tap into the economic benefits of a booming Asia by reducing regional perceptions of the U.S.S.R. as a brooding security threat. In line with these policies, confidence-building measures included the removal of SS-20s from the region in 1988 (INF agreement); and Gorbachev's Krasnoyarsk speech of the same year expressing Moscow's desire to improve relations with noncommunist powers. The combination of Soviet economic need and South Korea's nordpolitik initiatives led to a watershed crossing of the Cold War divide in the normalization of Seoul–Moscow relations in 1990. This would be followed in 1992 by China's normalization of relations with the ROK. These agreements in combination with the end of the Cold War rendered obsolete the bipolar structure of security in East Asia.

III. HOTSPOTS: POST-COLD WAR SECURITY TIERS IN EAST ASIA

How does one begin to fathom the ways in which the collapse of the Soviet Union has impacted East Asian security? One convenient analytical construct looks at this question in terms of the changes in traditional thinking about "hotspots" or security theaters engendered by the post-Cold War. As Morley has argued, the Cold War saw basically four primary theaters of concern: (1) the Sea of Okhotsk;

---

[21]These were: (1) Soviet troop drawdowns on the Chinese border; (2) withdrawal of support for the Vietnamese occupation of Cambodia; and (3) withdrawal from Afghanistan.

(2) the Korean peninsula; (3) the Taiwan Straits; and (4) the Sino-Soviet border.[22] The Soviet demise effectively reduced the salience of two of these as "first tier" potentialities of instability. The Sea of Okhotsk, for example, was home to the Soviet Pacific fleet; it was also key to the Cold War strategic balance as the region housed 30% of Soviet submarine-launched ballistic missile deployments (and therefore was critical in terms of second strike capabilities). With the end of the Cold War, however, the primary issue in this theater is the Northern territories. While the disputed sovereignty of these islands remains salient, the likelihood of armed conflict over this issue per se is low (discussed below). Similarly, while the post-Cold War has certainly not rendered Russian-Chinese border disputes obsolete, tension reductions as a result of the 1989 rapprochement and military drawdowns on the border have certainly defused this issue compared with the tension-filled 1970s.

Two theaters in which the post-Cold War has made less of a difference, however, are the Korean peninsula and Taiwan straits. The former remains the primary regional contingency in East Asia, and presents a varied set of problems. Although the post-Cold War did see some improvement in North–South Korean relations in 1991, the two regimes remain locked in one of the world's most heavily militarized standoffs, without a peace treaty, and steeped in zero-sum attitudes that are averse to conciliatory dialogue. This situation is exacerbated by the North's potential nuclear weapons program, support of terrorism, and cruise and ballistic missiles program. In addition, the issue of unification, both in terms of the process (i.e., hard or soft landing) and outcome, weigh heavily in the future balance of power in the region. A less immediate but potentially more consequential "first-tier" theater in terms of an actual outbreak of conflict is the Taiwan straits. The dispute over "one China" or "one China, one Taiwan" outlives the Cold War. Although the status quo has held for decades, there are two cross-cutting forces that weigh in the outcome. On the side of instability is a Chinese bid to retake the island as a result of increasing power capabilities and/or domestic-political developments in Taiwan that lead Taipei to an assertion of de jure independence. On the side of the status quo, however, are the growing trade and investment links being established between the two economies that help mitigate against conflict. In the present, another factor mitigating against conflict is China's operational limitations in carrying out a full-fledged military operation to absorb the island.

A. THE SECOND TIER

In addition to this first tier of security challenges, the post-Cold War has made salient a second tier.[23] Some of the issues in this category are new; others

---

[22] James Morley, Ed., *Security Interdependence in the Asia-Pacific* (Lexington: DC Heath, 1986), 4–26.

[23] For a similar although more basic categorization of Korea, Taiwan, and the South China Sea contingencies, see Robert Manning, "Security in East Asia," in William Carpenter and David Wiencek, *Asian Security Handbook* (Armonk, NY: M.E. Sharpe, 1996). Manning however does not term these "tiers," nor does he delve into the third tier of nontraditional security factors (discussed below).

have always existed but remained submerged in the currents of the Cold War. A new development in the former vein is arms acquisitions. Contrary to global trends, East Asia is arming itself at an accelerated pace. While defense expenditures among NATO and former Warsaw Pact countries have declined by 20% over the past decade, those of East Asia have increased by 25%. The region now generates about 34% of the global demand for weapons systems; in addition, of the top 15 conventional arms importers, 7 are from the Asia-Pacific region.

This arms buildup exhibits two basic characteristics. The first is the emphasis on *technology* and *autonomy*. In the past, East Asian powers built their militaries through the importation of finished weapons and the development of weapons maintenance and spare parts facilities largely with equipment and training from the exporting country. In the post-Cold War, the focus has shifted to acquiring key weapons components, defense technologies, and licensing agreements. This reflects a new-found desire in the region for more self-sufficient and indigenously produced militaries in all but the most advanced weapons, intelligence-gathering, and communications systems. The second characteristic is modernization. East Asian powers are replacing old systems with new ones; but more important, in the process of modernizing, they are also reconfiguring militaries for the capacity to *project power.* While the force structures of most East Asian militaries during the Cold War were designed for local ground conflicts and counterinsurgencies, they are increasingly being retooled for regional contingencies. This penchant for force projection is most clearly reflected in the aspirations of several powers in the region for blue-water navy capabilities. For example, Taiwan and South Korea are in the midst of naval buildup programs, the latter with an emphasis on submarine capabilities. Japanese plans include the purchase of new submarines, destroyers, and long-range tanker transports ship. China has expressed strong interests in purchasing an aircraft carrier, and has already acquired Russian in-flight refueling technology and long-range aircraft (e.g., Backfire bomber, SU-27, Mig-31). These trends reflect East Asia's increased interest in militaries as instruments for exerting influence rather than merely for local defense.

East Asian arms behavior stems from the region's unique combination of wealth, insecurity, and lack of controls. High rates of economic growth have given rise to a set of states with the resources to spend on new weapons systems. These weapons are seen as necessary to hedge against potential threats in the region, particularly if there is a reduction in the U.S. security presence (discussed below). Of not insignificant importance, these systems are also symbols of prestige in the regional status hierarchy. Economic factors also motivate the increased interest in indigenous defense capabilities as potential dual-use and spin-off technologies can further fuel economic growth and industrial innovation. This situation is exacerbated by supply-side factors as well. The cash-strapped former Soviet republics have been the source of a new, cheap supply of weapons and technicians. In addition, the competitive pressures of an increasingly bear global arms market in the post-

Cold War have caused many defense industries to sell cutting-edge technologies and systems at bargain-basement prices. Finally, the absence of regionwide arms control regimes adds to the unencumbered nature of the buildup.

Although the arms buildup in East Asia is a cause for concern, it is a second-tier issue because the likelihood of a destabilizing arms race is still not apparent. One must be careful not to characterize the current activities in the region as a "race" for supremacy. The dynamics behind the buildup do not resemble an arms race in the sense of states matching one another system for system, and depleting their budgets to do so (i.e., the implication being that cash-strapped states may be tempted to undertake preventive strikes when they hold a temporary lead over a rival). At the same time, however, these buildups are not occurring in a vacuum, and states are certainly acquiring arms with a suspicious eye toward their neighbors. As a result, what we see in the region is neither a bonafide race nor self-contained purchases, but a *latent competition* in acquisitions that has the potential to escalate into a race.[24]

One aspect of the arms issue in Asia of more immediate first-tier concern is missile proliferation. In particular, the growth of missile arsenals, particularly among rogue states like North Korea, pose destabilizing concerns for the region. The North has indigenous production capabilities in both cruise and ballistic missiles. While current designs of the Scud B and C only have short-range capabilities (300–500 km), the North has tested newer programs (No-dong 1 and 2) capable of targeting Japanese cities (1000–1500 km), and has plans for systems (Taepo-dong 1 and 2) that would reach Guam, Hawaii, and Alaska. Moreover, should the North in the future seek to resume its nuclear weapons program, the mating of these two programs would, in theory, provide the delivery capabilities for such weapons. The consequence of this scenario would almost certainly be an accelerated push up the arms ladder by North Korea's neighbors (e.g., South Korea, Japan), potentially leading to nuclearization of the region.

Another second-tier issue relates to the South China Sea and the Spratly Islands. Composed of hundreds of islets, reefs, rocks, sandbars, and underwater features, the Spratlys are the object of sovereignty disputes among a number of powers in the region including China, Vietnam, Taiwan, Malaysia, Philippines, and Brunei. While claims to the islands are couched in the rhetoric of nationalism, the primary driver of behavior is the resources (e.g., fish, water, seabed minerals) and in particular, the potential oil deposits in the region (some have estimated a capacity greater than that of Great Britain in the North Sea). Control of the area also provides access to key sealanes (e.g., the Malacca Straits) for defense as well as commercial purposes.

Settlement of these disputed claims by international law does not appear likely. Logistically, the drawing of water boundaries in the area is extremely complicated;

---

[24]For a debate on arms races versus arms acquisitions in the region, see Michael Klare, "The Next Great Arms Race," *Foreign Affairs* 72.3 (Summer 1993); and Desmond Ball, "Arms and Affluence: Military Acquisitions in the Asia-Pacific Region," *International Security* 18.3 (Winter 1993/4).

moreover, even if this feat could be accomplished, many of the protagonists (particularly, China and Vietnam) oppose a legal settlement as this would effectively undermine many of their claims. As a result, the issue has settled on an uneasy consensus to suspend sovereignty issues in the interim and focus on joint resource development. Nevertheless, the primary concern among the protagonists is Chinese intentions. Beijing's past interaction with others over the islands has been punctuated by a series of conflicts. These included naval clashes with Vietnam on three separate occasions (1974, 1988, 1994); and the contracting of oil expeditions in areas not claimed by China (e.g., Crestone's expeditions in areas claimed by Vietnam). Beijing's 1992 enactment of a law laying claim to the entire region shows an ominous ambition to dominate. Moreover, its recent seizure of Mischief Reef in 1995 (claimed by the Philippines) and its claims to Natuna (in dispute with Indonesia) have amplified these concerns.

Although the South China Sea has received a great deal of attention, this is a second-tier security issue because certain factors mitigate against an outbreak of hostilities in the near term. First, the oil potential in the region has not yet been fulfilled. With the exception of modest findings by the Philippines, expeditions by various powers have not yielded much success.[25] Until such findings are made, interaction over the islands will be limited to minor disputes such as the building of weather stations on already-occupied islands rather than open conflicts over attempts to change the status quo. Second, the gap between the current military capabilities of the protagonists and the nature of a conflict in the region mitigates against near-term instability (although as noted above, this gap is closing). Sustained fighting in the region requires force projection capabilities that many of the protagonists do not yet possess. For example, many of the reefs and islands in the South China Sea are beyond the range of bombers; they are also incapable of supporting airstrips/bases long enough for military aircraft; and none of the protagonists have acquired aircraft carriers or in-flight refueling technology (with the recent exception of China regarding the latter). Finally, in spite of certain aggressive actions in the past, Chinese intentions, until oil is found, appear to focus on preserving a right to claims in the future rather than immediate domination, yet at the same time, utilizing the issue as the rationale for development of blue water naval capabilities.

In a similar vein as the South China Sea, numerous other territorial disputes in the region fall within the second tier of security concerns. The most prominent of these are the Northern territories (southern Kuriles), the Sino-Japanese dispute over the Senkaku (Diaoyu) islands, and the Japanese–South Korean dispute over Tokdo (Takeshima) islets.[26] Although each of these disputes are historically based,

---

[25]In addition, the geography of the region shows that oil deposits, if found, will be extremely difficult to excavate. See United States Institute of Peace, *The South China Sea Dispute: Prospects for Preventive Diplomacy, Special Report of the United States Institute of Peace* (August 1996).

[26]The Senkaku/Diaoyu are seven islands north of Taiwan in the East China Sea. Although the sovereignty dispute dates back to the 1895 Sino-Japanese war and Treaty of Shimonoseki, the more im-

they stem more immediately from ambiguities regarding the postwar settlement with defeated Japan in 1945. All are important symbols of nationalism and potential sources of conflict now that overarching Cold War imperatives are gone. For example, Japanese–Korean quarrels over Tokdo/ Takeshima in the spring 1996 led to ROK naval patrols around the islets and the near-canceling of a scheduled summit meeting between the two countries' leaders. In 1992, Tokyo protested China's sovereign claim over the Senkaku/Diaoyu in its territorial sea law, and in 1996, the two governments clashed on several occasions over Chinese attempts to land on the islands occupied by Japanese.

Like the South China Sea, territorial claims remain as secondary causes of instability in post-Cold War East Asia. In spite of the nationalist sentiments that fuel these issues, the powers are not likely to go to war solely over them. Moreover, because each dispute operates primarily at the bilateral level, conflagrations in one case are not likely to escalate into regionwide conflicts. This does not mean that territorial disputes are irrelevant to the security landscape. Such disputes could very well be the *proximate* cause of conflict if certain *permissive* conditions exist, the latter being a deterioration of relations in any of the major and middle power dyads over other issues. Thus, for example, neither Japan nor China would see as profitable a second Sino-Japanese war over the Senkakus per se, but they could see such a struggle as necessary if it were embedded in intense bilateral competition for regional hegemony. In this sense, contested sovereignty claims could be the "Archduke Ferdinands" of East Asia. They may be the efficient cause of instability, but only as a result of deeper underlying causal forces for conflict.[27]

B. THE THIRD TIER

In addition to the above two tiers, East Asia faces a third tier of security challenges. These are more nontraditional in nature, and are a function of both the end of Cold War bipolarity and the region's economic dynamism. Numerous issues fall under this category, including terrorism, health, sustainable resources, refugees, and piracy. For example, terrorism as a post-Cold War concern was made evident by

mediate source of the problem was Japan's postwar renunciation of Taiwan but retention of the Senkakus. Tokdo/ Takeshima refers to two small rocks/islets about 200 meters apart that sit between Japan and Korea. Koreans have historically claimed these islands based on ancient cartographic evidence. Japanese claims center on their absorption of the islands after the defeat of Russia in 1905. After the Second World War, Korea unilaterally claimed sovereignty (1952 Rhee line) during Japan's postwar occupation, but the two sides later agreed to shelve the issue at normalization in 1965.

[27]The analogy refers to the assassination of Archduke Ferdinand by a Serbian nationalist which was the proximate cause of World War I. The permissive condition however was the spiraling balance of power dynamics in Europe and security dilemmas that increasingly propelled the states toward conflict. On the distinction between efficient and permissive conditions, see Kenneth Waltz, *Man, the State, and War: A Theoretical Analysis* (NY: Columbia, 1954).

the March 1995 nerve gas subway attack in Japan. The spread of disease in India, China, Thailand, and Burma (the WHO forecasts that by 2000, Asia will account for one-third of world's HIV cases) affects not only the nature of the domestic regime but also its interaction with other states as a result of population flows across borders. Maritime piracy in the South and East China Seas is a small but growing problem that has prompted nations like Japan, Russia, and South Korea to use armed escorts for commercial vessels. This naturally increases the chances for miscalculation, inadvertent naval clashes, and conflict escalation. The most disturbing of third-tier factors is long-term competition for resources, in particular, energy. The region's demand for energy is growing at a rate double that of the rest of the world.[28] At the same time, there are few indigenous resources (Asia accounts for 10% of global oil production and 4% of total reserves), and existing reserves (e.g., Indonesian Sumatra wells and Chinese Taching fields in Northern Manchuria) have been drying up.[29] Formerly an energy exporter, China is now a net importer; furthermore, its transformation to a consumer economy ensures that future energy demands will increase exponentially. As an illustration of the scale of this demand, should China reach oil dependency levels similar to that of the average newly industrializing economy, its gross oil consumption would double that of the United States. While China does have untapped resources to fulfill some of its mammoth needs, the geology of these deeply situated pockets of oil make them extremely difficult and costly to excavate.[30]

As a result of this situation, the potential for destabilizing competition among regional powers for indigenous energy supplies is not insignificant. This might be the case if major oil reserves were found in the South China Sea. It has already been manifest in the disputes over the Natuna natural gas fields. While Indonesia exports these reserves to Japan and South Korea, China has made sovereignty claims on the area. Energy-related resources in the Russian Far East could be another arena of competition among the Northeast Asian powers, particularly if needs are acute and Russia remains weak.[31] The competition for energy resources also could have destabilizing feedback effects on issues in other security tiers. For ex-

[28]For example, Japan is dependent on oil imports for 85% of its energy needs (compared with the United States at 18%); the South Korean economy is growing at 8% while energy consumption is growing at 20%; and Taiwan's energy import bill has increased an exponential 45 times over the past two decades (see Kent Calder, *Pacific Defense: Arms, Energy, and America's Future in Asia* (NY: William Morrow and Co., 1996), Chapter 3.

[29]*BP Statistical Review of World Energy 1996* (London: British Petroleum, 1996), 4–19.

[30]For example, one area of touted oil potential is the Tarim Basin in Western Sinkiang; however, drilling expeditions thus far have been relatively unsuccessful.

[31]One distant but not entirely implausible scenario might be a Russian Far East that becomes increasingly integrated with China, Japan, and Korea. The national loyalties of the population in this region (many of whom are not of Russian ancestry) to a capital 7000 miles away in Moscow is weak; moreover, the weak Russian state can do little to reign in this distant constituency. The incentive for either China or Japan, both with historical territorial disputes with Russia, to seek occupation of the region for resource and nationalist reasons is not insignificant (I am indebted to David Hale for this scenario).

ample, energy needs make imperative states' capabilities to operate off-shore, thereby fueling arms competition in the region and especially the acquisition of blue-water navies. The discovery of oil deposits in the region could also turn overlapping sovereignty claims on islands into disputes over territorial waters, continental shelfs, and exclusive economic zones. In this sense, islets and rocks that were once valuable only as enduring symbols of nationalism, suddenly become intrinsically precious possessions that delineate the vital resource areas and energy interests of states. These tangible factors would weigh most heavily as a primary cause of conflict. Thus, a Sino-Japanese dispute over the Senkaku/Diaoyu islands would have less to do with national pride and more to do with the 40,000 square kilometers of surrounding continental shelf and exclusive economic zones at stake. Similarly, sovereignty disputes between Japan and South Korea over Tokdo/Takeshima would have less to do with historical animosity and more with 63,600 square kilometers of maritime boundaries entitled to the rightful possessor of these islets. In sum, energy and resource needs, rather than nationalism, could have the effect of elevating second tier issues to the status of major regional contingencies.

IV. HORIZON: THE MAJOR POWERS

The degree to which issues in the three security tiers will be sources of post-Cold War instability is inextricably intertwined with the future behavior of the major powers in the region, China, Japan, and the United States. In each case, there exists a spectrum of plausible outcomes, ranging from ones that would generate uncertainty and insecurity spirals, to those that would enhance stability and transparency, which would directly impact the salience of concerns in each of the tiers.

Regarding China, the key concern is how its economic growth affects security intentions. China currently registers annual growth rates in the range of 13%, and based on purchasing power parity is already the third largest economy in the world. Compared with other great economic powers (e.g., Japan), China boasts a more expansive domestic market as well as superior resource endowments. This gives it a degree of self-sufficiency and invulnerability to external attempts to control its behavior. China's economy is complemented also by the overseas minority populations in Southeast Asia, many of whom hold disproportionately large shares of wealth in their respective economies, and provide the Mainland with connections and ties that contribute to a "Greater China" regional economy. The extent to which this phenomenal growth will be a stabilizing or destabilizing element in the post–Cold War security landscape depends greatly on the manner in which these economic capabilities affect Chinese security intentions and ambitions.[32]

---

[32]For destabilizing scenarios in this vein, see Denny Roy, "Hegemon on the Horizon? China's Threat to East Asian Security," *International Security* 19.1 (Summer 1994). For a counterargument, see Michael Gallagher, "China's Illusory Threat to the South China Sea," *International Security* 19.1 (Summer 1994).

At one end of the spectrum, economic growth could have aggrandizing effects on Beijing's behavior. Among all the major powers in the region, China is least satisfied with the status quo. It has territorial and irredentist disputes with most of the region, and has seen itself as a power historically victimized because of its relative weakness. In this regard, an elevation of China's position in the regional status hierarchy spurred by economic growth could make Chinese foreign policy more assertive. Historically, a state's desires to exert influence have been most pronounced in periods coinciding with rapid economic expansion and industrialization.[33] Early evidence of this in China's case has been its unilateralist tendencies in shunning compliance with multilateral arms control regimes; its liberal use of force to make political points (e.g., Tiananmen, Taiwan); and its sovereignty claims over disputed territories. Should economic growth lead China to hegemonic aspirations to reclaim its perceived rightful place in the region, this would have a destabilizing impact on several issues in the first and second security tiers (e.g. Taiwan, the Senkaku islands, and the South China Sea).

On the other hand, economics may have a mollifying effect on Chinese intentions. Borrowing one scholar's terminology, economic growth may make China not muscular and ambitious, but fat and happy.[34] Prosperity could have the effect of soothing festering resentments and any revisionist motivations stemming from historical injustices. In addition, the need to maintain economic growth may elicit more cooperative Chinese behavior. As financial, trade, and diplomatic ties deepen with other economic partners, the incentive to undertake acts that might disrupt these links would substantially lessen. Economic interdependence would also increase China's desires to embed itself in the norms, rules and procedures of international organizations and regimes in order to provide for a transparent environment conducive to continued economic progress. Growth could also engender a more cooperative China through its transforming effects on the nature of the domestic regime. As the cases of Taiwan and South Korea have shown, economic development in authoritarian states often unleashes the democratic forces that ultimately lead to the regime's demise. In this sense, China's growth may enhance political liberalization, as well as the prospects of a "democratic peace" in the region.[35] Therefore, at this end of the spectrum of potential Chinese behavior, the forces for interdependence and democracy could supplant the aggrandizing effects of economic growth. This, in turn, would greatly defuse tensions in the three tiers of security.

[33]For example, this was the case with Britain, France, Germany, Japan, the Soviet Union, and the United States (see Samuel Huntington, "America's Changing Strategic Interests," *Survival* 33.1 [January/February 1991], 12).

[34]The metaphors are borrowed from Richard Betts, "Wealth, Power, and Instability: East Asia and the United States after the Cold War," *International Security* 18.3 (Winter 1993/94), 50 (although Betts does not necessarily agree with the more optimistic view of Chinese economic growth).

[35]For a set of discussions on the viability of the argument that democracies rarely go to war against one another, see Michael Brown, Sean Lynn-Jones, and Steven Miller, Eds., *Debating the Democratic Peace* (Cambridge: MIT Press, 1996).

The primary impact of Japan on future security outcomes in the region centers on the issue of rearmament. Japan attained great power economic status in the 1980s, and has thus far been hesitant to assume global leadership roles and responsibilities commensurate with its economic capabilities. This hesitance has been the object of criticism by some (e.g., the United States), and relief by others wary of renewed Japanese militarism and ultranationalism. However, as the end of the Cold War raises questions about the continued viability of Japan's security dependence on the United States (discussed below), the assertion of a more independent stance, entailing the acquisition of military capabilities typical of a "normal" power, grows more likely. Moreover, it would take relatively little time for Japan to transform itself in this manner. The MSDF (Maritime Self-Defense Forces) are among the most modernly equipped in the region, and as noted above, naval buildup plans for the 1990s seek to substantially augment these forces. Japan currently produces and deploys its own cruise missile arsenal (ASM-1, 2 and SSM-1).[36] While it does not have a ballistic missile arsenal, the space launch vehicle program (SLV) demonstrates a proven capacity in intermediate and long-range ballistic missiles (e.g., M-3, H-1, H-2 rockets) as well as independent satellite reconnaissance and intelligence-gathering. Japan's plutonium stockpiles, while for civilian energy usages, also show a latent nuclear weapons capability.

The impact of a "normal" Japan on regional stability will be a function of both Tokyo's intentions and the regional powers' threat perceptions.[37] Again, at one end of the spectrum, a rearmed Japan could be extremely destabilizing for the region. In conjunction with its economic capabilities and technological prowess, rearmament would make Japan the most prominent power in the region, and this could have an aggrandizing effect on its interests and intentions. This, in turn, could have adverse effects on issues particularly in the second tier (e.g. territorial disputes with Korea, China, Russia). Even if the latter did not occur, heightened threat perceptions about renewed Japanese militarism among the neighboring powers could give rise to anti-Japan balancing coalitions that might in fact *compel* Japan toward more assertive behavior. Along these same lines, the notion of a rearmed Japan that still remained tied to the U.S.-Japan alliance would do little to alleviate regional threat perceptions. Alliance loyalties and obedience often are a function of power distributions, and as Japan acquires new military capabilities, there is no guarantee that it will not become less enamored with its subordinate position in the alliance.

At the other end of the spectrum of potential outcomes, a rearmed Japan could enhance regional stability. The relevant dynamic here is that Japan's new military capabilities would be embedded within both the U.S. alliance and multilateral

---

[36]Japan also deploys three versions of the American-made Harpoon cruise missile.

[37]For two interesting overviews of Japanese security, see Barry Buzan, "Japan's Defense Problematique," and Tsuneo Akaha, "Japan's Security Agenda in the Post-Cold War Era," both in *Pacific Review* 8.1 (1995).

security cooperation. Regarding the former, any assertive aspirations that might be engendered by Japan's new power status would be channeled into a reshaping of the U.S.-Japan alliance. This would accord Tokyo greater responsibilities as well as rewards within the context of a U.S.-Japanese great power "bigemony" that sought to uphold the status quo. In addition, regional threat perceptions of Japanese intentions would be mollified by putting Japanese rearmament in the context of UN peace-keeping operations rather than as a unilateral buildup. Under this view, rearmament will certainly make Japan more confident and independent; however, rather than this leading to an assertive and destabilizing Japan, it would enhance stability by making Japan a contributing and cooperative member of the security community. As another scholar characterized the two views, the pessimistic outlook likens Japanese rearmament to giving an alcoholic a drink; the optimistic outlook reasons that it is better for Japan to drink socially than drink alone.[38]

Whether the optimistic or pessimistic outcome prevails with regard to Japanese rearmament and Chinese growth may ultimately depend on the final and most important piece in the post-Cold War security puzzle in East Asia, the United States. As the dominant power in the region, the United States remains the one stabilizing influence on security perceptions among the middle and major powers. Its presence as both the region's security undergirder and honest broker provides, as one scholar put it, the "oxygen" that saves East Asia from suffocating spirals of insecurity.[39] In spite of this, the post-Cold War rationale for this expansive presence has come under fire. Domestic economic demands for "peace dividends" as well as a resurgence of traditional American isolationist sentiments augur a substantial scaling back of this presence. This was first evident in acts such as the closing of U.S. bases in the Philippines in 1991, and following this, the enactment of the Defense Department's East Asian Security Initiative (EASI). In line with the dictates of the Nunn-Warner bill, EASI called for the systematic reduction of the U.S. security presence in the region beginning with a phased reductions of forces on the Korean peninsula. The first phase of the plan was carried out with the withdrawal of 7000 ground and air personnel from 1990 through 1992[40]; however, the Bush administration postponed the plan indefinitely in conjunction with the North Korean nuclear dispute. Since then, the Clinton administration has consistently reaffirmed the U.S. security commitment to the region. In spite of these U.S. reassurances, an uneasy concern pervades governments in Asia that a reduced U.S. security presence in the post-Cold War is inevitable.

---

[38]The references are to comments by Lee Kuan Yew and Jack Snyder, cited in Betts, "Wealth, Power, and Instability," 57.

[39]Joseph Nye, "The Case for Deep Engagement," *Foreign Affairs* 74.4 (July/August 1995).

[40]See Lawrence Grinter, "East Asia and the United States into the 21st Century," *CADRE Report* November 1991, Maxwell Air Force Base, Alabama; and *Pacific Stars and Stripes,* April 6, 1990 and October 23, 1991.

The primary causal dynamic for regional stability with regard to the United States is therefore how changes in the nature and form of the U.S. presence affect threat perceptions and feelings of insecurity among the regional powers. Again on the more optimistic end of the spectrum, a reduced U.S. presence, while initially raising concerns among the powers, may not substantially destabilize the region. Governments in the region realize that a relatively less dominant U.S. presence in the post-Cold War is somewhat inevitable. Although in absolute terms, American trade and investment are growing, and its military capabilities are still the strongest in the world, the relative narrowing of both gaps (particularly the former) presage a decline in U.S. status from that of a superpower to one of a mere major power in the region. This may not result in tremendous instability if, for example, both the decline of American presence and the rise of Japanese influence remain within the context of the U.S.-Japanese bigemony. Other powers in the region, including China, might feel less insecure knowing that suspected Japanese ambitions were still curtailed by the U.S. presence, albeit a reduced one. In fact, since the end of the Cold War, Chinese officials while publicly maintaining their opposition to the alliance, are increasingly in private expressing support for the restraining effect the alliance has on renewed Japanese militarism. The obverse security perception would also hold true. As long as the U.S.-Japan alliance remained intact, Japan, too would experience less acute insecurities about an assertive China. Another possible outcome might be the formation of broad multilateral security cooperation as a result of a regionwide consensus for the need to preserve "oxygen" in the wake of a U.S. departure. Admittedly difficult to imagine at present, U.S. disengagement may provide the incentive for states to regionally organize and overcome historical antagonisms for the broader goal of preserving economic prosperity. In this regard, organizations like APEC and ARF may provide the springboard for greater security dialogue, confidence-building measures, and defense exchanges that make each other's defense doctrines, procurement plans, and overall intentions more transparent.

At the more pessimistic end of the spectrum, the more widely held view is that a U.S. withdrawal would have acutely destabilizing effects on the region. The primary consequence of American disengagement (or regional perceptions of disengagement) is not that this will directly lead to a struggle for a new hegemon, but that it will give rise to *uncertainty*. The various ways in which states deal with this uncertainty could set off dynamics that disturb peace. For example, as noted above, hedging against uncertainty for many states already has meant the increased acquisition of arms. Moreover, the nature of these capabilities are more offensive- and force projection-oriented than in the past. This, in turn, sets off insecurity spirals among powers with regard to the intentions behind these new-found capabilities, resulting in destabilizing arms races. In addition, the confidence that comes with new arsenals, coupled with the historical antagonisms, may make the major powers (i.e., China and Japan) more willing to check each other's ambitions, the spark for conflict being sovereignty disputes over territories like the Senkaku/Diaoyu islands (tier 2). Moreover, even if China's and/or Japan's enhanced security capabilities were benignly intended (i.e., building up for purely defensive purposes), balancing coalitions could form between one of these and the middle powers in the region against the other (e.g., Korea-China vis-à-vis Japan, or Japan-ASEAN vis-à-vis China), which would raise encirclement fears and press the isolated power into destabilizing behavior. Another distant but not inconceivable possibility could be a disengaging United States that still seeks the same level of influence despite its reduced presence in the region. Asian governments might grow resentful at an overbearing United States that increasingly leverages its security contribution to the region as a domestic jobs issue, causing the United States to be seen less as a security undergirder and more, as Winston Lord put it, "an international nanny, if not bully."[41]

V. CONCLUSION

Horizon-gazing exercises of East Asian security could entertain a plethora of scenarios in addition to the ones covered above. However, the basic point remains the same. The dynamics surrounding Chinese economic growth, Japanese rearmament, and U.S. engagement are the three determinants of the future security landscape in the region. Although we have looked at each of these discretely, outcomes in any one are naturally linked to developments in the other. For example, the degree to which Japan rearms, as well as regional perceptions of this rearmament, greatly depends on the future viability of the U.S.-Japan alliance and America's continued engagement in the region. Similarly, U.S. attitudes toward engagement or disengagement will be influenced by the degree to which China's economic growth has aggrandizing or satisficing effects on its security ambitions. The causal arrows among the three dynamics can potentially run in several different directions; however, the two most likely causal catalysts are Chinese growth and American engagement. The former largely because China's past behavior with regard to issues like human rights and arms control reflects a clear penchant for unilateralism regardless of trends in the region. As a result, its choice of a "muscular and ambitious" or "fat and satisfied" foreign policy may be made independent of other factors. The latter because East Asian perceptions of a diminished post-Cold War American presence have already driven some of the behavior among states in the region. The extent and nature of Japanese rearmament on the other hand, would largely be in response to either of these two prior trends.

[41]Manning, "Security in East Asia," 29.

Moreover, the spectrum of outcomes, ranging from pessimistic to optimistic, with regard to these three powers has direct bearing on the likelihood of conflict over issues in any of the three tiers of security. Whether it be conflict in Korea or Taiwan, territorial disputes, competition for energy resources, or competitive arms buildups, the uncertainty and insecurity spirals that would result from a pessimistic outcome to any of the major power scenarios would exacerbate tensions and increase the likelihood of conflict. However, the realization of one of the optimistic scenarios would substantially ease some of the uncertainties and suspicions in the region. Which of these will be East Asia's future path is of course difficult to predict. However, this chapter's delineation of specific tiers of issues, and specific issues with regard to the major powers, at least offers a first cut at marking some of the critical signposts and forks on East Asia's horizon.

CHAPTER 3

The Export-Oriented Industrialization of Pacific Rim Nations and Their Presence in the Global Market

Ichiro Numazaki
Faculty of Arts and Letters
Tohoku University
Kawauchi, Sendai 980–8576
Japan

I. INTRODUCTION

This chapter explores the patterns and processes of export-oriented industrialization (EOI) of the Pacific Rim nations, and analyzes their structural positions in the global market from both macro- and microperspectives. Focusing on the Four Asian Tigers—South Korea, Taiwan, Hong Kong, and Singapore—in general and on South Korea and Taiwan in particular, this chapter examines the context and consequences of EOI in the "Pacific Rim" economy.

The concept of "Pacific Rim" and its synonyms such as "Pacific Basin" and "Asia-Pacific" are rather dubious and are often loaded with highly ideological meanings (Dirlik, 1993). In this chapter, I shall use the term "Pacific Rim" as a purely geographic shorthand for the region containing the Four Asian Tigers, the ASEAN nations, China, Japan and the United States.[1]

The economies of South Korea, Taiwan, Singapore, and Hong Kong are characterized by a steady and high growth rate of GNP, rapid expansion of the manufacturing sector, heavy reliance on foreign trade, nearly full employment,

[1]This chapter focuses primarily on the "Asian" side of the Pacific Rim and excludes the "American" side, except for the United States. My omission of the Latin American NICs in particular by no means belittles their significance in the Pacific Rim economy. For an interesting comparison of the Asian and American sides of the rim, see Castillo and Acosta (1993) and Palacios (1995).

relatively egalitarian income distribution, and so on. The economies of Indonesia, Malaysia, the Philippines, and Thailand are following a similar path. The new "socialist market economy" of China also aims at EOI and is increasingly linked to the world economy. The Asian side of the Pacific Rim as a whole is growing fast and gaining a larger and larger share in the global market.

It has become the accepted wisdom by now that the Four Asian Tigers are the champions of economic development and that the secret of their success is the effective policies of EOI devised and implemented by strong developmental states (Deyo, 1987; Hughes, 1988; Amsden, 1989; Wade, 1990; Vogel, 1991; World Bank, 1993). Scholars differ, however, in their favorite "causes" and "secrets" of the EOI in the Four Tigers: some emphasize the role of the free market (Balassa, 1971, 1978; Porter, 1990; World Bank, 1993); others stress the role of the state (Amsden, 1979, 1985, 1989; Gold, 1986; Deyo, 1987; Appelbaum and Henderson, 1992); still others highlight the role of culture (Hofheinz and Calder, 1982; Berger, 1986; Clegg and Redding, 1990; Redding, 1990).

This chapter is not intended as yet another attempt at discovering "the secret of success" of EOI in the Pacific Rim. Rather it explores the context and consequences of EOI in the Pacific Rim in general and for the Four Tigers in particular. To do so, I focus on the interrelationship between the economies, both developed and developing, in the region and I examine the patterns of interaction between these economies.

I shall first trace the trajectories of EOI in the Pacific Rim and outline its overall pattern. I shall then examine the major structural features of EOI in the region by analyzing the interaction between the developing economies, the United States, and Japan. Finally, I shall explore the differences in the processes and outcomes of EOI in the Four Asian Tigers and describe their new roles in the changing context of the 1990s.

II. THE TRAJECTORY OF EOI IN THE PACIFIC RIM

A. The World's Fastest-Growing Economies

The Four Tigers of South Korea, Taiwan, Singapore, and Hong Kong experienced phenomenal economic growth in the past three decades. As shown in Table 1, the Four Tigers achieved average annual growth rates of from 8.6 to 10% during the 15 years between 1965 and 1980. Their rate of growth slowed down slightly in the 1980s due to recessions in the industrialized nations, but the four economies still managed to grow at the relatively high pace of from 6.1 to 9.7% per year. Their annual growth rates of from 5.2 to 8.3% in the first half of 1990s are still very impressive.

Between 1983 and 1993, South Korea and Taiwan quadrupled their per capita GNP, while Singapore and Hong Kong tripled theirs. The Four Tigers have

Table 1

**Average Annual Growth Rates of GDP (percent) and Per Capita GNP (US$)
in Pacific Rim Economies**

	Growth rate of GDP			Per capita GNP	
	1965–1980	1980–1990	1990–1994	1983	1993
Four Tigers					
South Korea	9.9	9.7	7.0	2010	7670
Taiwan	9.9	7.5	6.5	2670	10850
Singapore	10.0	6.1	8.3	6620	19310
Hong Kong	8.6	7.1	5.2	6000^b	17860^b
Four ASEAN nations					
Indonesia	7.0	5.3	7.6	560	730
Malaysia	7.4	4.9	8.6	1870	3160
Philippines	5.9	0.7	1.8	760	830
Thailand	7.3	7.0	9.0^a	820	2040
China	6.9	9.7	10.7^a	300	490

Source: Watanabe and Kim, 1996, 69; Asian Development Bank, 1995, 16.
[a]Average for 1990–1993.
[b]Refers to GDP.

achieved a level of economic development close to that of the advanced industrial countries.

The Four Tigers, however, were not alone in their rapid economic growth. Although they were less striking than the Four Tigers, developing countries in the southeastern region of the Rim, organized as the Association of Southeast Asian Nations (ASEAN) also attained comparatively high level of growth. Between 1965 and 1980, the four ASEAN nations of Indonesia, Malaysia, the Philippines, and Thailand grew at an average annual rate of from 6 to 7%. In the 1980s, the economic growth of the four ASEAN nations also slowed down a little, but these countries, except for the politically troubled Philippines, still managed to achieve an annual growth rate of from 5 to 7%. In the 1990s, the four ASEAN nations picked up their pace of growth again. Indonesia, Malaysia, and Thailand show growth rates higher than those in the 1965–1980 period.

Per capita GNP did not change much between 1983 and 1993 for Indonesia and the Philippines, but showed a substantial increase for Malaysia and Thailand. Malaysia in 1993 surpassed the level of South Korea and Taiwan in 1983 and Thailand in 1993 came quite close to that level.

China was another rapidly growing economy in the region. Although isolated from the outside and shaken by the upheaval of the Cultural Revolution, China accomplished a remarkable annual growth rate of 6.9% between 1965 and 1980. As the country adopted an open door policy and engaged in market-oriented economic reforms beginning in 1978, it has quickened its pace of growth. China attained the average annual growth rate of 9.7% in the 1980s and 10.7% in the early 1990s. In the past 15 years, therefore, China was the fastest growing economy in the region. The performance of these Pacific economies was among the best in the world. In the 15 years between 1965 and 1980, the average annual growth rate of developing countries was 5.8% and that of the industrialized nations in the Organization for Economic Cooperation and Development (OECD) was 3.8%; in the 1980s, the figures were just 3.8% for developing countries and 3% for the OECD nations (Watanabe and Kim, 1996, 69).

The Asian side of the Pacific Rim as a whole, and not just the Four Tigers, then, experienced extraordinary economic growth in the past three decades.

B. INDUSTRIALIZATION AS THE ENGINE OF GROWTH

The economic growth of these Pacific Rim nations was brought about by successful industrialization. These countries were able to transform their economies from an agrarian-based one to a manufacturing one.

As Table 2 indicates, the Four Tigers, the four ASEAN nations, and China achieved high rates of growth in the manufacturing sectors. In the period from 1965 through 1980 South Korea, Taiwan, Singapore, Indonesia, Malaysia, and Thailand attained the average annual growth rate of more than 10%, with South Korea and Taiwan leading at 18.7% and 15.5%, respectively. In the same period, Japan's average annual growth rate of manufacturing sector was 8.2% and the OECD nations' 6.6% (Watanabe and Kim, 1996, 70).

The manufacturing sector of these countries continued to grow in the 1980s, although at somewhat slower pace. Hong Kong, which registered relatively low rate of growth in the manufacturing sector in the earlier period, picked up its pace of growth and achieved an annual growth rate of 18.2%, the highest among the Four Tigers, in that decade. China also showed a high growth rate of 9.5% in the manufacturing sector in the 1960s and 1970s, and an even higher rate of 14.5% in the 1980s.

As a result, by 1990 the Four Tigers, the four ASEAN nations, and China all attained a level of industrialization comparable to that of Japan as measured by the ratio of industrial products to GNP as shown in Table 3. South Korea, Taiwan, and China, in particular, surpassed Japan in terms of the rate of industrialization. Singapore, Indonesia, and Thailand are not far behind. Except for Hong Kong, the ratios of industrial products to GNP increased by 1.2 to 2.8 times between 1965 and 1990. The decreasing rate of industrialization in Hong Kong, which was rather highly industrialized already in 1965, is mainly due to the higher growth of the service sector and thus represents postindustrialization that is similar to Japan.

As a whole, then, the Asian side of the Pacific Rim transformed itself into a powerful industrial base in the past three decades—and a big one at that.

Table 2

Average Annual Growth Rates of Industrial and Manufacturing Sectors
in Pacific Rim Economies (percent)

	All industry[a]		Manufacturing only	
	1965–1980	1980–1990	1965–1980	1980–1990
Four Tigers				
South Korea	16.4	12.4	18.7	13.1
Taiwan	14.8	10.8	15.5	10.7
Singapore	11.9	5.0	13.2	5.9
Hong Kong	6.2	14.4	5.6	18.2
Four ASEAN nations				
Indonesia	11.9	5.3	12.0	12.7
Malaysia	9.6	6.5	12.3	8.0
Philippines	8.0	−0.8	7.5	0.5
Thailand	9.5	8.1	11.2	8.1
China	10.0	12.6	9.5	14.5
Japan	7.4	5.2	8.2	6.7

Source: Watanabe and Kim, 1996, 69.
[a]Includes mining, manufacturing, construction, and utilities.

Table 3

Shares of Industrial and Manufacturing Sectors in GNP (percent)

	All industry[a]		Manufacturing only	
	1965	1990	1965	1990
Four Tigers				
South Korea	25	44	18	26
Taiwan	30	44	22	36
Singapore	24	37	15	26
Hong Kong	40	28	24	21
Four ASEAN nations				
Indonesia	13	37	8	17
Malaysia	25	40	9	24
Philippines	28	33	20	22
Thailand	23	38	14	21
China	39	48	31	34
Japan	44	41	34	30

Source: Watanabe and Kim, 1996, 69.
[a]Includes mining, manufacturing, construction, and utilities.

C. Exports as the Market for Growth

The economic growth realized by the rapid industrialization of the developing economies of the Pacific Rim was driven not by the growth of domestic consumption but by the rapid expansion of exports. This is why this industrialization is called "export-oriented." Table 4 shows that the developing economies of the Pacific Rim increasingly engaged in foreign trade, and they continue to do so.

Table 5 indicates that the significance of exports increased sharply in the 1970s for the Four Tigers and in the four ASEAN nations, except for the Philippines and Thailand. The average ratio of exports to GNP in the Four Tigers and in the four ASEAN nations in 1982 and 1983 "was over 50 percent, while the ratios of the United States and Japan were 8 and 16 percent, respectively" (Naya, 1988, 64).

Note here that not only exports but also imports increased rapidly in the 1970s in the Four Tigers and in the four ASEAN nations. The EOI in these economies was accompanied by a rise in imports as well, a point to which I shall return later.

The 1970s saw the rapid growth of exports from the Four Tigers and the four ASEAN nations as shown in Table 6. South Korea's total exports, for example, grew by almost 40% annually. Taiwan's total exports grew by about 30% a year, and its exports of manufactured goods grew even faster. The four ASEAN nations also experienced very rapid growth in total exports and a very impressive increase in manufactured exports.

The exports from the developing economies in the Pacific Rim continued to expand in the 1980s. South Korea and Taiwan averaged annual growth of 22.0% and 21.7%, respectively, in total exports for the 25 years from 1965 to 1990, while

Table 4

Foreign Trade as Percent of GNP

	1975	1985	1994
Four Tigers			
South Korea	59.4	67.4	52.6
Taiwan	73.0	80.5	73.0
Singapore	236.1	267.8	289.6
Hong Kong[a]	146.7	175.2	240.9[b]
Four ASEAN nations			
Indonesia	40.8	34.4	n.a.
Malaysia	82.2	95.1	179.3
Philippines	40.9	33.7	54.5
Thailand	36.9	42.8	67.8[b]

Source: Asian Development Bank, 1995, 37.
[a]Percent of GDP.
[b]Refers to 1993.

Thailand, Malaysia, and China averaged annual growth of more than 10% in total exports during the 1980s (Watanabe and Kim, 1996, 70). In the 1970s, exports from these countries accounted for only a fraction of world trade. As shown in Table 7, however, the amount of exports and its share of total world exports increased substantially in the 1980s and early 1990s. Between

Table 5

Exports and Imports as Percent of GNP

	Exports		Imports	
	1970–1971	1982–1983	1970–1971	1982–1983
Four Tigers				
South Korea	15.0	42.0	25.3	45.8
Taiwan	32.6	48.9	31.3	40.5
Singapore	79.9	138.3	127.8	182.7
Hong Kong[a]	68.9	76.1	80.5	84.1
Four ASEAN nations				
Indonesia	13.9	34.5	16.5	26.4
Malaysia	41.7	49.8	35.7	48.8
Philippines	19.0	18.2	19.5	24.9
Thailand	17.0	17.8	21.0	25.2
Japan	11.8	16.3	10.0	14.9

Source: Naya, 1988, 66.
[a]Percent of GDP.

Table 6

Annual Growth Rate of Total and Manufactured Exports from the Developing Economies in the Pacific Rim, 1970–1979 (percent)

	Total exports	Manufactured exports
Four Tigers		
South Korea	37.9	29.7
Taiwan	30.8	34.2
Singapore	28.0	33.0
Hong Kong	22.1	22.0
Four ASEAN nations		
Indonesia	34.9	47.4
Malaysia	23.3	38.0
Philippines	17.6	33.8
Thailand	25.2	47.1
World	20.6	19.7

Source: Naya, 1988, 69.

Table 7

Exports from the Developing Economies in 1981, 1991 and 1994 (US$ million)

	1981	1991	1994
(A) Four Tigers	86580	305587	436702
South Korea	21268	71870	96013
Taiwan	22518	76115	92833
Singapore	20967	59025	96457
Hong Kong	21827	98577	151399
(A)/(E)%	4.6	8.9	10.8
(B) Four ASEAN nations	46711	101087	154829
Indonesia	22260	29543	39497
Malaysia	11765	34349	58147
Philippines	5655	8767	12124
Thailand	7031	28428	45061
(B)/(E)%	2.5	2.9	3.8
(C) China	22007	71910	104672
(C)/(E)%	1.2	2.1	2.6
(D) (A)+(B)+(C)	155298	478584	696203
(D)/(E)%	8.3	13.9	17.3
(E) World	1875200	3441900	4030800

Source: Asian Development Bank, 1995, 32.

1981 and 1991, the combined share of the Four Tigers in world exports nearly doubled from 4.6% to 8.9%, and they reached 10.8% in 1994. Between 1981 and 1994, that of the ASEAN nations increased from 2.5% to 3.8%, and China's share grew from 1.2% to 2.6%. In 1994, therefore, 17.3% of the world exports originated from the nine developing Asian economies.

Table 8 presents changes in the composition of exported goods from the Four Tigers and the four ASEAN nations between 1970 and 1981. South Korea and Taiwan increased the share of manufactured goods from about 70% to more than 80%, and Singapore from less than 30% to more then 40%. Primary products still accounted for the bulk of exports from the four ASEAN nations in the 1970s, but the ratio of manufactured good rose sharply for Malaysia, the Philippines, and Thailand.

By 1990, manufactured exports reached 95% of total exports from South Korea and Taiwan, 32% from Indonesia, 44% from Malaysia, 62% from the Philippines, 54% from Thailand, and 70% from China, which became a major exporter in the 1980s (Watanabe and Kim, 1996, 70).

It was this expansion of the market for exports, especially for manufactured exports, that pulled the Four Tigers and the four ASEAN nations as well as China through the turbulent years of the 1970s and 1980s. Clearly, the economic growth of the Pacific Rim was led by exports.

Table 8

Composition of Exports from the Developing Economies
in the Pacific Rim, 1970 and 1981 (percent of total exports)

	Four Tigers				Four ASEAN nations			
	South Korea	Taiwan	Singapore	Hong Kong	Indonesia	Malaysia	Philippines	Thailand
Primary commodities								
1970	24.9	27.4	69.0	7.5	98.6	92.8	89.5	89.5
1981	18.2	13.1	51.5	7.9	96.8	80.0	55.4	71.6
Manufactured exports								
1970	75.1	72.3	28.0	92.2	1.2	6.3	6.4	5.2
1981	81.3	86.7	41.1	91.4	2.9	19.5	22.8	24.8

Source: Naya, 1988, 70, 77.

Table 9

Destinations of Exports from the Developing Economies
in the Pacific Rim (percent of total exports)

	Four Tigers			Four ASEAN nations		
	1970	1979	1983	1970	1979	1983
Total Pacific	63.8	62.7	62.9	73.9	76.0	75.1
U.S.A.	31.8	26.5	31.5	19.6	19.3	18.7
Japan	11.7	13.1	9.1	28.4	33.1	30.3
Australia	2.3	2.5	2.2	1.8	1.4	1.2

Source: Naya, 1988, 69.

Where is the market for exports from the developing economies of the Pacific Rim? As Table 9 shows, the answer is the Pacific Rim itself in general and the United States in particular. In the 1970s and early 1980s, between 26% and 32% of total exports from the Four Tigers and between 18% and 20% of total exports from ASEAN countries were directed to the U.S. market. From the 1970s through the mid-1980s, the Four Tigers shipped some two-thirds of all exports to other parts of the Pacific, with almost half of these going to the United States. In particular, the bulk of manufactured exports from the Four Tigers found their way to the U.S. market: in the clothing category, 48.5% in 1970 and 39.5% in 1981; in the electrical machinery category, 61.9% in 1970 and 39% in 1981; and in the miscellaneous manufactures category that includes such items as handbags, toys, various plastic goods, and so on, 58.2% in 1970 and 40.9% in 1981 (Naya, 1988, 74). Overall, 41% of total manufactured exports from the Four Tigers were destined to the United States in 1970, and 31.9% in 1981 (Naya, 1988, 74).

South Korea and Taiwan were especially dependent on the U.S. market. U.S. market share for South Korean exports climbed from less than 20% in 1961 to more than 50% in 1968, and it fluctuated between 25% and 50% during the 1970s and 1980s (Hattori and Sato, 1996a, 8). U.S. market share for total exports from Taiwan was below 5% in 1955, it reached a record high of 48% in 1985, and it remained at more than 30% in the 1980s (Hattori and Sato, 1996a, 8).

The Four Tigers were thus successful in gaining ground in the U.S. market. However, they faced difficulties in penetrating the Japanese market. In 1970, Japan received only 7% of exports of clothing, 5.3% of electrical machinery, and 3.7% of miscellaneous manufactures (Naya, 1988, 74). The figures for 1981 hardly changed: 8.3% of clothing, 5.1% of electrical machinery, and 5.8% of miscellaneous manufactures (Naya, 1988, 74). A mere 7.1% of total manufactured exports from the Four Tigers in 1970 went to Japan, and just 6.9% in 1981 (Naya, 1988, 74). The four ASEAN nations also exported heavily within the Pacific Rim, but Japan was the largest market and the United States was the second largest market.

The Japanese and U.S. markets differed from each other by their nature. Japan was more important as the market for primary commodities, while the United States was important as the market for manufactured exports. As for the exports of primary commodities from the four ASEAN nations, 36.4% in 1970 and 44.9% in 1981 went to Japan, while 13.5% in 1970 and 16.2% went to the United States (Naya, 1988, 80). As for manufactured exports, by contrast, 6.7% in 1970 and 6.9% in 1981 went to Japan, while 28.6% in 1970 and 27.9% in 1981 went to the United States (Naya, 1988, 80). In the 1970s and early 1980s, therefore, the United States was the most important market for the industrial producers not only in the Four Tigers but also in the four ASEAN nations. In the late 1980s and early 1990s, the U.S. market still remained the single most important market for the developing economies in the Pacific Rim, as I shall discuss shortly.

Japan, on the other hand, was not as open a market for the manufacturers in the Four Tigers and the four ASEAN nations in the 1970s and early 1980s. The situation started to change since the mid-1980s, however, when the Japanese yen appreciated sharply against the U.S. dollar. Japan now imports more manufactured products from the developing economies in the Pacific Rim than it used to, as many Japanese corporations have shifted their production sites to these economies and have started to engage in international sourcing. Later, I shall examine this change in more detail.

III. THE STRUCTURE OF EOI IN THE PACIFIC RIM

In the previous section I demonstrated that the EOI of developing economies in the Pacific Rim was aimed primarily at the U.S. market. What created the strong demand for the Pacific products in the U.S. market? How were the Pacific economies able to respond to the U.S. demand? Who supplied capital, technology, and other necessities for EOI to the Pacific Rim nations? In short, what was the underlying structure of the EOI on the Pacific scale?

To answer these questions, this section sheds some light on the patterns of EOI in the Pacific Rim and on the complex networks of production and procurement that underlie and interlink the "national" economies in the region.

A. Product Cycles on an International Scale

The pattern of EOI in the developing economies of the Pacific Rim shows what Bruce Cumings calls the "classic product-cycle industrialization pattern" (Cumings, 1987, 45; also Vernon, 1971). Furthermore, these economies followed the product-cycle industrialization in succession. Different countries passed through similar stages of industrialization at different points in time. This is evident in Tables 10 and 11.

In 1970, labor-intensive and low-skilled products of light industries were the mainstay of exports from the Four Tigers. As shown in Table 10, clothing, textiles, and miscellaneous manufactures combined—"classical trio" as Naya (1988, 72) puts it—accounted for 66.2% of the total manufactured exports from South Korea, 59.3% from Taiwan, 31.1% from Singapore, and 68.8% from Hong Kong. Resource-based manufactures that include such simple merchandises as leather, rubber, wood, and cork products, and so on, accounted for more than 10% of the manufactured exports from South Korea, Taiwan and Singapore.

By 1981, however, the "classical trio" decreased its share in the manufactured exports by between 14% and 20% in all Four Tigers. Technologically simple resource-based manufactures also decreased in relative importance in the Four Tigers.

In contrast, more capital-intensive and technologically advanced products such as electrical and nonelectrical machinery increased their share in the manufactured exports from the Four Tigers in 1981. Singapore, for instance, more than doubled exports of electrical machinery between 1970 and 1981. Hong Kong tripled its exports of precision instruments in the same period. South Korea increased the export of transport equipment (mainly ships) by seven times, thanks to the government-promoted and *chaebol*-led development of heavy industry in the 1970s. South Korea also increased its export of iron and steel from 1.6% of total exports in 1970 to 8.6% in 1981.

Table 10 also shows that the four ASEAN nations were just developing the less-skilled and labor-intensive light industries from which the Four Tigers were "graduating." Indonesia, for example, dramatically increased the export of resource-based manufactures from near zero in 1970 to 37% in 1981. Resource-based manufactures were already the backbone of the manufactured exports from the three other ASEAN nations: 40.5% in Malaysia, 68.8% in the Philippines, and 40.4% in Thailand. But in 1981, resource-based manufactures were no longer the mainstay of rapidly growing manufactured exports from the three ASEAN nations. In

Table 10

Composition of Manufactured Exports from the Developing Economies in the Pacific
Rim, 1970 and 1981 (percent of total manufactured exports)

	Four Tigers				Four ASEAN nations			
	South Korea	Taiwan	Singapore	Hong Kong	Indonesia	Malaysia	Philippines	Thailand
Resource-based manufactures								
1970	16.7	13.2	11.3	6.3	—	40.5	68.8	40.4
1981	10.0	8.3	6.6	4.0	37.0	11.8	18.9	20.0
Miscellaneous manufactures								
1970	18.6	19.6	11.3	26.7	—	4.8	9.3	7.7
1981	10.0	14.9	6.6	16.1	3.4	2.6	12.7	6.9
Textiles								
1970	13.5	19.1	12.9	11.9	16.7	6.3	7.8	23.1
1981	14.2	10.4	3.4	11.0	6.9	6.1	5.2	19.8
Clothing								
1970	34.1	20.6	6.9	30.2	—	4.7	—	1.9
1981	22.4	14.5	5.1	27.3	13.8	1.4	26.8	19.8
Transport equipment								
1970	1.5	1.2	12.0	0.7	—	9.5	—	5.8
1981	11.9	4.2	10.2	2.3	10.3	1.5	3.1	0.8
Chemicals								
1970	1.8	3.3	10.3	4.3	41.7	11.1	7.8	7.7
1981	3.7	2.8	8.7	3.9	10.3	3.6	7.9	3.2
Electrical machinery								
1970	7.0	17.1	14.2	9.9	—	4.7	—	1.9
1981	13.2	18.7	35.5	14.9	10.3	55.9	8.3	18.1
Nonelectrical machinery								
1970	1.3	4.7	15.7	1.6	25.0	11.1	1.6	3.8
1981	2.9	6.5	17.0	5.6	3.4	5.1	0.9	1.6
Precision instruments								
1970	0.5	0.6	2.3	3.1	—	1.6	—	3.8
1981	2.2	2.6	3.8	10.6	—	1.5	2.2	2.0

Source: Naya, 1988, 70, 77.

Malaysia, electrical machinery became the major category of manufactured exports.
In the Philippines, clothing accounted for more than a quarter of manufactured exports. And in Thailand, clothing and electrical machinery became two other important categories of manufactured exports.

Table 11 shows that in the 1980s and early 1990s the Pacific Rim economies
dominated the U.S. market, the most important destination for exports, in many
fields of consumer and capital goods. Some two-thirds of clothing and footwear,
more than three-fourths of office equipment, more than half of audio-visual equip-

Table 11

Changing Shares of Pacific Rim Nations' Products in the U.S. Market,
1983 and 1991 (percent)

		Four Tigers			ASEAN nations				
Japan	South Korea	Taiwan	Singapore	Hong Kong	Indonesia	Malaysia	Thailand	China	Total

Clothing (SITC 84)
1983	3.47	17.14	18.54	2.02	23.20	0.82	0.98	2.44	8.06	76.66
1991	0.52	10.47	10.14	2.30	15.45	2.28	2.69	2.17	14.74	60.77

Footwear (SITC 85)
1983	0.56	21.25	30.16	0.00	0.01	0.00	0.02	0.40	0.89	53.29
1991	0.07	20.52	12.19	0.00	1.11	4.39	0.04	3.19	26.81	68.32

Metal processing machinery (SITC 74)
1983	24.18	0.67	6.82	1.58	4.07	0.00	0.01	0.00	0.28	37.62
1991	27.14	2.24	5.98	1.79	0.40	0.05	0.53	0.52	2.18	40.84

General industrial machinery (SITC 75)
1983	48.48	2.13	5.54	10.02	7.28	0.00	0.40	0.04	0.01	73.90
1991	39.48	3.96	12.60	15.35	2.60	0.00	1.57	1.95	0.97	78.49

Office equipment (SITC 76)
1983	50.36	7.81	12.93	4.19	5.35	0.00	1.25	0.00	0.09	81.97
1991	40.03	7.46	5.17	5.11	1.77	0.30	7.43	2.87	6.51	76.65

Audio-visual equipment (SITC 77)
1983	23.48	6.09	6.70	5.92	4.67	0.00	9.65	1.20	0.02	57.75
1991	26.84	6.91	6.45	4.45	2.36	0.12	5.04	1.77	2.59	56.52

Other electrical equipment (SITC 78)
1983	41.56	0.12	0.71	0.03	0.00	0.00	0.01	0.00	0.01	42.43
1991	40.78	1.78	1.17	0.04	0.01	0.01	0.01	0.02	0.16	43.98

Source: Watanabe and Kim, 1996, 74.

ment and nearly half of other electrical appliances came from the Asian side of the Rim. Many industrial goods such as machine tools also originated in the Pacific Rim.

Moreover, a comparison of 1983 and 1991 figures reveals that the upgrading of industry through product cycle continued in the 1980s. As for clothing and footwear, the market share of the Four Tigers declined as that of Indonesia, Thailand, and China increased. Clothing and footwear were once the mainstay of Japanese exports to the United States. The production of these goods originally shifted from Japan to the Four Tigers in the 1960s. Now the industry moved to ASEAN countries and then to China.

A similar trend is observed in other sectors as well. Japan still dominates the export of metal-processing machine tools that include such precision instruments as numerically controlled machines. But South Korea is increasing its share of exports in this area. In the field of general industrial machinery, Japan is being replaced by Taiwan and Singapore. In the office equipment category, both Japan and the Four Tigers are losing their market share while Malaysia and China are rapidly increasing their share. The EOI in the Pacific Rim therefore has taken the form of successive and ever-extending product-cycle industrialization aimed primarily at the U.S. market.

Temporally, each economy goes through a similar chain of product cycles starting with less-skilled and labor-intensive industries to more-skilled and capital-intensive industries. As the economy moves through the product cycles, the level of technological development is upgraded.

Spatially, production sites "travel" from the center to the periphery. Production of footwear, for instance, started in Japan, moved first to South Korea and Taiwan, and then to ASEAN nations and China. Production of textiles, clothing, electrical machinery, and so forth followed a similar pattern.

This is the hallmark of the so-called "miracle" in the Pacific Rim. The Asian side of the Rim as a whole is going through successful "product-cycle industrialization."

B. AMERICAN OUTSOURCING

As the above analysis shows, this "product-cycle industrialization" was sustained by the strong demand for imports in the U.S. market. It was American buyers who ruled the EOI on the Asian side of the Pacific Rim.

The main reason for this strong U.S. demand for Asian products is the increasingly active "global sourcing" by large U.S. retailers as well as by transnational manufacturers (Gereffi, 1993, 1994). According to Gereffi, in recent years U.S. firms have externalized production processes through subcontracting and networking on an international scale. Thus, "global commodity chains" emerged that link firms and factories across the Pacific ocean.

The global sourcing by big U.S. buyers started in the garments industry. Cheap made-in-Japan clothing showed up in American department stores and supermarkets in the 1960s. Then, in the 1970s and especially in the 1980s, made-in-Taiwans and made-in-Koreas started to show up on the floor of J. C. Penneys and K-Marts. Now, made-in-Chinas are displayed and sold in these stores.

The cycle of global sourcing was repeated in electronics and home appliances in the 1970s and 1980s. First came toyish Japanese-made transistor radios, then more high-quality Sonys and Toshibas. As things made in Japan shifted to the higher-end market, things made in South Korea and Taiwan entered the cheaper sectors. Now, however, the lower end products come from Malaysia, Thailand and China among others.

One of the important characteristics of this "buyer-driven" commodity chain is that it is "demand-responsive" (Gereffi, 1994). That is to say, it is the buyers who specify design and quality of the finished goods they want to sell. The buyers then look for manufacturers who can meet their specifications and they subcontract with them. The manufacturers simply respond to the buyers' specific demand.

Gereffi (1993, 53) distinguishes two kinds of global subcontracting: *commercial subcontracting* by "large-volume retailers" who import finished goods and "market the goods under private labels or in their own retail outlets," and *component supply subcontracting* by "original equipment manufacturers," or OEMs, who import high-tech component parts for their final products, which they sell under their own brand name.

Commercial subcontracting started in and still is most common in garments and footwear industries, which traditionally involved "a highly labor intensive activity with low capital and technology requirements" (Gereffi, 1993, 55), a kind of activity that was easy to relocate to the developing economies with cheap labor. In recent years, however, "industrial flexibility" became a more important factor for international commercial subcontracting (Gereffi, 1993, 56). Fashion changes every year, and demand for specific items fluctuates seasonally. Life cycles of consumer goods are becoming shorter and shorter. As a result, the U.S. buyers demand frequent change in the style and quantities of the goods they order.

American manufacturers were not responsive to such demands. For example, Liz Claiborne, a famous American fashion house, engaged in global sourcing "because of the difficulty of finding capable domestic suppliers who were willing to give Claiborne the variety of fabrics and the careful tailoring she wanted" (Gereffi, 1993, 56). However, Chinese entrepreneurs in Hong Kong and Taiwan were more adaptable. Taiwanese "bosses" in particular have successfully met the fluctuating demand of the large U.S. retailers through their flexible network of subcontractors (Shieh, 1992). Similarly, Nike, Reebok, L.A. Gear, and other fashionable athletic shoes companies rely on inexpensive and flexible subcontractors in East Asia.

Component subcontracting is more common in the home appliance, personal computer, and automobile industries. In the personal computer sector today, Taiwanese manufacturers supply 80% of "mother boards"—circuit boards with a microprocessing unit—to the world market (Asamoto, 1996, 123). American OEMs such as Compaq and Dell rely heavily on these component subcontractors. Taiwanese auto parts makers are also strong in the market of add-on accessories and spare parts (Gereffi, 1993, 58). Component subcontractors also need to meet constantly changing specifications demanded by the OEMs, as life cycles of personal computers and peripherals are shortening rapidly.

Today, global sourcing seems to be the norm rather than exception. Besides garments and home electronics, personal computers, automobiles, and even airplanes are produced through global networks of production (Dicken, 1992; Gereffi and Koreniewicz, 1994; Chen and Drysdale, 1995). Because of this ever-increasing "global sourcing" by major U.S. retailers and OEMs, the U.S. market manifests a very strong demand for imports from suppliers in the developing economies in the Pacific Rim. American outsourcing, therefore, is one of the principal factors that accounts for the EOI in the Pacific Rim nations.

C. THE IMPORT-DEPENDENT EOI

The product-cycle industrialization of the Pacific Rim nations was dependent not only on the U.S. market as discussed above but it was also dependent on Japan for imports. As Japan itself went through the product cycles, labor-intensive industries traveled to the Four Tigers and then to ASEAN countries and China. These labor-intensive industries brought some direct capital investments and technology transfer to the host nations but they did not bring the basic industries that supplied materials and tools for them. Producers in the Pacific Rim nations therefore were forced to import such materials and tools from Japan. As a result, as exports to the United States increased, so did imports from Japan.

Between 1974 and 1984, while exports from the Four Tigers and the four ASEAN nations to the United States increased by 470% to $44.9 billion, imports from Japan to the Tigers and ASEAN nations also increased by 340% to $35.0 billion (Tu, 1987, 39–40). In 1993, exports to the United States stood at $115.1 billion and imports from Japan at $121.6 billion (calculated from the data in Asian Development Bank, 1995). In 1993, therefore, the Four Tigers and the four ASEAN nations together imported more from Japan than they exported to the United States.

As indicated in Table 12, the Four Tigers and the four ASEAN nations generally enjoyed a trade surplus with the United States but suffered a trade deficit with Japan in the 1980s and early 1990s. The Four Tigers in particular consistently reg-

Table 12

Asian Developing Economies' Trade Balance with Japan and the U.S. for the Developing Economies in the Pacific Rim in 1980, 1985, 1990, and 1994 (Billions of U.S. Dollars)

	Japan				U.S.A.			
	1980	1985	1990	1994	1980	1985	1990	1994
Four Tigers								
South Korea	−2.8	−3.0	−5.9	−11.9	−0.3	+4.2	+2.5	−1.0
Taiwan	−3.2	−2.1	−7.7	−14.6	+2.1	+10.0	+9.1	+6.3
Singapore	−2.8	−2.3	−7.6	−13.1[a]	−1.0	+0.8	+1.4	+1.1[a]
Hong Kong	−4.2	−5.6	−8.6	−17.8	+2.5	+6.5	+13.2	+23.6
Four ASEAN nations								
Indonesia	+7.4	+5.9	+5.5	+4.0	+2.9	+2.3	+0.8	+2.6
Malaysia	+0.5	+1.0	−2.5	−8.2	+0.5	+0.1	0.0	+2.2
Philippines	−0.1	+0.1	−0.8	−2.2[a]	−0.4	+0.3	+0.6	+0.8[a]
Thailand	−1.0	−1.5	−6.2	−7.7[a]	−0.5	+0.3	+1.6	+2.6[a]
China	−1.1	−9.1	+1.6	−7.5[a]	−2.8	−2.9	−1.3	+6.3[a]

Source: Asian Development Bank, 1995.
[a]Refers to 1993.

Table 13

South Korea's Trade Balance (Annual Average) with Japan

	Imports from Japan (Millions of U.S. dollars)	Ratio to total imports (percent)	Balance (Millions of U.S. dollars)
1965–1970	619	41.6	−491
1971–1975	1,752	37.6	−850
1976–1980	5,104	33.1	−2,510
1981–1985	6,623	23.9	−2,735
1986–1990	15,295	29.9	−4,903
1991–1993	20,197	24.5	−8,357

Source: Watanabe and Kim, 1996, 238.

istered an increasing trade deficit with Japan, while they usually had a trade surplus with the United States. Taiwan and Hong Kong show the pattern most clearly. Among the four ASEAN nations, only oil-exporting Indonesia had a consistent trade surplus with Japan, but the margin is decreasing. Malaysia and the Philippines began to have a trade deficit with Japan in the 1990s as they increased their trade surplus with the United States. Thailand shows the clearest trend of a growing deficit with Japan and an increasing surplus with the United States throughout the 1980s and 1990s.

The "success" of EOI by the Four Tigers and the four ASEAN nations as well as China, then, was a costly one. Their EOI was coupled with a rapid increase in imports from Japan. In order to produce for the U.S. market, the Asian developing economies had to purchase tools and parts from Japan. Even South Korea, the country with most comprehensive and advanced basic materials industry among the Four Tigers, relied heavily on Japan for capital goods. As Table 13 indicates, South Korea's trade deficit with Japan worsened as Japanese imports steadily increased beginning in the 1960s. The share of Japanese imports, although declining over the years, still stood at about 25% in the early 1990s. A similar trend for Taiwan is shown in Table 14. Japan accounted for some 30% of Taiwan's total imports in 1990.

The commodities that South Korea imported from Japan were mostly the materials and tools necessary for the production of export goods. Japan accounted for 42.4% of the capital goods imported to South Korea in 1990, and 38.9% in 1993 (Watanabe and Kim, 1996, 239). In 1993, South Korea imported from Japan $3.2 billion of industrial chemical products, $3.4 billion of electrical and electronic parts, $4.1 billion of general machinery, and $1.1 billion of precision machinery (Watanabe and Kim, 1996, 241). The situation is similar if not worse for the other three Tigers, which do not have well-developed basic materials industry.

Table 14
Taiwan's Trade Balance with Japan

	Imports from Japan (Millions of U.S. dollars)	Ratio to total imports (percent)	Balance (Millions of U.S. dollars)
1955	61	30.5	+12
1960	105	35.3	−43
1965	221	39.8	−83
1970	653	42.8	−437
1975	1,812	30.6	−1,118
1980	5,353	27.1	−3,180
1985	5,549	27.6	−2,088
1990	15,998	29.2	−7,660

Source: Sumiya, Liu, and Tu, 1992, B6.

D. JAPANESE OUTPROCESSING

The dependency on Japanese imports is a consequence of Japanese "outprocessing." It was Japanese manufacturers and trading houses that created this dependency as they extended their production systems into the developing economies in the Pacific Rim.

Since the 1960s, Japan has faced higher labor costs and shortages in the course of its postwar "miracle." In response, Japanese exporters of textiles, clothing, and footwear, many of them small- and medium-scale firms, gradually shifted production to South Korea and Taiwan through direct investments, joint ventures, and technology transfer (Yoshihara, 1978; Ozawa, 1979; Gold, 1988). Large trading houses (*sogo shosha*) that handled the bulk of Japanese exports to the United States also started sourcing outside of Japan, by shifting their suppliers from Japan to South Korea and Taiwan.

The Japanese government, unlike the West German government, hesitated at bringing cheap foreign laborers into Japan for "security reasons." Not until the mid-1980s when the Japanese yen appreciated sharply against the U.S. dollar, did Japanese society face an increasing number of foreign guest workers. Consequently, Japanese exporters themselves moved outside Japan in search of cheap labor. Guided and organized by large *sogo shosha*, which "knew" the host countries, many small- and medium-scale firms that produced goods for the U.S. market began moving to South Korea and Taiwan in the mid-1960s.

The first wave of Japanese investment was made mainly in the textile, garment, and apparel industries in Hong Kong, South Korea, and Taiwan. The Japanese accounted for the largest share of foreign investment in textiles in all Four Tigers (Haggard and Cheng, 1987, 100).

The second wave of Japanese investment focused on electronics and home appliances. The newly developed export processing zones (EPZs), the first of which opened in Taiwan in 1965, attracted Japanese companies that were ready to move their labor-intensive assembly plants to the neighboring developing economies.

Matsushita, known under its brand name Panasonic, started its overseas operations in Thailand and Taiwan, where it produced batteries in the early 1960s; Matsushita then opened a factory in the Philippines in the late 1960s, it built assembly plants in Malaysia and Singapore in the 1970s, it expanded its Malaysian facilities in the 1980s, and it began production of electrical devices in China in the late 1980s (Itoh and Shibata, 1995, 194–195). In 1993, Matsushita's overseas production reached 14% of its total production (Itoh and Shibata, 1995, 194).

Sanyo, another home electronics producer, began its offshore production in Taiwan, Malaysia and Thailand in the 1960s, it built assembly plants in Hong Kong and Singapore in the early 1970s and in South Korea in the late 1970s, and it established Chinese subsidiaries in the early 1980s (Itoh and Shibata, 1995, 195). In 1993, 25% of Sanyo's total production came from these foreign establishments (Itoh and Shibata 1995, 195).

And the list goes on. Through direct investments and joint ventures, Japanese manufacturers brought capital and technology to the nascent Tigers and made them dependent on Japanese imports, for Japanese invested firms tended to rely on the suppliers back in Japan.

Malaysia's electrical/electronics industry is a case in point. For instance, Malaysia's Penang Island was developed as an export processing zone that catered to the electronics industry, to which many Japanese, U.S., and European multinationals came (Palacios, 1995). Malaysia's export of electrical machinery to Japan was worth just $55 million in 1985, but it grew more than 18 times to $1 billion in 1993. At the same time, however, Malaysia's imports from Japan in the same category also increased more than 6 times from $561 million to $3.7 billion. Of this, the import of semiconductors and integrated circuits accounted for $1.5 billion, and other parts for audio-visual and domestic equipment accounted for $0.6 billion (Itoh and Shibata, 1995, 197). In short, about 57% of Malaysia's imports of Japanese electrical machinery consisted of parts and key components.

Japanese trading houses also linked the Tigers to the U.S. market. The accepted wisdom in Taiwan is that about half of its foreign trade is handled by the Japanese. Japanese *sogo shosa* also nurtured local manufacturers through subcontracting. A Taiwanese entrepreneur recalls that he was approached by a manager of a Japanese *sogo shosha* who told him that his company would offer him "an American market" if he was interested in export (Wu, 1987). The Japanese trading houses often provided loans and technical assistance as well as marketing skills to the local subcontractors. This also enhanced local entrepreneurs' reliance on Japanese-made parts and tools. The magnitude of subcontracting by the Japanese trading houses, however, is hard to measure.

As a result, both Japanese-invested and local manufacturers in South Korea and Taiwan, and later in other Asian developing countries, became dependent on Japan for capital goods. This dependency was further enhanced as the Four Tigers and ASEAN nations developed more capital- and technology-intensive industries such as electrical machinery, personal computers, and automobiles. The import of tools and key components from Japan increased in quantity and in price.

I am not arguing here that Japanese-affiliated firms were the primary factor in the EOI of the Four Tigers or the ASEAN nations. The relative importance of EPZs was limited and short-lived in South Korea and Taiwan (Haggard and Cheng, 1987, 93). What I do maintain, however, is that not just Japanese affiliates but more importantly domestic enterprises in the Four Tigers depended on Japanese imports for basic materials and industrial tools.

It was Hyundai, the big Korean *chaebol,* that assembled compact cars for export to the U.S. market in the late 1980s. But, the much-publicized Hyundai "pony" was produced under a technical assistance agreement with Mitsubishi and it carried a Mitsubishi-made engine. There are thousands of local Taiwanese small factories that today assemble "mother boards" for personal computers worldwide. But nearly every mother board made in Taiwan contains Japanese-made memory chips.

The EOI of the developing economies in the Pacific Rim, therefore, was systematically linked to the internationalization of Japanese manufacturers and it was sustained by the increasing import of capital goods from Japan.[2] Japanese outprocessing, then, was as important a factor in the EOI in the Pacific Rim nations as American outsourcing.

E. EOI as Fragmentary Industrialization

If the newly industrializing Asian economies depended heavily on the United States as "the" market for EOI, they also depended heavily on Japan as "the" supplier of the means and materials needed for EOI. The so-called "miracles" through EOI in fact created the "double dependency": dependency on American buyers and dependency on Japanese producers.

The developing economies in the Pacific Rim take part only partially in the "global commodity chains" that extend between Japan and the United States. The EOI in the Pacific Rim, therefore, did not result in the balanced development of all industries. No Tiger achieved "full-range industrialization" comparable to that in Japan or the United States (Kojima Kiyoshi's term cited in Watanabe and Kim, 1996, 246). The outcome of EOI in the Four Tigers was the disproportionate and limited development of particular segments of the economy, a "partial industrial-

---

[2]U.S. and European manufacturers also engage in worldwide outprocessing. While U.S. and European firms export more to their home markets, the Japanese tend to export to markets other than Japan. U.S. and European outprocessing thus increases not only imports from but also exports to their home markets. The Japanese, in contrast, only increased imports from Japan and exports to the U.S.

ization" as Watanabe and Kim (1996, 247) call it. As successful and remarkable as it is, EOI in the Pacific Rim remains "fragmentary" at best.

IV. THE ROLES OF THE FOUR TIGERS IN THE 1990s

So far this chapter has analyzed some general features common to the EOI in the Four Tigers as well as in the four ASEAN nations and China. In this section, I turn to the features that distinguish the Four Tigers from one another and I examine the different roles they play in the Pacific Rim economy in the 1990s.

A. SOUTH KOREA: THE BASE OF INDEPENDENT EXPORTERS

South Korea perhaps is the only Tiger that attempted to develop an integrated "national economy" through EOI (Hattori and Sato, 1996b, 348–349). The ideology of "unification" as well as the urgency of building a domestic defense industry were important motivations for the South Korean political/military elite. The "united Korea" will be comparable in population to Britain, France, or Germany, all of which have strong national economies of their own. Under the military threat from the North, building a domestic defense industry was deemed necessary and the heavy industry was to be the foundation of a strong defense industry. Hyundai not only makes compact cars for the U.S. market but also builds tanks for the South Korean army.

Especially under the dictatorial regime of Park Chung Hee who assumed power in 1961 through a military coup, the South Korean state launched a series of economic policies aimed at the development of such heavy industries as petroleum, chemical, iron and steel, automobiles, and shipbuilding, and implemented them strongly and coercively (Amsden, 1989; Song, 1990; Cho and Kim, 1991). Today, South Korea is the world leading exporter of ships and is the only non-Western, non-Japanese nation that exports a large number of automobiles.

The state decided the target industries, it set the export target, and it selected a few existing large enterprises and nurtured them through subsidies and privileges into large-scale mass producers in becoming "Asia's next giant" (Amsden, 1989). As pointed out earlier, even South Korea is dependent on Japan for a variety of capital goods and it still suffers from "fragmentary" industrialization. Yet, South Korea is the Tiger that has made the greatest strides toward building an integrated national economy.

Thanks to the state's selective support and protection, large and vertically integrated business groups called *chaebols* emerged in South Korea (Kim, 1991; Hattori, 1996). Modeled after Japanese business groups, each South Korean *chaebol* attempted to contain a "full set" of enterprises from heavy industries to general trading companies.

The South Korean *chaebol,* like large Japanese corporations, also strived to build its own brand name in the world market. Names such as Hyundai (automobiles), Samsung and Lucky-Goldstar (both in home electronics), and Leading Edge (personal computers) are now well known in the United States.

South Korean *chaebols* produce export goods by themselves under their own brand names and they market them by themselves through their own sales network. Large *chaebols* with their vertically integrated production systems were able to achieve efficiency through economies of scale and to build worldwide distribution networks through general trading companies.

The role of South Korea in the 1990s, then, is the base of new "independent exporters" who "control export and distribution networks in global commodity chains, in addition to attaining a high degree of productive efficiency" (Gereffi, 1993, 54). There are many companies that engage in component and/or commercial subcontracting as well. Nevertheless, South Korea is the only Tiger that was able to foster the growth of private businesses big enough to possess financial, industrial, and marketing resources needed for independent exporters. To the extent that no other Tiger was able to do so, South Korea stands out as the base of independent exporters.

B. Taiwan: The Home
of Internationalizing Subcontractors

In Taiwan, 30 years of EOI resulted in an industrial organization sharply different from that in South Korea. Small- and medium-scale entrepreneurs dominate the private sector, especially the export sector, of the island economy (Sumiya, Liu, and Tu, 1992). Through personal relationships and contacts, Taiwanese "bosses" have developed complex horizontal and vertical subcontracting networks that are flexible and responsive to the changing demands of large foreign buyers (Shieh, 1992; Numazaki, 1997).

This does not mean that the Nationalist state on Taiwan was weak or that large-scale corporations are absent in Taiwan. Since the 1940s, the Nationalist state has owned and controlled large public corporations in such basic materials industries as petroleum and chemicals and in communication and transportation. The government also tried to develop such heavy industries as steel and shipbuilding through public enterprises in the 1970s. Nevertheless, those large public corporations are oriented primarily to the domestic market. Large private corporations also emerged since the 1960s, and loosely knit business groups called *guanxiqiye* appeared in the 1970s and 1980s (Numazaki, 1991, 1992, 1993), but they are also geared toward the domestic market (Sumiya, Liu, and Tu, 1992; Numazaki, 1992).

Taiwanese businesses in the export market primarily are small independent entrepreneurs who act as subcontractors of some sort. As subcontractors, they remain largely anonymous. Much of the merchandise displayed in U.S. retail outlets is marked "made in Taiwan," but usually it carries the brand name of an OEM. Athletic shoes "made in Taiwan" are still called Nike and L. A. Gear. Taiwanese exporters are either component subcontractors or commercial subcontractors who supply component parts or finished products to OEMs abroad.

The personal computer industry is a good example. In 1993, Taiwan surpassed Japan in terms of the number of personal computers produced. In 1994, Taiwan produced more than 5 million personal computers, or 10% of total world production, and more than 11 million mother boards, or 80% of total world production (Asamoto, 1996, 123). And yet, most of them are not sold under original brand names but are supplied to OEMs such as Compaq and Dell. Acer, which produces and markets computers under its own brand name, is a rare exception.

The new development in the 1990s is that increasing numbers of these global subcontractors are extending their production networks overseas into China, Malaysia, the Philippines, and most recently Vietnam. In response to the sharp appreciation of the New Taiwan dollar against the U.S. dollar and the rising cost of labor in Taiwan, Taiwanese entrepreneurs are rapidly internationalizing their operation (Asamoto, 1996). The number of foreign direct investments was just 97 cases for the period between 1980 and 1986, but increased to 1424 cases during the period between 1987 and 1993, excluding the investments in China (Asamoto, 1996, 164, 167). As for China, gradual relaxation of trade restrictions by Taiwan and active courting of Taiwanese investors by China contributed to the rapid increase of Taiwanese investments in China beginning in the late 1980s. In 1994 alone, Taiwanese investments in China amounted to 934 cases worth $962 million, the second largest total after Hong Kong (Asamoto, 1996, 179).

Taiwan in the 1990s, therefore, is the home of "internationalizing subcontractors." Taiwanese entrepreneurs who first created extensive subcontracting networks in Taiwan are extending their networks beyond the island through joint ventures and direct investments in Southeast Asia and China.

C. SINGAPORE: THE CENTER
FOR INTERNATIONAL PROCUREMENT

Singapore, a city–state at the heart of Southeast Asia, has achieved EOI primarily through the activities of foreign transnational corporations (TNCs). In 1972, for instance, wholly or partially foreign owned firms accounted for 84% of manufactured exports, and in 1980 the figure reached 92.9% (Haggard and Cheng, 1987, 93). Unlike their counterparts in Taiwan and Hong Kong, small- and medium-scale Chinese firms in Singapore are not the main actor in the export sector (Tu, 1988, 182).

TNCs moved into Singapore first as manufacturers. They invested in 14 industrial zones created by the Singaporean state and assembled export goods as they did in the EPZs in the other Tigers.

Singapore's unique location with its well-developed financial sector and good communications and transportation facilities, however, gave it a new role in the late 1980s: the center for "international procurement."

Both outsourcing and outprocessing require sophisticated procurement activities on a global scale. Outsourcing necessitates coordination and management of a number of subcontractors and suppliers, often in several different countries. Outprocessing involves arranging and executing complex intra- and interfirm transactions in raw materials, half-finished components, and finished goods across national borders, often "just in time."

As they increased their outsourcing and outprocessing in Southeast Asia, both U.S. and Japanese TNCs established international procurement offices (IPOs) at locations close to the source of supplies to facilitate the growing volume of transactions overseas. IPOs in electronics industry, for example, not only procure parts and components but also "buy a wide range of other products including primary commodities, chemicals, furniture, garments and a variety of consumer goods" (Yue, 1995, 244). IPOs thus also boost local economic activities.

A TNC may establish its own buying office or it may rely on an independent "buying agent" or it may simply assign the procuring role to an existing manufacturing plant (Yue, 1995, 244). IPOs that have trading company status "also handle vender qualification and quality assurance, business planning, international logistics, after-sales service support and finance" (Yue, 1995, 244).

In the mid-1980s the Singaporean government introduced new tax incentives to persuade major TNCs to set up IPOs in Singapore (Yue, 1995, 244). In 1992, 106 IPOs in Singapore together purchased more than $4 billion in goods mainly from Pacific Rim nations and redistributed them across the region (Yue, 1995, 243–247). Nearly half of the purchases were made in Singapore itself, but about 15% were made in the other three Tigers, some 16% in the four ASEAN nations, and another 14% in Japan, while the destination of purchases ranged from Singapore itself (38.8%) and the four ASEAN nations (13.8%), to the United States (19.8%), Europe (14.2%), and Japan (4.9%) (Yue, 1995, 245).

TNCs then are increasingly centralizing their procurement activities in Singapore, a regional business center with sophisticated financial and other institutions. The role of Singapore in the 1990s therefore seems to be as the center for international procurement.

D. Hong Kong: The Hub of the Greater South China Economic Zone

Hong Kong's EOI was characterized by the predominance of small- and medium-scale Chinese firms in labor-intensive light industries such as textiles, clothing, toys, and various plastics products. In textiles, relatively large manufacturers—mainly émigré entrepreneurs from Shanghai—played a major role in the 1950s and 1960s (Wong, 1988). In the other industries, however, small- and medium-scale enterprises prevailed (Sit and Wong, 1989).

Small manufacturers in Hong Kong, like their cousins in Taiwan, relied heavily on subcontracting and have developed flexible networks of production in the colony that churned out garments, footwear, toys, travel goods, handbags, and so on, for the export market (Sit and Wong, 1989).

As China adopted the "open door" policy and started to develop special economic zones that catered to foreign investors, Hong Kong exporters who faced rising labor costs at home and growing competition abroad began moving their factories to China in order to tap into the pool of cheap labor in nearby Guangdong Province, especially in the special economic zones of Shenzhen and Zhuhai (Sit and Wong, 1989; Chen, 1993; Sung, 1995). Hong Kong exporters increasingly engaged in outprocessing in Southern China. It is estimated that today Hong Kong enterprises employ some 3 million workers in Guangdong, while the manufacturing labor force in Hong Kong itself peaked at about 900,000 workers in 1984 and declined to about 500,000 in 1993 (Sung, 1995, 64).

Outprocessing by Hong Kong exporters in China generated heavy trade between Hong Kong and China. China imports raw materials and half-processed goods from and through Hong Kong. Hong Kong in turn imports Chinese products, then further processes them and packages them for export to the consumer market abroad.

As discussed earlier, Taiwanese manufacturers recently also started to move their productive facilities to China. The lack of formal ties between the governments in Beijing and Taipei and the Taipei's ban on direct linkage with China forced these Taiwanese entrepreneurs to invest in and trade with China through Hong Kong (Chen, 1993; Sung, 1995).

Finally, large TNCs are now setting up regional headquarters in Hong Kong to coordinate production and procurement in the South China region as a whole. Nike, for instance, places orders to Chinese-Taiwanese joint ventures in Guangdong and Fujian, which import most of the raw materials from Taiwan through Hong Kong, and which keeps Taiwanese supervisors in Chinese factories as well as managing staff in Hong Kong that takes care of designing, testing, and shipping of products bound for the U.S. market (Chen, 1993, 101–102). NEC, to take another example, has an office in Hong Kong with "a staff of 26 production engineers" who "travel around the region coordinating production" of dot matrix printers in "six to eight factories in southern China" as well as other products in Taiwan and Southeast Asia (Simon and Jun, 1995, 219).

In recent years, Hong Kong is becoming a key node in the global commodity chain that "stretches across the Pacific Ocean through the United States, Taiwan, Hong Kong, and China" (Chen, 1993, 102). The role of Hong Kong in the 1990s, therefore, is the "hub" in the so-called "Greater South China Economic

Zone" (Chen, 1993) and it serves as the center of "subregional economic integration" (Sung, 1995). Hong Kong was "handed over" to China on July 1, 1997. The long-term impact of reunification with China on the economic role of Hong Kong remains uncertain. The short-term effect, however, is believed to be small.

V. CONCLUSION

This chapter describes the overall pattern of EOI in the Asian side of the Pacific Rim, it examines the structural linkages between the developing economies of the region, Japan, and the United States, and it explores the emerging role of the Four Tigers in the changing global market of the 1990s.

The overall pattern of EOI is clear and is similar for the Four Tigers as well as for the four ASEAN nations and China. Rapid economic growth was achieved through rapid industrialization, mostly in labor-intensive light industries that produced consumer goods for export mainly to the U.S. market. A comparison of the developing economies shows that each went through similar stages of product cycles at different points of time and at a different pace. The EOI in the Pacific Rim followed a "classic product-cycle industrialization pattern."

The EOI of the developing economies in the region, however, created a "double dependency," that is, a dependency on the U.S. market for exports and on Japanese industry for imports. As the Tigers and ASEAN nations increased their exports to the United States, their imports from Japan also climbed. Taiwan and Hong Kong, for example, show a chronic trade surplus with the United States and a chronic trade deficit with Japan. This double dependency was brought about by fragmentary industrialization, a consequence of American outsourcing and Japanese outprocessing. American retailers subcontracted out certain portions of the global commodity chain to Asian manufacturers, while Japanese producers shifted limited segments of the production process to the developing economies in East and Southeast Asia. Consequently, no developing economy in the Pacific Rim was able to industrialize in a full range. The EOI resulted in a fragmentary industrialization that was dependent on the United States and Japan. Phenomenal as it was, EOI in the Pacific Rim was but an integral part of structural changes in the global economy.

In the 1990s, the Four Tigers assumed new roles and captured new niches in the changing global market. South Korea, with its vertically integrated *chaebols,* is becoming the base for new independent exporters. Taiwan, with its numerous entrepreneurs, is turning into the home of internationalizing subcontractors who are willing to extend their network of production into Southeast Asia and China. Singapore and Hong Kong are becoming the regional nodes in the increasingly extensive networks of global commodity chains—Singapore as the center for international procurement in Southeast Asia and Hong Kong as the hub in the Greater South China Economic Zone.

Such adjustments and adaptations notwithstanding, the basic structural context in which the Four Tigers are embedded remains the same. They still rely strongly on the demand generated by the U.S. market and they still depend heavily on the import of parts and tools from Japan. Even South Korea, which came closest to developing an integrated national economy, suffers from the "fragmentary" nature of its industry and continues to face the double dependency inherent in the EOI. Although the Four Tigers succeeded in EOI, they have not yet found a solution to its negative consequences.

REFERENCES

Amsden, A. H. (1979). Taiwan's economic history: A case of "etatisme" and a challenge to dependency theory, *Modern China* **5**, 3, 341–379.

Amsden, A. H. (1985). The state and Taiwan's economic development, *in* "Bringing the State Back In" (P. Evans, D. Rueschemeyer, and T. Skocpol, Eds.), pp. 78–106. New York: Cambridge University Press.

Amsden, A. H. (1989). "Asia's Next Giant: South Korea and Late Industrialization." New York: Oxford University Press.

Appelbaum, R. P., and Henderson, J. (Eds.). (1992). "States and Development in the Asian Pacific Rim." Newbury Park, CA: Sage.

Asamoto, T. (1996). "Gendai Taiwan keizai bunseki" [An analysis of contemporary Taiwan economy]. Tokyo: Keiso Shobo.

Asian Development Bank. (1995). "Key Indicators of Developing Asian and Pacific Countries, 1995." Manila: Oxford University Press.

Balassa, B. (1971). Industrial policies in Taiwan and Korea. *Weltwirtschaftliches Archiv* **106**, 1, 55–77.

Balassa, B. (1978). Export incentives and export performance in developing countries: A comparative analysis. *Weltwirtschaftliches Archiv* **114**, 1, 24–61.

Berger, P. (1986). "The Capitalist Revolution: Fifty Propositions about Prosperity, Equality and Liberty." New York: Basic Books.

Castillo, V. M., and Acosta, R. J. R. (1993). Restructuring manufacturing: Mexican *Maquiladoras* and East Asian EPZs in the presence of the North American Free Trade Agreement, *in* "What Is in a Rim? Critical Perspectives on the Pacific Region Idea." (A. Dirlik, Ed.), pp. 69–88. Boulder, CO: Westview Press.

Chen, E. K. Y., and Drysdale, P. (Eds.). (1995). "Corporate Links and Foreign Direct Investment in Asia and the Pacific." Pymble, New South Wales: HarperEducational (Australia).

Chen, X. M. (1993). China's growing integration with the Asia-Pacific economy, *in* "What Is in a Rim? Critical Perspectives on the Pacific Region Idea." (A. Dirlik, Ed.), pp. 89–119. Boulder, CO: Westview Press.

Cho, L. J., and Kim, Y. H. (Eds.). (1991). "Economic Development in the Republic of Korea: A Policy Perspective." Honolulu: East-West Center.

Clegg, S. R., and Redding, S. G. (Eds.). (1990). "Capitalism in Contrasting Cultures." Berlin: Walter de Gruyter.

Cumings, B. (1987). The origins and development of the Northeast Asian political economy: Industrial sectors, product cycles, and political consequences, *in* "The political economy of the Asian industrialization" (F. C. Deyo, Ed.), pp. 44–83, Ithaca, NY: Cornell University Press.

Deyo, F. C. (Ed.). (1987). "The Political Economy of the New Asian Industrialism." Ithaca, NY: Cornell University Press.

Dicken, P. (1992). "Global Shift: The Internationalisation of Economic Activity." New York: Guilford Press.

Dirlik, A. (Ed.). (1993). "What Is in a Rim? Critical Perspectives on the Pacific Region Idea." Boulder, CO: Westview Press.

Gereffi, G. (1993). Global sourcing and regional division of labor in the Pacific rim, in "What Is in a Rim? Critical Perspectives on the Pacific Region Idea" (A. Dirlik, Ed.), pp. 51–68. Boulder, CO: Westview Press.

Gereffi, G. (1994). The role of big buyers in global commodity chains: How U.S. retail networks affect overseas production patterns, in "Commodity Chains and Global Capitalism" (G. Gereffi and M. Korzeniewicz, Eds.), pp. 95–122. Westport, CT: Praeger.

Gereffi, G., and Korzeniewicz, M. (Eds.). (1994). "Commodity Chains and Global Capitalism." Westport, CT: Praeger.

Gold, T. B. (1986). "State and Society in the Taiwan Miracle." Armonk, NY: M. E. Sharpe.

Gold, T. B. (1988). Entrepreneurs, multinationals and the state, in "Contending Approaches to the Political Economy of Taiwan" (E. A. Winkler and S. Greenhalgh, Eds.), pp. 175–205. Armonk, NY: M. E. Sharpe.

Haggard, S., and Cheng, T. J. (1987). State and capital in the East Asian NICs, in "The Political Economy of the New Asian Industrialism" (F. C. Deyo, Ed.), pp. 84–135. Ithaca, NY: Cornell University Press.

Hattori, T. (1996). Kankoku ni okeru "zaibatsu" teki kigyo hatten ["chabol"-led development of business in South Korea], in "Kankoku Taiwan no hatten mekanizumu" [The Mechanism of Development in South Korea and Taiwan] (T. Hattori and Y. Sato, Eds.), pp. 319–345. Tokyo: Ajia Keizai Kenkyusho.

Hattori, T., and Sato, Y. (1996a). Josho [Introduction], in "Kankoku Taiwan no hatten mekanizumu" [The Mechanism of Development in South Korea and Taiwan] (T. Hattori and Y. Sato, Eds.), pp. 3–32. Tokyo: Ajia Keizai Kenkyusho.

Hattori, T., and Sato, Y. (1996b). Shusho [Conclusion], in "Kankoku Taiwan no hatten mekanizumu" [The Mechanism of Development in South Korea and Taiwan] (T. Hattori and Y. Sato, Eds.), pp. 347–360. Tokyo: Ajia Keizai Kenkyusho.

Hofheinz, R., and Calder, K. E. (1982). "The Eastasia Edge." New York: Basic Books.

Hughes, H. (Ed.). (1988). "Achieving Industrialization in East Asia." Cambridge: Cambridge University Press.

Itoh, M., and Shibata, J. (1995). A study of the operations of Japanese firms in Asia: The electrical machinery industry, in "Corporate Links and Foreign Direct Investment in Asia and the Pacific" (E. K. Y. Chen and P. Drysdale, Eds.), pp. 187–202. Pymble, New South Wales: HarperEducational (Australia).

Kim, E. M. (1991). The industrial organization and growth of the Korean chaebol, in "Business Networks and Economic Development in East and Southeast Asia" (G. G. Hamilton, Ed.), pp. 272–299. Hong Kong: Centre of Asian Studies, University of Hong Kong.

Naya, S. (1988). The role of trade policies in the industrialization of rapidly growing Asian developing countries, in "Achieving Industrialization in East Asia" (Hughes, H., Ed.), pp. 64–84. Cambridge: Cambridge University Press.

Numazaki, I. (1991). The role of personal networks in the making of Taiwan's guanxiqiye (related enterprises), in "Business Networks and Economic Development in East and Southeast Asia" (G. Hamilton, Ed.), pp. 77–93. Hong Kong: Centre of Asian Studies, University of Hong Kong.

Numazaki, I. (1992). "Networks and Partnerships: The Social Organization of the Chinese Business Elite in Taiwan," Ph.D. dissertation, Michigan State University.

Numazaki, I. (1993). The Tainanbang: The rise and growth of a "banana-bunch-shaped" business group in Taiwan. Developing Economies 31, 4, 485–510.

Numazaki, I. (1997). The Laoban-Led Development of Business Enterprises in Taiwan: An Analysis of Chinese Entrepreneurship. Developing Economies 35, 4, 440–457.

Ozawa, T. (1979). "Multinationalism Japanese Style: The Political Economy of Outward Dependency." Princeton: Princeton University Press.

Palacios, J. J. (1995). Multinational corporations and technology transfer in Penang and Guadalajara, *in* "Corporate Links and Foreign Direct Investment in Asia and the Pacific" (E. K. Y. Chen and P. Drysdale, Eds.), pp. 153–186. Pymble, New South Wales: HarperEducational (Australia).

Porter, M. E. (1990). "The Competitive Advantage of Nations." London: Macmillan.

Redding, S. G. (1990). "The Spirit of Chinese Capitalism." Berlin: Walter de Gruyter.

Shieh, G. S. (1992). "'Boss' Island: The Subcontracting Network and Micro-Entrepreneurship in Taiwan's Development." New York: Perter Lang.

Simon, D., and Jun, Y. W. (1995). Technological change, foreign investment and the new strategic thrust of Japanese firms in the Asia Pacific, *in* "Corporate Links and Foreign Direct Investment in Asia and the Pacific (E. K. Y. Chen and P. Drysdale, Eds.), pp. 203–226. Pymble, New South Wales: HarperEducational (Australia).

Sit, V. F. S., and Wong, S. L. (1989). "Small and Medium Industries in an Export-Oriented Economy: The Case of Hong Kong." Hong Kong: Centre of Asian Studies, University of Hong Kong.

Song, B. N. (1990). "The Rise of the Korean Economy." New York: Oxford University Press.

Sumiya, M., Liu, J. J., and Tu, Z. Y. (1992). "Taiwan no keizai" [The economy of Taiwan]. Tokyo: Tokyo Daigaku Shuppankai.

Sung, Y. W. (1995). Subregional economic integration: Hong Kong, Taiwan, South China and beyond, *in* "Corporate Links and Foreign Direct Investment in Asia and the Pacific (E. K. Y. Chen and P. Drysdale, Eds.), pp. 56–86. Pymble, New South Wales: HarperEducational (Australia).

Tu, Z. Y. (1987). "Dochaku to kindai no nikkusu-asean" [The indigenous and modern economies of NICs and ASEAN]. Tokyo: Ochanomizu Shobo.

Tu, Z. Y. (1988). "Nikkusu" [NICs]. Tokyo: Kodansha.

Vernon, R. (1971). "Sovereignty at Bay: The Multinational Spread of U.S. Enterprises." New York: Basic Books.

Vogel, E. F. (1991). "The Four Little Dragons." Cambridge, MA: Harvard University Press.

Wade, R. (1990). "Governing the Market: Economic Theory and the Role of Government in East Asian industrialization." Princeton, NJ: Princeton University Press.

Watanabe, T., and Kim, C-N. (1996). "Kankoku keizai hatten ron" [A treatise on Korean economic development]. Tokyo: Keiso Shobo.

Wong, S. L. (1988). "Emigrant Entrepreneurs: Shanghai Industrialists in Hong Kong." Hong Kong: Oxford University Press.

World Bank. (1993). "The East Asian Miracle: Economic Growth and Public Policy." New York: Oxford University Press.

Wu, X. Q. (1987). "Rensheng qishi" [Seventy years of my life]. Taipei: Caituanfaren Wu Zunxian wenjiao gongyi jijinhui.

Yoshihara, K. (1978). "Japanese Investment in Southeast Asia." Honolulu: University Press of Hawaii.

Yue, C. S. (1995). The international procurement and sales behavior of multinational enterprises, *in* "Corporate Links and Foreign Direct Investment in Asia and the Pacific" (E. K. Y. Chen and P. Drysdale, Eds.), pp. 227–261. Pymble, New South Wales: HarperEducational (Australia).

PART II

The Actors and Institutions of Economic Development

CHAPTER 4

Commodity Chains and Regional Divisions of Labor in East Asia

Gary Gereffi
Department of Sociology
Duke University
Durham, North Carolina 27706

The newly industrializing economies (NIEs) of East Asia—South Korea, Taiwan, Hong Kong, and Singapore—have been the focus of considerable attention by academics and policy-makers alike for their outstanding economic record over the past four decades. In the 1960s, these nations launched the labor-intensive phases of their export-oriented development strategies. In the 1970s, South Korea and Taiwan added heavy and chemical industrialization drives to their policy agenda, while Hong Kong and Singapore consolidated their positions as regional production centers in apparel and electronics, respectively. In the 1980s, all of the NIEs began to upgrade their manufactured exports with products that contained significantly higher levels of knowledge, skill, and technology, and in the 1990s, they are continuing their quest for advanced industrial status via high-value manufactured exports, the diversification into service industries, the promotion of original brandname exports, and the expansion of outward investments to low-wage countries to consolidate their growing role in international production and trade networks.

Explanations of how the East Asian NIEs attained and sustained their competitive advantage, and the implications for other developing countries, are diverse. Neoclassical economists focus on low wages as the initial stimulus for labor-intensive export industries, coupled with government policies that have created free markets, stability, and openness to trade. The latter position is challenged by statist interpretations, which argue that significant government intervention is a key feature of East Asia's export success. The World Bank recently has tried to steer a middle course in this debate by claiming that East Asia has pursued "market friendly" economic growth, which combines an adherence to macroeconomic policy fundamentals with

The Four Asian Tigers: Economic Development and the Global Political Economy

selective state intervention. While the neoclassical and statist perspectives show that labor costs and government policies are key factors in the early stages of export-oriented development, they are not sufficient to account for the many changes that have occurred during the recent evolution of East Asia's export industries.

In an effort to move beyond the state versus markets debate, this chapter focuses on the organization of production as a major determinant of industrial transformation in East Asia. During the past several decades, East Asia's export industries have become increasingly diversified, internationalized, and regionally integrated. Whereas industrial upgrading from labor-intensive to capital- and technology-intensive industries has clearly occurred within Japan and the East Asian NIEs, by itself the industrial upgrading concept is inadequate because it retains the national economy as the central unit of analysis. Related perspectives such as the "flying geese" model of East Asian development and product life cycle theory, while more dynamic than comparative advantage explanations of economic growth, also fail to capture the significance of a network-centered view of the world economy. The successful export industries of Japan and the East Asian NIEs are part of a broader process of globalization in which international production and trade networks create hierarchical divisions of labor within and between regions. East Asian firms have mastered the art of using networks as a strategic asset. The technological and organizational learning that occurs within these networks is an essential feature of East Asia's ability to endogenize its international competitive edge.

In making these arguments, I utilize a global commodity chains approach to highlight the existence of overlapping regional divisions of labor in East Asia created by producer-driven and buyer-driven commodity chains. These contrasting forms of international economic organization coexist in Asia, they are sectorally differentiated, and they have very different implications for national and regional development. The apparel and electronics industries will be used to illustrate these phenomena. Even after considering the role of low wages, quotas, and other government policies, I conclude that organizational variables (such as types of commodity chains, the structure of networks, organizational learning, and conventions) are significant determinants of export growth, industrial upgrading, and other aspects of economic performance in East Asia.

I. STATES, MARKETS, AND NETWORKS IN EAST ASIA'S "ECONOMIC MIRACLE"

Japan and the East Asian NIEs have been dubbed "miracle economies" because of their unparalleled accomplishments in the latter half of the twentieth century. They registered record economic growth rates not only during the prosperous 1960s when international trade and investment were expanding rapidly, but they also managed to sustain their dynamism through the 1970s and 1980s in the face of several oil price hikes, a global recession, and rising protectionism in their major export markets. In addition, the exceptionally rapid economic growth of the East Asian economies has been accompanied by high and rising per capita incomes, relatively low levels of inequality in wealth and income distribution, and dramatic improvements in other dimensions of human welfare, such as education, health, and housing.

In 1993, the World Bank published its much heralded study entitled *The East Asian Miracle,* which argues for the uniqueness of East Asia's record of rapid and sustained economic growth with social equity. Prompted by Japan's vocal dissatisfaction with the World Bank's overemphasis on macroeconomic issues in Bank structural adjustment policy and by policy disagreements within the Bank itself, the *East Asian Miracle* study, whose $1.2 million price tag was funded mainly by the Japanese government, focuses on eight high-performing Asian economies (HPAEs): Japan, the "Four Tigers" (or East Asian NIEs), and the three newly industrializing economies of Southeast Asia (Malaysia, Thailand, and Indonesia). If one looks at economies between 1965 and 1990 that are characterized by high growth (annual increases in gross domestic product per capita above 4.0%) and low relative inequality (a ratio of less than 10 between the top quintile and the bottom quintile of household income), there are just seven high-growth, low-inequality countries in the world. All of them are in East Asia; only Malaysia, which is high-growth but has an inequality index of about 15, is excluded among the set of HPAEs (World Bank, 1993, 31).

The track record of the HPAEs is superior to that of any other region of the world since 1960. Between 1960 and 1990, the growth in per capita income in the HPAEs (an average annual increase of 5.5% for these three decades) was more than double that of the advanced industrial economies, roughly three times as fast as in Latin America and South Asia, and five times faster than in sub-Saharan Africa. High rates of investment, exceeding 20% of gross domestic product during the period from 1960 through 1990, especially private investment, were supported by a rapid increase in domestic savings. Indeed, the HPAEs are the only developing economies in which savings exceed investment, making them net exporters of capital (see World Bank, 1993, chap. 1; Page, 1994).

Exports are perhaps the most impressive measure of East Asian dynamism. The HPAEs have been steadily increasing their share of world exports, from 8% in 1965 to 13% in 1980 and 18% in 1990. These percentages are even higher for manufactured exports (21.3% of the world total in 1990), which represent well over 90% of all exports in Japan, South Korea, Taiwan, and Hong Kong. Excluding Japan, the remaining HPAEs account for three-quarters of the developing world's manufactured exports. Hong Kong and the People's Republic of China topped the list of developing country exporters in 1995 with $174 billion and $149 billion in overseas sales, respectively, followed by South Korea ($125 billion), Singapore ($118 billion), and Taiwan ($112 billion). In the next tier, several of the Southeast Asian

HPAEs (Malaysia, Thailand, Indonesia), along with Brazil and Mexico, all generated substantial exports, ranging from $45 to $80 billion (World Bank, 1993, 37–38; 1997, 242–243). Thus, the HPAEs (excluding Japan) and China account for eight of the top 10 exporters in the developing world.

How can we explain these differences in economic performance between East Asia and other regions of the Third World? The World Bank's *East Asian Miracle* report identifies three alternative views on the role of public policy in the HPAEs. The "neoclassical" view attributes East Asian success to limited government intervention and an export-oriented trade strategy. Unlike nations in Latin America and other regions that followed the protectionist path of import-substituting industrialization (ISI), the East Asian NIEs relied on export-oriented industrialization (EOI) since the mid-1960s to stoke global demand for their manufactured exports and to promote local industrial upgrading (see Gereffi and Wyman, 1990; Haggard, 1990). Neoclassical economists and prominent international financial institutions such as the World Bank loudly touted EOI as a successful development paradigm that the rest of the developing world should emulate. The explicit message directed at Latin America and the other countries pursuing ISI was that "the economic performance of the outward-oriented economies has been broadly superior to that of the inward-oriented economies in almost all respects," most notably increased exports, employment, and economic growth (World Bank,1987, 85).

The "revisionist" view is that East Asian governments actively "led the market" in critical ways via industrial policy and other measures (Wade, 1990). Interventionist states were central to East Asian success because of the presence of pervasive market failures, which governments remedied by altering incentives and deliberately "getting the prices wrong" to boost industries that otherwise would not have thrived (Amsden, 1989). The lessons to be learned from East Asia are still in dispute, as Amsden (1994, 627) wryly observes: "East Asia created competitiveness by subsidizing learning, whereas Bank policy emphasizes methods that effectively cut real wages." However, the key features of East Asia's success may lie less in the area of economic policy than in the region's dynamic institutional arrangements. The East Asian institutional model is characterized by: (a) local ownership and control in the leading export and intermediate goods industries (Gereffi, 1990); (b) substantial backward and forward linkages within the domestic economy involving a wide variety of local business groups and subcontracting networks (Hamilton and Biggart, 1988; Orrù *et al.,* 1991); (c) a high level of endogenous technological development, although few of these countries (with the exception of Japan) have made true innovative technological breakthroughs (Lall, 1994); and (d) "industrialization by learning," either by competitively benchmarking best practices or inventing them (Amsden, 1989; Sabel, 1994).

The "market-friendly" view advocated by the Bank is that economic growth resulted from functional interventions in "fundamentals," such as stable macroeconomic management, high investments in human capital (especially education), secure financial systems, limited price distortions, and openness to foreign technology and trade. Although selective interventions—such as mild financial repression (keeping interest rates positive, but low), directed credit, the promotion of specific industries, and export-push trade policies—were commonplace among the HPAEs, these industrial policies were considered by the Bank to be "largely ineffective" in promoting growth and enhancing productivity. Elsewhere in the report, the Bank qualifies its assessment, "Our judgment is that in a few economies, mainly in Northeast Asia, in some instances, government intervention resulted in higher and more equal growth than otherwise would have occurred. However, the prerequisites for success were so rigorous that policymakers seeking to follow similar paths in other developing economies have often met with failure" (World Bank, 1993, 312 and 6).

What is missing from the World Bank's market-friendly position is the realization that East Asia's "macroeconomic basics"—high saving and investment rates, expenditures on education, and exports—are supported by "microinstitutional foundations" that embed the development process in a local context. Social and economic networks are one of the microinstitutional pillars supporting East Asian development because they facilitate organizational innovations and technological learning at the domestic level. Primary consideration in this chapter will be given to transnational production and trade networks in East Asia's apparel and electronics commodity chains. In contrast to the erroneous image of placelessness often associated with globalization, these networks are grounded in highly endogenous forms of economic coordination held together by a variety of established and emergent conventions (Storper, 1995).

A network-centered perspective requires us to view East Asia as an interrelated regional economy. Malaysia, Thailand, and Indonesia—the southern tier of the HPAEs—enjoyed fast growth and an export boom in the 1980s without much in the way of selective industrial policies. The World Bank sees this as additional evidence of the beneficial effects of widespread liberalization. However, if the starting point of one's analysis shifts from internal determinants of national growth to external linkages, then regional "neighborhood" effects become a compelling alternative explanation for Southeast Asia's growth path. As noted by Wade (1994, 68), the rapid growth of the southern-tier HPAEs has actually been driven to an important extent by the industrial restructuring of the northern-tier economies: "The fact that Northeast Asian firms moving production offshore went to Southeast Asia rather than to Latin America or South Asia may be due less to the fact that Southeast Asia had better 'fundamentals' than other cheap labor sites (as the report would argue) and more to other, regionally specific factors [including] overseas Chinese networks, similarities in business practices, and the advantages of geographical proximity . . ." Furthermore, a closer look at the internationalization patterns of the East Asian NIEs reveals that their sourcing networks in labor-intensive industries like apparel and footwear also extend into Latin America, South Asia, and socialist economies like China and Vietnam. Thus, a global rather than exclusively regional framework is needed.

II. PRODUCER-DRIVEN AND BUYER-DRIVEN COMMODITY CHAINS

In global capitalism, economic activity is not only international in scope, it also is global in organization. "Internationalization" refers to the geographic spread of economic activities across national boundaries. As such, it is not a new phenomenon; indeed, it has been a prominent feature of the world economy since at least the seventeenth century when colonial empires began to carve up the globe in search of raw materials and new markets for their manufactured exports. "Globalization" is much more recent than internationalization because it implies the functional integration of internationally dispersed activities.

Globalization is not a frictionless web of arm's-length market transactions, as neoclassical economics might assert. Countries are incorporated into the global economy through international production, trade, and financial networks that are dominated by foreign capital. Globalization requires the agency of three kinds of international capital: (1) industrial capital—that is, vertically integrated transnational corporations that establish international production and trade networks through the activities of overseas subsidiaries; (2) commercial capital—that is, large retailers, merchandisers of brandname products, and trading companies that create and control global sourcing networks typically headquartered in developed countries, coordinated from semiperipheral locations (the NIEs), and with production concentrated in the low-wage periphery; and (3) finance capital—that is, commercial banks, official international lending institutions (such as the World Bank and the International Monetary Fund), and, to a lesser degree, portfolio investors that supply the short-term funds used to finance global production and trade.

Industrial and commercial capital have promoted globalization by establishing two distinct types of international economic networks, which we call "producer-driven" and "buyer-driven" commodity chains (Gereffi, 1994). Both types of global commodity chains have been prominent in East Asia's development. Producer-driven commodity chains are those in which large, usually transnational, manufacturers play the central roles in coordinating production networks (including their backward and forward linkages). This is characteristic of capital- and technology-intensive industries such as automobiles, aircraft, computers, semiconductors, and heavy machinery. The automobile industry offers a classic illustration of a producer-driven chain, with multilayered production systems that involve thousands of firms (including parents, subsidiaries, and subcontractors). The average Japanese automaker's production system, for example, comprises 170 first-tier,

4700 second-tier, and 31,600 third-tier subcontractors (Hill, 1989, 466). Florida and Kenney (1991) have found that Japanese automobile manufacturers actually reconstituted many aspects of their home-country supplier networks in North America. Doner (1991) extends this framework to highlight the complex forces that drive Japanese automakers to create regional production schemes for the supply of auto parts in a half-dozen nations in East and Southeast Asia. Henderson (1989) also supports the notion that producer-driven commodity chains have established an East Asian division of labor in his study of the internationalization of the U.S. semiconductor industry.

Buyer-driven commodity chains refer to those industries in which large retailers, designers, and trading companies play the pivotal role in setting up decentralized production networks in a variety of exporting countries, typically located in the developing world. This pattern of trade-led industrialization has become common in labor-intensive, consumer goods industries such as garments, footwear, toys, housewares, consumer electronics, and a variety of hand-crafted items (e.g., furniture, ornaments). Production is generally carried out by tiered networks of developing world contractors that make finished goods for foreign buyers. The specifications are supplied by the large retailers or designers that order the goods.

One of the main characteristics of the firms that fit the buyer-driven model, including retailers like Wal-Mart, Sears Roebuck, and J.C. Penney, athletic footwear companies like Nike and Reebok, and fashion-oriented apparel companies like Liz Claiborne and The Limited, is that these companies design and/or market, but do not make, the branded products they order. They are part of a new breed of "manufacturers without factories" that separate the physical production of goods from the design and marketing stages of the production process. Profits in buyer-driven chains derive not from scale, volume, and technological advances as in producer-driven chains, but rather from unique combinations of high-value research, design, sales, marketing, and financial services that allow the retailers and designers to act as strategic brokers in linking overseas factories and traders with evolving product niches in the main consumer markets.

Profitability is greatest in the relatively concentrated segments of global commodity chains characterized by high barriers to the entry of new firms. In producer-driven chains, manufacturers making advanced products like aircraft, automobiles, and computers are the key economic agents not only in terms of their earnings, but also in their ability to exert control over backward linkages with raw material and component suppliers, and forward linkages into distribution and retailing. The transnationals in producer-driven chains usually belong to global oligopolies. Buyer-driven commodity chains, by contrast, are characterized by highly competitive and globally decentralized factory systems. The companies that develop and sell brandname products exert substantial control over how, when, and where manufacturing will take place, and how much profit accrues at each stage of the chain. Thus, whereas producer-driven commodity chains are controlled by

Table 1

Main Characteristics of Producer-Driven and Buyer-Driven Global Commodity Chains

	Producer-driven chains	Buyer-driven chains
Drivers of global commodity chains	Industrial capital	Commercial capital
Core competencies	Research & development; production	Design; marketing
Barriers to entry	Economies of scale	Economies of scope
Economic sectors	Consumer durables Intermediate goods Capital goods	Consumer nondurables
Typical industries	Automobiles; computers; aircraft	Apparel; footwear; toys
Ownership of manufacturing firms	Transnational firms	Local firms, predominantly in developing countries
Main network links	Investment-based	Trade-based
Predominant network structure	Vertical	Horizontal

industrial firms at the point of production, the main leverage in buyer-driven industries is exercised by retailers and branded merchandisers at the marketing and retail end of the chain.

The main characteristics of producer-driven and buyer-driven commodity chains are highlighted in Table 1. Producer-driven and buyer-driven chains are rooted in distinct industrial sectors, they are led by different types of transnational capital (industrial and commercial, respectively), and they vary in their core competencies (at the firm level) and their entry barriers (at the sectoral level). The finished goods in producer-driven chains tend to be supplied by core country transnationals, while the goods in buyer-driven chains are generally made by locally owned firms in developing countries. Whereas transnational corporations establish investment-based vertical networks, the retailers, designers, and trading companies in buyer-driven chains set up and coordinate trade-based horizontal networks.

III. EXPORT ROLES AND INDUSTRIAL UPGRADING IN EAST ASIA

Countries are connected to global commodity chains through the goods and services they supply in the world economy. These trade linkages can be conceptualized as a set of five major export roles: (1) primary product exports, including processed "industrial commodities" and nontraditional agricultural exports; (2) the export-oriented assembly of traditional manufactured goods, such as apparel and electronics items, using imported components; (3) the production of components for export in relatively advanced industries, such as automobiles and computers, using substantial local inputs; (4) original equipment manufacturing (OEM), whereby contractors make goods to be sold under another company's brandname; and (5) original brandname manufacturing (OBM), whereby manufacturers make goods for export and sale under their own label.

These export roles are not mutually exclusive. In fact, most nations are tied to the world economy in multiple ways. The East Asian NIEs employed all five export roles from the 1960s to the mid-1990s, although they currently are focusing almost exclusively on component-supply manufacturing, OEM, and OBM. Most of the countries in Southeast Asia and Latin America are involved in the first three roles, the bulk of exports in South Asia and sub-Saharan Africa fit the first two roles, and many nations from Africa and the Middle East only have primary product exports (Gereffi, 1995).

The East Asian NIEs are generally taken as the archetype for industrial upgrading among developing countries. Hong Kong, Taiwan, South Korea, and Singapore appear to have moved smoothly and rapidly from assembly to component production to OEM to OBM. Each export role is progressively more difficult to establish because it implies a higher degree of domestic integration and local entrepreneurship; thus industrial upgrading is enhanced as countries move along this trajectory. However, a closer look at the experiences of the East Asian nations reveals considerable diversity in the sequences, content, and organizational dynamics of these export roles.

The East Asian NIEs made a rapid transition from the initial assembly phase of export growth (typically utilizing export processing zones located near major ports) to a more generalized system of incentives that applied to all export-oriented factories in their economies (Chen, 1994). The next stage for Taiwan, South Korea, Hong Kong, and Singapore was OEM production. Original equipment manufacturing, also known as specification contracting, has the following features: the supplying firm makes a product according to the design specified by the buyer; the product is sold under the buyer's brandname; the supplier and buyer are separate firms; and the supplier lacks control over distribution. East Asian firms became full-range "package suppliers" for foreign buyers, and thereby forged an innovative entrepreneurial capability that involved the coordination of complex production, trade, and financial networks.

The OEM export role has many advantages. It enhances the ability of local entrepreneurs to learn the preferences of foreign buyers, including prevailing international standards for the price, quality, and delivery of export merchandise. It also generates substantial backward linkages in the domestic economy because OEM contractors are expected to develop reliable sources of supply for many inputs. Moreover, expertise in OEM production increases over time, and it contributes to the development of local conventions (norms and practices) that are the glue in agglomeration economies (Storper, 1995). Particular places such as the East Asian

NIEs thus retain an enduring competitive edge in export-oriented development. However, East Asian producers confront intense competition from lower-cost exporters in various parts of the developing world, and the price of their exports to Western nations has been further elevated by sharp currency appreciations during the past decade. Under these circumstances, it is advantageous to establish forward linkages to developed-country markets, where the biggest profits are made in buyer-driven commodity chains. Therefore, a number of firms in the East Asian NIEs that pioneered OEM are now pushing beyond it to the OBM role by integrating their manufacturing expertise with the design and sale of their own brand-name merchandise.

South Korea is the most advanced of the East Asian NIEs in OBM production, with Korean brands of automobiles (Hyundai), computers (Leading Edge), and household appliances (Samsung and Goldstar), among other items, being sold in North America, Europe, and Japan. Taiwanese companies have pursued OBM in computers, bicycles, sporting equipment, and shoes, but not in apparel. Hong Kong has only been successful in apparel OBM. There have been significant reversals, however. Taiwan's Mitac Corporation, the main competitor to Acer in Taiwan's personal computer market, reduced its own-brand computers from 70% of its total sales in 1990 to 40% in 1993 (Selwyn, 1993), and Daewoo, Korea's third-largest appliance and consumer-electronics company (after Samsung and Goldstar), moved from years of brand-building back to the OEM game (*Asiaweek*, 1995a).

Why has the OEM role proven so resilient? To a large degree, the answer lies with core competencies and networks. C.S. Ho, the president of Mitac, says that his firm was more profitable when it concentrated on its core competencies: "We asked ourselves: What functions are we best at? Our strengths are in R & D, design and manufacturing. We are now focusing on designing and supplying products and key components for major OEM customers, whose brands are better-known but which have withdrawn from fully integrated manufacture" (Selwyn, 1993, 24). S.H. Bae, chairman and chief executive officer of Daewoo, says, "Our strength is in manufacturing. If our margins are adequate, we don't mind making products for others" (*Asiaweek*, 1995a, 56). Bae expects a shakeout in appliances and consumer electronics by the year 2000, and concludes that companies will have to become dominant producers in core products.

To keep OEM profitable under conditions of intense wage competition among developing countries and protectionism in Western markets, East Asian NIE companies have set up elaborate offshore production networks. Daewoo, for example, has 16 offshore plants in China, Vietnam, Central Asia, Europe, and Mexico. It is building more, even as it upgrades its factories in Korea. Through worker-training programs, Bae claims that "[Daewoo's] Vietnam plant is almost as efficient as local ones" (*Asiaweek*, 1995a, 57). Thus, the key to profitability in OEM production for East Asian NIEs seems to be manufacturing expertise (including substantial spending in research and development), and learning how to flexibly manage overseas production networks. This can be seen in Hong Kong's apparel manufacturers, Taiwan's footwear companies, and Singapore's computer firms. Network flexibility thus has become one of the major organizational assets utilized by the NIEs in their internationalization strategies.

IV. THE EMERGENCE OF REGIONAL DIVISIONS OF LABOR IN EAST ASIA: A COMMODITY CHAINS INTERPRETATION

There is a paucity of literature on regional divisions of labor in the East Asian context. Bernard and Ravenhill (1995) have written an important recent article on this topic that challenges the "flying geese" variant of product cycle theory adopted in a seminal essay by Cumings (1984). Both articles take the existence of an East Asian regional division of labor as their point of departure, and note the diffusion of key aspects of Japan's development model to the East Asian NIEs, Southeast Asia, and most recently China. In explaining Japanese economic leadership, Cumings highlights the protective mantle of U.S. hegemony and Cold War geopolitics, while Bernard and Ravenhill stress technological change and the instrumental character of Japanese foreign direct investment in the region.

Bernard and Ravenhill provide several salient critiques of the flying geese and product cycle approaches initially popularized by the Japanese and American economists, Akamatsu Kaname (1961) and Raymond Vernon (1971), respectively. The standard amalgam of Akamatsu's and Vernon's ideas claims that the development experience of Japan will be replicated in a series of economic sectors and countries throughout East Asia. Imports, domestic production, and exports are expected to follow one another in strict succession, as the product cycle is repeated for increasingly sophisticated goods. According to this statecentric view, the rise and fall of products mirrors the rise and fall of national economies, which the flying geese model takes as the appropriate unit of analysis for understanding economic change. Product cycle theory, in turn, posits an essentially "ahistoric" flow of individual products in isolation from larger industrial structures. Consequently, it omits the backward and forward linkages involving diverse networks of firms within economic sectors, and it overlooks differences in company strategies that can be used to alter the dynamics of product cycles.

Technological diffusion in East Asia has only been partial, at best, and is linked to ongoing Japanese innovation of components, machinery, and materials. Thus South Korea and Taiwan remain technologically dependent on Japan, which has never really exited so-called "mature" industries. In key sectors like electronics and automobiles, Japan has revitalized core technologies and restricted exports of finished products from the East Asian NIEs back into Japan. Southeast Asia, unlike

South Korea and Taiwan, lacked a substantial foundation of import-substituting industrialization (ISI), leading to "technologyless" industrialization with a heavy dependence on transnational subsidiaries for their manufactured exports (Bernard and Ravenhill, 1995, 196). Without an ISI base, indigenous capital goods sectors in Southeast Asia are weak, resulting in limited backward linkages and a foreign-dominated export sector.

While Bernard and Ravenhill advance our understanding of East Asian development on a variety of fronts, their article has two critical flaws. First, it has an undertheorized notion of East Asia's regional production hierarchy. There is no effort to distinguish between producer-driven and buyer-driven commodity chains, nor is there any discussion of the extensive literature by sociologists, economic geographers, and others on transnational production and trade networks. Second, the authors overstate the significance of Japan-centered networks in the political economy of East Asia because they look at a limited range of industry cases (mainly electronics, computers, and autos) that encompass only producer-driven chains. This leads them to miss the lead role played by U.S. buyers (and the absence of Japanese manufacturers) in the buyer-driven commodity chains that fueled East Asia's export drive from the 1960s to the 1980s, and also to neglect the challenge to Japanese networks posed by U.S. and European transnationals in producer-driven chains such as electronics. These theoretical blind spots distort our view of East Asia's regional division of labor, and misrepresent how East Asia is linked to other areas of the world.

From a commodity chains perspective, there are overlapping, and at times conflicting, networks involved in East Asia's export-oriented development. Producer-driven and buyer-driven chains coexist in each of the tiers of the Asian regional division of labor. While all the nations in the region have pursued strategies of EOI, the timing, products, and linkages involved have varied across the region.

- *Japan* was a significant exporter to the United States in buyer-driven commodity chains (BDCCs) such as apparel and footwear in the 1950s and 1960s, but then switched in the 1970s to producer-driven commodity chains (PDCCs) like automobiles, electrical machinery, and computers. Japan used its large trading companies (*sogo shosha*) to transfer BDCCs to the East Asian NIEs, while Japanese transnationals were the main mechanism employed in setting up and maintaining PDCCs in Southeast Asia.
- The *East Asian NIEs* became successful exporters in the late 1960s and 1970s primarily by mastering the dynamics of BDCCs. Apparel was a leading export sector for each of the four NIEs, toys for all but Singapore, footwear for South Korea and Taiwan, and so on. These countries moved quickly from assembly to OEM production in BDCCs. Unlike Southeast Asia, however, the East Asian NIEs (with the exception of Singapore) moved to PDCCs on the basis of exports by domestically owned firms, not transnational companies.

- *Southeast Asia* launched a different form of EOI than that of the East Asian NIEs. Southeast Asia's initial export industries—electronics (semi-conductors, disk drives, and computers) and automobiles—were organized in the 1970s and early 1980s as PDCCs. The drivers in these chains were Japanese, U.S., and European transnationals. In the late 1980s, a second generation of export industries was set up in Southeast Asia: these were the BDCCs (apparel, footwear, toys) that were no longer cost-competitive in the East Asian NIEs because of currency appreciation, rapid wage increases, and the difficulty in hiring workers domestically for labor-intensive production, even at prevailing high wage rates. Instead of core country transnationals (as in PDCCs) or U.S. and European buyers (as in the first-generation BDCCs set up in the NIEs), the main organizing agents in Southeast Asia's buyer-driven chains were investors from the East Asian NIEs who set up "triangle manufacturing" networks in the region to take advantage of lower labor costs and, in the case of apparel, available quotas.

- The *People's Republic of China* has emerged as the region's dominant player in BDCCs in the 1990s, but it currently has only a minor role in PDCCs. China is the world's biggest volume exporter of a wide range of consumer goods, including clothes, shoes, toys, watches, and bicycles. China's presence as a leading exporter in these global commodity chains is vulnerable to economic and political shifts. These range from economic recession in the North American and European economies that are the major markets for Chinese exports, to the possibility that the U.S. government will fail to renew China's most-favored-nation trade status. As a result, Chinese production is likely to be increasingly directed at Asian and other non-quota markets in the latter half of the 1990s.

The impact of producer-driven and buyer-driven commodity chains within East Asia's regional political economy suggests a hypothesis of *network isomorphism*. These two types of commodity chains give rise to overlapping and competing regional divisions of labor in East Asia that are based on different network structures, as follows:

> Producer-driven commodity chains transfer the hierarchical relations between transnational core firms and their subsidiaries into vertical, investment-based networks within East Asia; conversely, the core commercial companies (retailers and designers) in buyer-driven commodity chains convert their specification contracting or OEM relationship with suppliers in Asia into horizontal, trade-based networks that establish a distinctive division of labor within and between global regions.

Network isomorphism will be examined in greater detail in the next two sections of this chapter, which focus on the apparel and electronics sectors in East Asia.

In the case of apparel, U.S. buyers initially established direct OEM links with producers in Hong Kong, Taiwan, and South Korea. Eventually China and the nations of Southeast and South Asia were incorporated into the chain as lower-cost Asian production sites, with Hong Kong and Taiwan employing their cultural ties with the overseas Chinese business communities throughout the region to establish the three-tiered networks used in "triangle manufacturing." The intermediary role of the NIEs continued to evolve. In addition to supplying a growing number of regional exporters with apparel orders, fibers, textiles, financing, and quota brokerage services, the NIEs moved from OEM to OBM by developing their own brands of clothing for production and sale within Asia. Apparel has now become a leading export sector for nations at lower levels in Asia's regional production hierarchy, such as China, Thailand, Indonesia, Bangladesh, Pakistan, and Sri Lanka. As new countries turn to apparel to launch their export-oriented development strategies, the regional hierarchy deepens.

In the electronics commodity chain, Japan and the United States retain central roles through the activities of their transnational corporations. Low wages matter less than in buyer-driven chains, and quotas not at all. Compared to apparel, these networks are not very deep (i.e., they have fewer tiers) nor very dense (i.e., there are fewer countries in each tier). This regional division of labor relies on Singapore more than Hong Kong, and transnationals control the needed capital and technology. Japanese and U.S. transnationals have constructed networks with divergent characteristics (e.g., the former are relatively "closed" and the latter more "open"). Company strategies concerning local sourcing are a prime determinant in the organization of the networks. Southeast Asian nations like Malaysia and Thailand have occasionally leapfrogged the East Asian NIEs by making technologically more advanced products, although the backward linkages and product sophistication of the former are still limited.

V. THE TRANSFORMATION OF EAST ASIA'S APPAREL COMMODITY CHAIN

The world textile and apparel industry has undergone several major migrations of production during the past four decades and they all involve Asia. The first migration of the industry took place from North America and Western Europe to Japan in the 1950s and early 1960s, when Western textile and clothing production was displaced by a sharp rise in imports from Japan. Textiles and clothing, which accounted for about one-third of Japan's exports during the first half of the twentieth century, still represented 36% of its total exports and 22% of its manufacturing employment in the 1950s (Park, 1990, 96). The second migration of production was a shift from Japan to the "Big Three" Asian economies (Hong Kong, Taiwan, and South Korea), and allowed the latter group to dominate global textile and clothing exports in the 1970s and 1980s, especially in apparel. During the past 10 to 15 years, however, there has been a third migration of production from the Asian Big Three to a number of other developing economies. In the 1980s, the principal shift was to mainland China, but it also encompassed several Southeast Asian nations and Sri Lanka. In the 1990s, the proliferation of new suppliers included South Asian and Latin American apparel exporters, with new entrants like Vietnam waiting in the wings (Khanna, 1993; Tran, 1995).

There are several perspectives we can use to analyze these shifts: neoclassical economics, the statist perspective, the product-cycle model, and the organization of production (or networks) approach. These theoretical frameworks are complementary and interactive, rather than mutually exclusive. However, it is clear that economic and political models alone are not sufficient to account for the transformation of East Asia's textile and apparel complex.

Neoclassical economics has the simplest prediction: the most labor-intensive segments of the apparel commodity chain should be located in countries with the lowest wages. This theory is supported by the sequential shifts of textile and apparel production from the United States and Western Europe to Japan, the Asian Big Three, and China, since the entrants into each new tier of the production hierarchy had significantly lower wage rates than their predecessors. China, with apparel labor costs of U.S.$0.25 per hour, had become the largest supplier of textiles and clothing to the $34 billion U.S. import market by 1992 (up from fourth place in 1982, when China trailed only the Asian Big Three). China was also the largest volume supplier of textiles and clothing to the European Community in 1992, and in terms of value it ranked second only to Turkey (Khanna, 1993, 16–17). Furthermore, as the NIEs in East Asia were shifting into higher-value-added production in the 1980s and 1990s, clothing exports became a growth pole for other low-wage countries in the region. The Southeast Asian nations of Thailand, Indonesia, Malaysia, and the Philippines increased their share of global apparel exports more than fivefold (from 1.3% to 7.1%), while the South Asian economies more than doubled their portion of the global total (from 2.3 to 5.5%). In Bangladesh, Sri Lanka, and Mauritius, apparel exports climbed to about one-half or more of each economy's merchandise exports in 1995 (see Table 2).

Textiles and clothing, the preeminent export sector in the East Asian NIEs in the 1960s and 1970s, actually shrank as a proportion of these economies' total exports between 1980 and 1995. The share of global apparel exports represented by Hong Kong, South Korea, and Taiwan declined from 25% in 1980 to just over 11% in 1995 (Table 2). Rising incomes as a consequence of economic development pushed wages in South Korea and Taiwan to the point where the textile and apparel industries were becoming uncompetitive. The labor consequences of these shifts have been quite severe. In South Korea, textile and clothing employment fell from its peak of 784,000 in 1987 to 534,000 in 1991, a loss of 250,000 jobs in just 5 years. In Taiwan, there was a similar decrease of 150,000 jobs in the textile and

Table 2

Shifts in Asian Clothing Exports, 1980–1995

Countries	Apparel labor costs (US$ per hour)[a] 1993	Value (US$ millions)		Share in world exports (percent)		Share in economy's total merchandise exports (percent)				
		1980	1995	1980	1995	1980	1990[b]	1995	Δ 1980–1990[b]	Δ 1990–1995[b]
World		40,590	157,880	100.0	100.0	2.0	3.2	3.2	+1.2	0.0
Japan	10.64	488	530	1.2	0.3	0.4	0.2	0.1	−0.2	−0.1
East Asia										
Hong Kong	3.85	4,976	21,297	—	—	24.5	18.7	12.2	−5.8	−6.5
domestic exports		4,664	9,540	11.5	6.0	34.1	31.9	31.9	−2.2	0.0
re-exports		312	11,757	—	—	4.7	11.5	8.2	+6.8	−3.3
China[d]	0.25	1,625	24,049	4.0	15.2	8.9	15.6	16.2	+6.7	+0.6
South Korea	2.71	2,949	4,957	7.3	3.1	16.8	12.1	4.0	−4.7	−8.1
Taiwan	4.61	2,430	3,256	6.0	2.1	12.3	5.9	2.9	−6.4	−3.0
Macao	na[c]	422	1,372	1.0	0.9	78.4	65.6	69.1	−12.8	+3.5
Subtotal (w/ China)		*12,402*	*54,931*	*29.8*	*27.3*					
Subtotal (w/o China)		*10,777*	*30,882*	*25.8*	*12.1*					
Southeast Asia										
Thailand	0.71	267	4,620	0.7	2.9	4.1	12.2	8.2	+8.1	−4.0
Indonesia	0.28	98	3,367	0.2	2.1	0.4	6.4	7.4	+6.0	+1.0
Malaysia	0.77	150	2,272	0.4	1.4	1.2	4.5	3.1	+3.3	−1.4
Singapore	3.06	427	1,464	—	—	2.2	3.0	1.2	+0.8	−1.8
domestic exports		354	586	0.9	0.4	2.8	2.9	0.8	+0.1	−2.1
re-exports		73	878	—	—	1.1	3.3	1.8	+2.2	−1.5
Philippines	0.53	na[c]	1,065	na[c]	0.7	na[c]	8.4	6.1	na[c]	−2.3
Subtotal		*942*	*12,788*	*2.2*	*7.5*					
South Asia										
India	0.27	590	3,701[f]	1.5	2.3	6.9	14.1	14.8	+7.2	+0.7
Pakistan	0.27	103	1,611	0.3	1.0	3.9	18.1	20.2	+14.2	+2.1
Bangladesh	0.16	2	1,244[e]	0.0	0.8	0.2	35.0	54.8	+34.8	+19.8
Sri Lanka	0.35	109	1,474[f]	0.3	0.9	10.2	32.2	46.0	+22.0	+13.8
Mauritius	1.04	73	817	0.2	0.5	17.0	51.9	55.6	+34.9	+3.7
Subtotal		*877*	*8,847*	*2.3*	*5.5*					

[a] Including wages and social contributions.
[b] Δ 1980–1990 and Δ 1990–1995 refer to the increase or decrease in the percentage share of exports during the selected years.
[c] na = not available.
[d] Includes exports from processing zones.
[e] 1993.
[f] 1994.

Source: GATT, *International Trade* (1994); WTO, *Annual Report* (1996); ILO, *Recent Developments in the Clothing Industry* (1995), pp. 35–36.

apparel sector, from 460,000 workers in 1987 to only 310,000 workers in 1991 (Khanna, 1993, 23, 28). In both countries, the steepest fall in employment was in apparel, followed by textiles and man-made fibers. This job loss occurred despite the fact that wages were rising rapidly for textile and apparel workers. In Taiwan, apparel wages rose from U.S.$420 per month in 1987 to $630 per month in 1991, while the average monthly earnings of textile workers increased from $540 to $900 during the same period. In South Korea, the wages of apparel workers rose from $485 per month in 1991 to $550 per month at the beginning of 1992 (Khanna, 1993, 24, 28).

Hong Kong represents a special case among the NIEs. While Hong Kong's domestic apparel exports declined from 11.5 to 6% of the global total from 1980 to 1995, Hong Kong's re-exports of textiles and clothing have grown dramatically. In 1980 re-exports accounted for only 6% of Hong Kong's clothing exports, while in 1995 apparel re-exports were 55% of the Hong Kong total (Table 2). These re-exports are based primarily on imports from mainland China, which are shipped from Hong Kong to many other sites around the world. If we add the apparel exports from China together with Hong Kong's re-exports, apparel's share of Greater China's export total jumps from 14 to 24% between 1980 and 1995 (Table 3). Hong Kong's restoration to mainland China in 1997 will further consolidate China's domination of global textile and clothing exports.

The neoclassical cheap-labor argument does not hold up as well, however, when we get to the proliferation of new Asian suppliers, whose wage rates are often considerably higher than China's. As we can see in Table 2, the major apparel exporters have wide variations in their labor costs. Thailand's 1995 clothing exports are greater than Indonesia's, even though the former's labor costs are nearly three times as high. Sri Lanka's exports are about the same as those of Bangladesh, but Sri Lanka's wages are double those of its South Asian neighbor. Furthermore, even though the share of global apparel exports represented by Hong Kong, South Korea, and Taiwan declined from 25 to 11% between 1980 and 1995, these NIEs still rank among Asia's top five apparel exporters in the latter year, despite having the highest apparel labor costs in the region (excluding Japan).

The statist perspective, which argues that government policies will play a major role in shaping the location of apparel export activities, helps to explain these discrepancies. We need to distinguish at least three kinds of government policies: macroeconomic policies that affect the entire economy, industrial policies that target particular sectors, and protectionist policies in the advanced industrial countries that seek to dampen the impact of imports. All three types of government policy have affected the performance of apparel exporters in Asia. As discussed in the first section of this article, the East Asian NIEs clearly got their macroeconomic fundamentals right. Since the mid-1960s, they have had relative stability in their exchange and interest rates, they have invested heavily in human capital formation, they have promoted exports, and they have encouraged private investment and

Table 3

Relative Importance of Textiles and Clothing in the Total Exports
of East Asia's Main Economies, 1980–1995

East Asian economies	Segment of apparel commodity chain	Share in economy's total merchandise exports (percent)				
		1980	1990	1995	Δ 1980–1990	Δ 1990–1995
Taiwan	Textiles	9.0	9.1	10.7	+0.1	+1.6
	Clothing	12.3	5.9	2.9	−6.4	−3.0
	T&C	21.3	15.0	13.6	−6.3	−1.4
South Korea	Textiles	12.6	9.3	9.8	−3.3	+0.5
	Clothing	16.8	12.1	4.0	−4.7	−8.1
	T&C	29.4	21.4	13.8	−8.0	−7.6
Hong Kong	Textiles	6.6	7.5	6.1	+0.9	−1.4
(domestic exports)	Clothing	34.1	31.9	31.9	−2.2	0.0
	T&C	40.7	39.4	38.0	−1.3	−1.4
Hong Kong	Textiles	13.0	11.3	8.3	−1.7	−3.0
(re-exports)	Clothing	4.7	11.5	8.2	+6.8	−3.3
	T&C	17.7	22.8	16.5	+5.1	−6.3
China	Textiles	14.0	11.6	9.4	−2.4	−2.2
	Clothing	8.9	15.6	16.2	+6.7	+0.6
	T&C	22.9	27.2	25.6	+4.3	−1.6
Greater China	Textiles	27.0	22.9	17.7	−4.1	−5.2
(China plus Hong	Clothing	13.6	27.1	24.4	+13.5	−2.7
Kong re-exports)	T&C	40.6	50.0	42.1	+9.4	−7.9

Δ 1980–1990 and Δ 1990–1995 refer to the increase or decrease in the percentage share of exports
during the selected years.
Source: GATT, International Trade (1994) and WTO, Annual Report (1996).

domestic competition. The most important factor in the sharp decline of Taiwan's and
South Korea's apparel exports in the late 1980s, however, was not their rising wage
rates, but the sharp appreciation of their local currencies vis-à-vis the U.S. dollar after
the Plaza Agreement was signed in 1985. Between 1985 and 1987, the Japanese yen
was revalued by close to 40%, the New Taiwan dollar by 28%, and from 1986 to 1988
the Korean won appreciated by 17% (Bernard and Ravenhill, 1995, 180).

The East Asian NIEs tended not to use specific industrial policies to promote
the booming exports of light manufacturing sectors like apparel, footwear, and toys.
The government's role was more indirect. In South Korea and Taiwan, a key factor that facilitated clothing exports was the establishment of upstream (petrochem-
icals, synthetic fibers) and midstream (spinning, weaving, dyeing, finishing, and
knitting) industries that strengthened the overall textile and apparel complex. In
these cases, as well as Hong Kong, the major investors were in the private sector,
not state firms. State credit, trade, and labor policies were supportive, but not determining. By contrast, in high-tech industries like semiconductors and computers,

the state in the East Asian NIEs has played a more active role in industrial upgrading through the creation of research centers and science-based industrial parks, as well as by designating these sectors as "strategic industries" that are entitled to a variety of special benefits.

The most important policies that shape apparel exports in East Asia are quotas and preferential tariffs imposed by the importing countries. The impact of quotas is very clear in the textile sector. Prior to 1962, when the Long-Term Arrangement that restricted international trade in cotton textiles was established, Korean and Taiwanese textile firms concentrated almost exclusively (90% or more) on cotton textile production. The Long-Term Arrangement, supplemented by the more comprehensive Multifiber Arrangement in the early 1970s, encouraged these firms to switch from cotton to synthetic fibers. By the early 1980s, synthetic textiles accounted for 70% of South Korea's textile output and 78% in Taiwan (Park, 1990, 106). This dramatic increase in synthetic textile capacity also shaped each economy's downstream export niches in apparel. Thus, whereas Hong Kong and China are both very strong global competitors in cotton textiles and cotton apparel items, South Korea and Taiwan have specialized in apparel made from synthetic fibers (polyester, nylon, and rayon).

Industrial upgrading in the NIEs was one of the major consequences of import quotas for apparel since they permitted successful Asian exporters to maximize the foreign exchange earnings and the profitability of quantitative restrictions on trade. Although the clear intent of these policies was to protect developed-country firms from a flood of low-cost imports that threatened to disrupt major domestic industries, the result was exactly the opposite: protectionism heightened the competitive capabilities of developing world manufacturers. Protectionism by core countries had a second consequence as well: the diversification of foreign competition. The imposition of quotas on an ever-widening circle of Third World exporters led producers in Japan and the East Asian NIEs, who had to contend with escalating labor costs and U.S.-mandated currency appreciations, to open up new satellite factories in low-wage countries that offered either quota or labor advantages.

The product-cycle model predicts that over time exporters will lose their competitive edge in mature products, and become importers. One way to counter this liability is to move from simple to more sophisticated items within an export niche. Furthermore, we should also expect that high-cost exporters will shift from the labor-intensive segments of the apparel commodity chain (clothing) to the more capital- and technology-intensive segments (textiles and fibers). These expectations are quite well supported in East Asia. In response to rapidly growing demand in the domestic apparel market, clothing imports in South Korea rose by 150% in 1989 and 100% in 1990. Similarly, Taiwan's textile and clothing imports more than doubled from U.S.$1.2 billion in 1986 to $2.6 billion in 1991 (Khanna, 1993, 25, 29). One of the reasons the Asian Big Three have continued to be significant apparel exporters despite their relatively elevated wages is that they are able to make better quality apparel items that low-wage countries like China and Indonesia cannot yet handle. In addition, the Big Three have gained the confidence of Western buyers for their expertise in OEM production, which leads them to be the logical choices for coordinating offshore production networks.

Generally speaking, the downstream sectors (clothing and accessories) in the apparel commodity chain in the East Asian NIEs have lost international competitiveness relative to midstream (textiles) and upstream (man-made fiber) sectors. There is clear evidence that the NIEs are making the transition from finished apparel exports to becoming textile and fiber suppliers for affiliated downstream producers in China, Southeast Asia, and South Asia. Taiwan is a classic example of this process. From 1985 to 1996, Taiwan's exports of clothing declined from 56 to 20% of its textile and apparel total, while the share represented by intermediate goods (textile fibers, yarn and fabrics) rose from 44 to 80% (Gereffi and Pan, 1994, 130, supplemented by more recent data from the Taiwan Textile Federation). The trend in South Korea is the same as in Taiwan: textiles have displaced apparel as the export leader in the apparel commodity chain (see Table 3).

What the product cycle model does not explain is how the East Asian NIEs have moved from OEM to OBM production in apparel. Nor does it identify the reasons why the NIEs have such markedly different geographic profiles in their offshore networks. While low wages, quotas, and product cycles all play significant roles in accounting for the production migrations among Asia's apparel exporters, by themselves they do not adequately account for either industrial upgrading or patterns of internationalization in the East Asian NIEs. A key element in the NIEs' successful transition from short-lived comparative advantage based on low labor costs to sustainable forms of competitive advantage that depend on upgrading and outsourcing are the organizational networks and strategies of the firms that actually do the investing, manufacturing, and exporting in East Asia. We thus need to adopt a firm-centered perspective to understand how, when, and where the trade and investment networks in East Asia's apparel commodity chain are changing

One of the most important mechanisms facilitating the shift to higher-value-added activities for mature export industries like apparel in East Asia is the process of "triangle manufacturing." The essence of triangle manufacturing, which was initiated by the East Asian NIEs in the 1970s and 1980s, is that U.S. (or other overseas) buyers place their orders with the NIE manufacturers they have sourced from in the past, who in turn shift some or all of the requested production to affiliated offshore factories in low-wage countries (e.g., China, Indonesia, or Guatemala). These offshore factories can be wholly owned subsidiaries of the NIE manufacturers, joint-venture partners, or simply independent overseas contractors. The triangle is completed when the finished goods are shipped directly to the overseas buyer under the U.S. import quotas issued to the exporting nation. Triangle manufacturing thus changes the status of NIE manufacturers from established suppliers for U.S. retailers and designers to "middlemen" in buyer-driven commodity chains that can include as many as 50 to 60 exporting countries (Gereffi, 1994).

Triangle manufacturing networks are socially embedded. Each of the East Asian NIEs has a different set of preferred countries where they set up their new factories. Hong Kong and Taiwan have been the main investors in China; South Korea has been especially prominent in Indonesia, Guatemala, the Dominican Republic, and North Korea; and Singapore is a leading force in Southeast Asian sites, such as Malaysia and Indonesia. These production networks are explained in part by social and cultural factors (e.g., ethnic or familial ties, common language), as well as by unique features of a country's historical legacy (e.g., Hong Kong's British colonial ties gave it an inside track on investments in Mauritius and Jamaica). However, as the volume of orders expands in new low-wage production sites, the pressure grows for the large U.S. buyers to eventually bypass their East Asian intermediaries and deal directly with the factories that fill their orders.

In each of the East Asian NIEs, a combination of domestic supply side constraints (labor shortages, high wages, and high land prices) and external pressures (currency revaluation, tariffs, and quotas) led to the internationalization of the textile and apparel complex by the late 1980s and early 1990s. Typically, the internationalization of production was sparked first by quotas, but the process was greatly accelerated as supply-side factors became adverse. Quotas determined *when* the outward shift of production began, while preferential access to overseas markets and social networks determined *where* the firms from the East Asian NIEs went. In this international division of labor, labor-intensive activities are relocated and skill-intensive activities are retained. In the apparel sector, the activities associated with OEM production that tended to remain in the NIEs were jobs such as product design, sample making, quality control, packing, warehousing, transportation, quota transactions, and local financing through letters of credit. These provided relatively high gross margins or profits.

The internationalization of Hong Kong's firms was triggered by textile import restrictions imposed by the United Kingdom in 1964, which led Hong Kong manufacturers in the late 1960s to shift production to Singapore, Taiwan, and Macao. The Chinese population in these three countries had cultural and linguistic affinities with Hong Kong investors. In addition, Macao benefited from its proximity to Hong Kong, while Singapore qualified for Commonwealth preferences for imports into the United Kingdom. In the early 1970s, Hong Kong apparel firms targeted Malaysia, the Philippines, and Mauritius. This second round of outward investments again was prompted by quota restrictions, coupled with specific host-country inducements. For example, Mauritius established an export processing zone in an effort to lure Hong Kong investors, particularly knitwear manufacturers who directed their exports to European markets that offered preferential access in terms of low tariffs.

The greatest spur to the internationalization of Hong Kong's textile and apparel companies was the opening of the Chinese economy in 1978. At first, production was subcontracted to state-owned factories, but eventually an elaborate outward-processing arrangement with China was set up that relied on a broad assortment of manufacturing, financial, and commercial joint ventures. Trading companies have replaced export-oriented factories as the key economic agent in Hong Kong's internationalization. Total manufacturing employment fell in Hong Kong during the late 1980s, due in large part to the relocation of industry to the Chinese mainland. In 1991, 47,000 factories were employing 680,000 workers in Hong Kong, a figure 25% below the peak of 907,000 manufacturing jobs recorded in 1980. While manufacturing declined, trading activities in Hong Kong grew to encompass approximately 70,000 firms and 370,000 jobs in 1991, a fivefold increase in the number of firms and a fourfold increase in the number of workers in the trading sector compared to 1978 (Khanna, 1993, 19). In 1995, Hong Kong entrepreneurs operated more than 20,000 factories employing an estimated four-and-a-half to five million workers in the Pearl River Delta alone in the neighboring Chinese province of Guangdong (De Coster, 1996, 96). Considering that total employment in Hong Kong industry had shrunk to 386,000 in 1995, or just over 15% of the Hong Kong workforce (Berger and Lester, 1997, 9), Hong Kong manufacturers in effect increased their domestic labor force well over tenfold through their outward processing arrangement with China.

As in Hong Kong, the internationalization of South Korea's and Taiwan's apparel producers began as a response to quota restrictions. Korean garment firms lacking sufficient export quotas initially set up production in quota-free locations like Saipan, a U.S. territory in the Mariana Islands. More recent waves of internationalization have been motivated by the domestic constraints of rising wages and worker shortages. The low-wage regions that have attracted the greatest number of South Korean companies are Latin America, and Southeast and South Asia. The preference of Korean firms for investment in Latin America (Guatemala, Honduras, the Dominican Republic, etc.) is stimulated by its proximity to the U.S. market and easy quota access. The pull of Asian nations such as Indonesia, Sri Lanka, and Bangladesh comes mainly from their wage rates, which are among the lowest in the world (see Table 2).

When Taiwanese firms moved offshore in the early 1980s, they also confronted binding quotas. While Taiwan's wages in the late 1970s and early 1980s were still relatively low, quota rents were high. Firms had to buy quota (whose value in secondary markets fluctuated widely) in order to be able to expand exports, thereby causing a decrease in profitability for firms without sufficient quota (Appelbaum and Gereffi, 1994). This led to a growing emphasis on nonquota markets by Taiwan's textile and apparel exporters. Quota markets (the United States, the European Community, and Canada) accounted for more than 50% of Taiwan's textile and apparel exports in the mid-1980s, but this ratio declined to 43% in 1988 and fell further to 35% in 1991. The United States, which had been Taiwan's largest export market for years, claimed one-quarter of Taiwan's textile and apparel exports in 1991, the European Community 8%, and Canada just 2%. The main nonquota markets, which

Table 4

Regional Trade Patterns in World Exports of Textiles and Clothing

	1980	1984	1987	1990	1993	1995
Textiles						
World (US$ billions)	$ 55.6	$ 53.9	$ 80.2	$104.8	$115.4	$152.6
World (percentages)	100.0	100.0	100.0	100.0	100.0	100.0
Intra-Western Europe	40.1	34.9	40.0	41.4	32.8	30.9
Intra-Asia	13.1	17.4	18.2	20.6	26.6	28.4
Asia to Western Europe	1.6	4.6	5.9	5.6	5.8	5.5
Western Europe to C./E.						
Europe/Baltic States/CIS★	na	na	na	2.3	3.1	4.0
Asia to North America	2.9	5.4	4.9	3.6	4.3	3.7
Asia to the Middle East	na	na	na	2.2	3.0	2.9
Western Europe to Asia	1.6	2.4	2.0	3.0	2.6	2.9
Western Europe to North America	1.6	3.2	2.9	2.4	2.3	1.9
Other	39.1	32.1	26.1	18.9	19.5	19.8
Clothing						
World (US$ billions)	$ 41.8	$ 48.2	$ 81.9	$106.4	$133.0	$157.9
World (percentages)	100.0	100.0	100.0	100.0	100.0	100.0
Intra-Western Europe	36.6	29.3	33.7	35.2	28.7	27.7
Asia to North America	14.8	26.8	22.5	19.5	19.6	16.8
Intra-Asia	4.3	6.2	6.0	8.8	10.5	12.8
Asia to Western Europe	14.4	11.0	13.2	12.9	13.6	11.7
Latin America to North America	1.7	2.1	2.3	2.4	3.9	4.6
C./E. Europe/Baltic States/CIS						
to Western Europe★	na	na	na	na	na	3.9
Africa to Western Europe	1.9	1.2	2.1	na	3.0	na
Other	26.3	23.4	20.2	21.1	20.7	22.5

★Includes Central and Eastern Europe, the Baltic States, and the Confederation of Independent States.
na = not available.
Source: GATT, *International Trade*, and WTO, *Annual Report*, various years.

in total absorbed nearly two-thirds of Taiwan's textile and apparel exports in the early 1990s, are Hong Kong (30%), Japan (6%), and Singapore (3%) (Khanna, 1993, 29–30). Hong Kong, now Taiwan's leading export market, is mainly a conduit for shipping yarns, fabrics, and clothing to China for further processing and re-export.

Two trends—the shift from OEM to OBM, and the growing importance of nonquota markets for the NIEs—point to an important fact: production and trade networks in the apparel commodity chain are becoming increasingly concentrated in Asia. Table 4 indicates a sharp decline in Asian clothing exports to North America (from 27% of the global total in 1984 to 17% in 1995), a drop in Asian textile and apparel exports to Western Europe, and a striking increase in intra-Asian trade in apparel (from 4% in 1980 to 13% in 1995). This rise in intra-Asian trade is even stronger in textiles, where it increased from 13% of the world total in 1980 to 28%

in 1995. Asia's growing prominence as a market for its own textile and apparel output, and the continuing migration of production to low-cost supply sites around the world, suggest a general movement may be underway toward a regionalization of the apparel commodity chain within Asia, North America, and Europe. The emerging supply relationships that are being fashioned with nearby low-cost producers in each area (Vietnam and North Korea in Asia, Central America and the Caribbean vis-à-vis North America, and North Africa and Eastern Europe for the European Union) are likely to strengthen intraregional trade and production networks in the apparel commodity chain, thereby giving rise to new forms of economic coordination and competition among local as well as global firms.

VI. COMPETING U.S. AND JAPANESE PRODUCTION NETWORKS IN THE ASIAN ELECTRONICS COMMODITY CHAIN

There are opposing images of U.S. and Japanese production networks in East Asia's electronics sector. U.S. networks are considered to be relatively open and conducive to local development in host countries, while Japanese networks are perceived as closed and hierarchical with activities confined within affiliates that are tightly controlled by the parent company. Borrus (1994) argues that this contrast in network structures is the main reason why Japanese companies have faltered in industrial electronics in the 1990s and why leadership in the electronics sector has been restored to U.S. firms:

> In Asia today, beneath the superficial similarity engendered by aggregate trade and investment data and macro-analyses, lie distinctly different electronics production networks under the control of U.S. versus Japanese multinationals. The U.S. networks tend to be open to outsiders, fast and flexible in decision-making and implementation, structured through formal, legal relationships and capable of changing contour (and patterns) as needs change—in an image: open, fast, flexible, formal, and disposable. Their activities are centered in the NICs, especially Singapore and Taiwan, but increasingly reach into the rest of Asia and China. By contrast, the Japanese networks tend to be relatively closed to outsiders, slower to make and implement decisions that are generated from Japan, and structured on stable, long-term business and *keiretsu* relationships—that is, closed, slow, rigid, long-term and stable. They are most definitely centered in Japan.
> (Borrus, 1994, 142)

As we will see below, these U.S. and Japanese electronics networks in East Asia utilize distinct supply bases, they boast different product mixes, and, most significantly, they have established competing divisions of labor within the same geographic space.

The development of Asian production networks in electronics can be traced through three stages. In the first stage (late 1960s–1970s), the investment of most

U.S. electronics firms in Asia was motivated by their search for cheap production locations, while Japanese investments in Asia were primarily aimed at supplying nascent local markets behind high tariff walls. Although the assembly-oriented nature of both Japanese and U.S. investments in this first stage may appear similar on the surface, the contrasting export strategies of the core firms led these networks to evolve differently. "Because their Asian affiliates were integrated into a production operation serving advanced country markets, U.S. firms upgraded their Asian investments in line with the pace of development of the lead market being served, the U.S. market. In essence, they upgraded in line with U.S. rather than local product cycles. By contrast, Japanese firms were led to upgrade the technological capabilities of their Asian investments only at the slower pace necessary to serve lagging local markets" (Borrus, 1994, 134–135).

During the second stage (1980–1985), U.S. affiliates in Asia began to source more parts and components domestically. The networks of U.S. transnationals made increasingly sophisticated industrial electronics products such as hard-disk drives, personal computers, ink-jet printers, and telecom devices. The Japanese networks supplied consumer audio-visual electronics such as television sets and video-cassette recorders, as well as appliances. As the U.S. industry shifted from consumer to industrial electronics, local producers in places such as Taiwan began to follow. A new supply base thus emerged in the East Asian NIEs under the control of U.S. and local, but not Japanese, capital. Meanwhile, Japanese investment created a dual production structure premised on traditional product cycles: Japanese firms supplied both the domestic and U.S. markets with sophisticated items made in Japan, while local Asian markets received simple low-end products made by Japanese subsidiaries in the region.

In the third stage (1985–early 1990s), the division of labor between U.S. affiliates and local producers in East Asia deepened significantly. U.S. electronics transnationals set up Asian networks based on a "complementary" division of labor: U.S. firms specialized in "soft" competencies (the definition of standards, designs, and product architecture) and the Asian firms specialized in "hard" competencies (the provision of components and basic manufacturing stages). The Asian affiliates of U.S. firms developed extensive subcontracting relationships with local manufacturers, who in turn became increasingly skilled suppliers of components, subassemblies and, in some cases, entire electronics systems. By contrast, Japanese networks were characterized by market segmentation and significant production redundancies: electronics firms in Japan made high-value, high-end products, while their offshore subsidiaries in Asia continued to make low-value, low-end products (Borrus, 1994, 143). While the U.S. networks maximized the contributions from their Asian affiliates, Japanese networks minimized the value added by their regional suppliers.

Apple Computer provides a good illustration of the Asian sourcing networks set up by U.S. firms (Borrus, 1994, 138–139). Apple Computer Singapore (ACS) opened a printed circuit board assembly plant for the Apple II personal computer in

1981. By 1990, ACS was expanded and upgraded to include final assembly of a variety of Apple computer models for the world market. Virtually all components were sourced in Asia (except the U.S.-made microprocessor), and ACS's network of local suppliers grew from 9 firms in 1983 to 130 companies by 1990. In 1993, ACS set up a design center for Macintosh's high-volume desk-top products (Apple's only hardware design center outside the United States), and in 1994, ACS became the distribution, logistics, sales, and marketing center for the Asia-Pacific region. Regional sourcing amounted to $2 billion, with Japan accounting for one-half of the total (liquid crystal displays, peripherals, memory, hard disk drives), and Singapore for one-quarter. Taiwan made from $250 to $500 million worth of merchandise for ACS (OEM supply of low-end desktops, printed circuit boards, a Powerbook model, and chips), while Korea's Samsung supplied some of the monitors.

The geography of the electronics commodity chain in Asia has changed over time. Henderson (1989) found that Hong Kong was the regional and technological core of East Asia's U.S.-dominated semiconductor industry in the late 1960s. By the mid-1980s, however, Singapore had displaced Hong Kong as the favored location in East Asia for technologically advanced electronics investments, such as wafer fabrication plants, 4- and 16-megabit DRAMs, hard disk drives, and some microprocessors (Lim and Pang, 1991; Henderson, 1994). Furthermore, Southeast Asia has begun to challenge South Korea and Taiwan as the favored Asian production site for new as well as mature electronics products.

Southeast Asia is enjoying some of the "advantages of lateness" vis-à-vis the East Asian NIEs, but this occurs in distinct ways in Japanese and U.S. production networks. Southeast Asian subsidiaries of Japanese electronics transnationals often are preferred over their Korean and Taiwanese competitors, in part because the Southeast Asian affiliates have access to the latest production technologies used by their Japanese parent firms. Between 1989 and 1991, for example, Japanese imports of color television sets from Korea and Taiwan fell from 1.6 to 1.3 million units, while Japan's imports of color televisions from Malaysia during this same period soared from 2000 to 385,000 units. By 1991, Malaysia had replaced Taiwan as the second largest supplier of color television imports to Japan, and Malaysia became the largest exporter of radio cassette recorders to the Japanese market (Bernard and Ravenhill, 1995, 198). The advantages for Southeast Asia in this case may be more apparent than real, since the Southeast Asian companies in Japan's production networks are subsidiaries of Japanese transnationals, whose ultimate loyalty is to their home economy, while their Korean and Taiwanese competitors are local manufacturers with more substantial domestic linkages in the NIEs.

Whereas Japanese networks benefited Southeast Asia by displacing Korean and Taiwanese sales of a mature product (color television sets) in Japan, U.S. networks have moved in the opposite direction: they produce more sophisticated exports in Southeast Asia than those available in the East Asian NIEs. In the early 1980s, Malaysia, Singapore, and the Philippines were the main manufacturing sites for relatively advanced metal oxide semiconductor (MOS) digital integrated circuits (ICs), while U.S. transnationals in South Korea and Taiwan used much simpler technology to export lower value-added bipolar digital ICs and linear ICs (UNCTC, 1986, 350–351). The reason these Southeast Asian nations leapfrogged South Korea and Taiwan in advanced semiconductor production involves issues of timing and organizational path dependence in U.S. electronics networks. The emergence of MOS as the predominant technology in the 1970s coincided with the rapid expansion of U.S. transnationals into the lower-cost assembly locations of Southeast Asia. The new entrants into the offshore assembly business—Malaysia, Singapore, and the Philippines—received the largest share of U.S. transnational investments using the MOS technology, while the earlier NIE entrants—Hong Kong, Taiwan, Korea, and Mexico—continued to make the mature semiconductor products they began with in the 1960s (Grunwald and Flamm, 1985, 70–71).

Company strategy is a key variable in the evolution of both U.S. and Japanese electronics production networks. Particular companies often are responsible for creating significant export niches for national suppliers. Barbados, for instance, had an unusually high average unit value for its semiconductor exports to the United States in the 1980s. The explanation in this case was straightforward: the overwhelming share of U.S. imports of ICs from Barbados consisted of high-value MOS memories and microprocessors assembled within Intel's new subsidiary there (UNCTC, 1986, 353). Thus the "Barbados effect" was really an "Intel effect." Similarly, Dieter Ernst, who believes that Japanese electronics firms are likely to switch to more open regional production networks in Asia, bolsters his argument by reference to the strategies of leading Japanese companies. Hitachi and NEC are taking the initiative in establishing more extensive local procurement networks in East Asia, with NEC's Hong Kong subsidiary in charge of redesigning the motherboard so it can use more of the cheaper, standard components available from South Korean, Taiwanese, and perhaps even Chinese suppliers (Ernst, 1994, 43). This trend suggests the possibility of a partial convergence in the production strategies of Japanese and U.S. transnationals.

Product cycle dynamics vary in apparel and electronics because trade networks operate quite differently in the two sectors. In the "triangle manufacturing" arrangement that characterizes East Asia's apparel commodity chain, U.S. companies typically supply orders, not inputs; manufacturers in the East Asian NIEs act as intermediaries by passing these orders, and frequently material and service inputs, to contractors in Southeast Asia and China who make the goods on an OEM basis. The exports are then shipped back to the originating country (the United States), utilizing where needed the quotas of the exporting nation. In this fashion, the product cycle is completed in buyer-driven chains. In the electronics commodity chain, there is a different mechanism known as "trade triangles" (Bernard and Ravenhill, 1995). Inputs are purchased from Japan (or more recently, South Korea and Taiwan), processed in the NIEs (and increasingly Southeast Asia and China), and exported to third-country markets rather than Japan. The product cycle in this case fails to go full circle because firms in the originating country (Japan) have not exited from the market. Instead, Japanese companies supply the core technologies and continue to be involved in the production of consumer goods.

VII. CONCLUSION

Recent studies of international competitiveness in East Asia have been hampered by their inability to move beyond the increasingly sterile debate about the role of states versus markets, and to come to grips with new trends in the organization of production on a world scale. This chapter argues that the global commodity chains perspective introduces a critical axis of variation in understanding the evolution of East Asia's evolving regional divisions of labor. Producer-driven and buyer-driven commodity chains are based on different types of production and trade networks, they are driven by different types of lead firms, they incorporate different sets of countries into their regional hierarchies, and they have different consequences for industrial upgrading in Asia's various subregions.

The electronics commodity chain in East Asia, which embodies the producer-driven type, is held together in large part by Japanese and U.S. transnationals. These companies have orchestrated regional production hierarchies in which Singapore, South Korea, and Taiwan are prominent in the second tier, well below Japan's core status, and Malaysia, Thailand, and the Philippines are growing third-tier suppliers. While Japanese transnationals have been the leaders in consumer electronics commodity chains, U.S. transnationals are the frontrunners in industrial electronics. Furthermore, the dynamics of the trade networks set up by the Japanese and U.S. electronics transnationals are quite distinct. The Japanese networks perpetuate a dualistic system in which electronics production in Japan serves developed-country markets, while the output from Japanese affiliates in Asia serve developing-country markets. By contrast, U.S. electronics transnationals have upgraded the capabilities of their suppliers in the East Asian NIEs and Southeast Asia to meet the sophisticated demand emanating from the U.S. market. This strategy tends to maximize the local value added by Asian contractors in U.S. electronics networks and to promote industrial upgrading in the second and third tiers of the region. In Japan's regional electronics networks, the Asian contribution has been minimized and Japan remains a key supplier of components and new technologies.

The apparel commodity chain, which is buyer-driven, operates very differently. The core companies are not manufacturing transnationals, but U.S. and European buyers that have set up elaborate specification contracting or OEM supply systems encompassing dozens of countries in virtually every corner of the globe. Within Asia, the apparel commodity chain is centered in Hong Kong and China, which together represent more than one-fifth of world clothing exports. These two countries play relatively minor roles, however, as exporters in Asia's producer-driven chains. The regional hierarchy for textile and apparel production in Asia has many levels, with Hong Kong, Taiwan, and South Korea being the principal intermediaries for U.S. and, to a lesser degree, European retailers and designers. These East Asian NIEs, in turn, subcontract the majority of their orders and provide a wide range of inputs to clothing factories in Southeast Asia, South Asia, Central America, the Caribbean, and other parts of the world. The double shift in the role of East Asian NIE suppliers in the apparel commodity chain—from finished to intermediate goods exporters, and from OEM to OBM producers—has led to a substantial rise in the intra-Asian share of global textile and clothing exports, thereby contributing to greater regional closure of the apparel commodity chain within Asia.

The OEM process itself works differently in these producer-driven and buyer-driven chains. In producer-driven chains, transnational manufacturers use numerous subsidiaries and subcontractors to make both components and finished goods, but these core companies also are concerned with safeguarding their proprietary technologies from potential competitors. Japanese electronics transnationals dealt with this problem through "closed" networks with very little technology transfer to their Southeast Asian affiliates, while U.S. transnationals relied on "open" networks to tap the relatively advanced technological and manufacturing skills of their subcontractors in the East Asian NIEs. The possibility for an OEM supplier to improve its position in producer-driven chains is enhanced if the technology gap with the lead transnationals is small (rather than large), if it produces unique (rather than standard) components, if it makes sophisticated (rather than simple) finished products, and if the subcontractor complements (rather than duplicates) the capabilities of the core firm. The rapid industrial upgrading experienced by the Korean and Taiwanese firms in the production networks of U.S. electronics transnationals derives from the fact that they made specialized components and high-end finished products for the U.S. market, and these two NIEs had the ability to form local subcontracting networks which the U.S. transnationals could not duplicate. These factors allowed South Korea and Taiwan to reduce (but by no means eliminate) the technological gap with leading Japanese as well as U.S. companies, and thus enhance their production and export options.

In buyer-driven chains, there appears to be more opportunity for learning and entrepreneurship by contractors in the OEM relationship. A number of successful East Asian producers eventually became major brandname competitors to their U.S. clients. Well-known cases include the Fang Brothers in Hong Kong, a large apparel manufacturer that now competes at the retail level in Asia and the United States with its main U.S. customer, Liz Claiborne, and the Giant bicycle company in Taiwan that made most of Schwinn's bikes on an OEM basis before coming out with its own nameplate in the late 1980s, a move that eventually helped drive Schwinn into bankruptcy. The opportunity for producers in other regions, like Latin America, to move from OEM to OBM is extremely limited because the lower-tier contractors there are only entrusted with recruiting workers and assembling finished goods using imported inputs. Therefore these manufacturers do not develop the skills nor can they count on the diversified array of local collaborators utilized by East Asia's full-package suppliers (Gereffi and Hempel, 1996).

Commodity chains in Asia encompass coherent trade and investment networks that lie "below" the aggregate picture for the entire region but "above" the interactions between states. Nonetheless, these production systems must be grounded in local contexts. In this regard, the shared understandings embodied in institutionalized conventions are extremely important. When we look closely at the multiplicity of industrial, commercial, and financial networks that make up East Asia's highly successful form of OEM production, it is evident that numerous conventions underpin the functioning of both the micro and macro institutions and routines that allow this system to operate. The importance of conventions grows in direct proportion to the spatial and cultural distances implied by globalization. Understanding East Asian development requires far more than a "market friendly" environment, export promotion, and selective state interventions. International competitiveness by East Asian firms has been spurred by organizational learning through networks and it is anchored in conventions that are an amalgam of Western and Asian institutions, norms, and practices. New and potential entrants into the apparel and electronics commodity chains that link East Asia with the rest of the world are likely to find that the unwritten conventions of these product worlds are every bit as important as modern technologies and regulatory frameworks in accounting for economic success.

REFERENCES

Akamatsu, K. (1961). A theory of unbalanced growth in the world economy. *Weltwirtschaftliches Archiv* **86**(2), 196–217.

Amsden, A. H. (1989). "Asia's Next Giant: South Korea and Late Industrialization." New York: Oxford University Press.

Amsden, A. H. (1994, April). Why isn't the whole world experimenting with the East Asian model to develop?: Review of *The East Asian Miracle. World Development* **XXII** (4), 627–633.

Appelbaum, R. P., and Gereffi, G. (1994). Power and profits in the apparel commodity chain, *in* "Global Production: The Apparel Industry in the Pacific Rim" (E. Bonacich, L. Cheng, N. Chinchilla, N. Hamilton, and P. Ong, Eds.), pp. 42–62. Philadelphia, PA: Temple University Press.

Asiaweek. (1995a, May 12). What's in a name? After years of building a brand, Daewoo's back to the OEM game, pp. 56–57.

Asiaweek. (1995b, May 12). Prying open Pyongyang: North Korea experiments with a free trade zone, p. 58.

Berger, S., and Lester, R. K. (1997). "Made By Hong Kong." New York: Oxford University Press.

Bernard, M., and Ravenhill J. (1995, January). Beyond product cycles and flying geese: Regionalization, hierarchy, and the industrialization of East Asia. *World Politics* **47**(2), 171–209.

Borrus, M. (1994). Left for dead: Asian production networks and the revival of U.S. electronics, *in* "Japanese Investment in Asia: International Production Strategies in a Rapidly Changing World" (E. M. Doherty, Ed.), pp. 125–146. San Francisco, CA: The Asia Foundation and the University of California's Berkeley Roundtable on the International Economy (BRIE).

Chen, X. (1994, Fall). The changing roles of free economic zones in development: A comparative analysis of capitalist and socialist cases in East Asia. *Studies in Comparative International Development* **29**(3), 3–25.

Cumings, B. (1984, Winter). The origins and development of the Northeast Asian political economy: Industrial sectors, product cycles, and political consequences. *International Organization* **38**(1), 1–40.

De Coster, J. (1996, November). Productivity: a key strategy of the Hong Kong textile and clothing industry. *Textile Outlook International* **68**, 80–97.

Doner, R. F. (1991). "Driving a Bargain: Automobile Industrialization and Japanese Firms in Southeast Asia." Berkeley, CA: University of California Press.

Ernst, D. (1994, November). "Carriers of Regionalization: The East Asian Production Networks of Japanese Electronics Firms." BRIE Working Paper 73. Berkeley, CA: University of California's Berkeley Roundtable on the International Economy (BRIE).

Florida, R., and Kenney, M. (1991, June). Transplanted organizations: The transfer of Japanese industrial organization to the United States. *American Sociological Review* **LVI** (3), 381–398.

General Agreement on Tariffs and Trade (GATT). (1994). "International Trade: Trends and Statistics 1994." Geneva: GATT.

Gereffi, G. (1990). Big business and the state, *in* "Manufacturing Miracles" (G. Gereffi and D. L. Wyman, Eds.), pp 90–109. Princeton, NJ: Princeton University Press.

Gereffi, G. (1994). The organization of buyer-driven global commodity chains: How U.S. retailers shape overseas production networks *in* "Commodity Chains and Global Capitalism" (G. Gereffi and M. Korzeniewicz, Eds.), pp. 95–122. Westport, CT: Praeger.

Gereffi, G. (1995). Global production systems and Third World development, *in* "Global Change, Regional Response: The New International Context of Development" (B. Stallings, Ed.), pp. 100–142. New York: Cambridge University Press.

Gereffi, G., and Hempel, L. (1996, Jan./Feb.). Latin America in the global economy: Running faster to stay in place. *NACLA Report on the Americas* **29**(4), 18–27.

Gereffi, G. and Pan, M.-L. (1994). The globalization of Taiwan's garment industry, *in* "Global Production: The Apparel Industry in the Pacific Rim" (E. Bonacich, L. Cheng, N. Chinchilla, N. Hamilton, and P. Ong, Eds.), pp. 126–146. Philadelphia, PA: Temple University Press.

Gereffi, G. and Wyman, D. L. (Eds.). (1990). "Manufacturing Miracles: Paths of Industrialization in Latin America and East Asia." Princeton, NJ: Princeton University Press.

Grunwald, J. and Flamm, K. (1985). "The Global Factory: Foreign Assembly in International Trade." Washington, D.C.: The Brookings Institution.

Haggard, S. (1990). "Pathways from the Periphery: The Politics of Growth in the Newly Industrializing Countries." Ithaca, NY: Cornell University Press.

Hamilton, G. G., and Biggart, N. W. (1988). Market, culture, and authority: A comparative analysis of management and organization in the Far East. *American Journal of Sociology* **XCIV** (Supplement), S52–S94.

Henderson, J. (1989). "The Globalisation of High Technology Production: Society, Space and Semiconductors in the Restructuring of the Modern World." New York: Routledge.

Henderson, J. (1994). Electronics industries and the developing world: uneven contributions and uncertain prospects, *in* "Capitalism and Development" (L. Sklair, Ed.), pp. 258–288. London: Routledge.

Hill, R. C. (1989, September). Comparing transnational production systems: The automobile industry in the USA and Japan. *International Journal of Urban and Regional Research* **XIII**(3), 462–480.

International Labor Organization (ILO). (1995). "Recent Developments in the Clothing Industry," Report I. Geneva: ILO.

Khanna, S. R. (1993, September). Structural changes in Asian textiles and clothing industries: The second migration of production. *Textile Outlook International* **49**, 11–32.

Lall, S. (1994, April). The East Asian miracle: Does the bell toll for industrial strategy? *World Development* **22**(4), 645–654.

Lim, L. Y. C., and Fong, P. E. (1991). "Foreign Direct Investment and Industrialization in Malaysia, Singapore, Taiwan and Thailand." Paris: OECD Development Centre.

Orrù, M., Biggart, N. W., and Hamilton, G. G. (1991). Organizational isomorphism in East Asia, *in* "The New Institutionalism in Organizational Analysis" (W. W. Powell and P. J. DiMaggio, Eds.), pp. 361–389. Chicago, IL: University of Chicago Press.

Page, J. M. (1994, April). The East Asian miracle: An introduction. *World Development* **XXII** (4), 615–625.

Park, Y. (1990, Fall.) A sequential development of the textile and clothing industries in Northeast Asia and China's effect on world markets. *Pacific Focus* **5**(2), 91–113.

Sabel, C. F. (1994). Learning by monitoring: The institutions of economic development, *in* "The Handbook of Economic Sociology" (N. J. Smelser and R. Swedberg, Eds.), pp. 137–165. Princeton, NJ: Princeton University Press.

Selwyn, M. (1993, August). Radical departures. *Asian Business,* 22–25.

Storper, M. (1995, Summer). Territorial development in the global learning economy: The challenge to developing countries. *Review of International Political Economy* **2**(3), 394–424.

Tran, A. N. (1995). "Can the Vietnamese State Play a Developmental Role? Integrating the Vietnamese Textile and Garment Industries into the Global Economy." Paper presented at the Association for Asian Studies annual meeting, Washington, D.C., April 6–9.

UNCTC (United Nations Centre on Transnational Corporations). (1986). "Transnational Corporations in the International Semiconductor Industry." New York: UNCTC.

Vernon, R. (1971). "Sovereignty at Bay: The Multinational Spread of U.S. Enterprises." New York: Basic Books.

Wade, R. (1990). "Governing the Market: Economic Theory and the Role of Government in East Asian Industrialization." Princeton, NJ: Princeton University Press.

Wade, R. (1994). Selective industrial policies in East Asia: Is *The East Asian Miracle* right? *in* "Miracle or Design? Lessons from the East Asian Experience," by A. Fishlow, C. Gwin, S. Haggard, D. Rodrik, and R. Wade. Washington, DC: Overseas Development Council.

World Bank. (1987). "World Development Report 1987." New York: Oxford University Press.

World Bank. (1993). "The East Asian Miracle: Economic Growth and Public Policy." New York: Oxford University Press.

World Bank. (1997). "World Development Report 1997." New York: Oxford University Press.

CHAPTER 5

State Autonomy and Its Social Conditions for Economic Development in South Korea and Taiwan

Hee-Yeon Cho
Department of Sociology
SungKongHoe University
Seoul 152-716, South Korea

Eun Mee Kim
Department of Sociology
University of Southern California
Los Angeles, California 90089 and
Graduate School of International Studies
Ewha Woman's University
Seoul 120-750, South Korea

I. INTRODUCTION

East Asia has received much attention from scholars and policymakers due to the region's tremendous economic development in the past few decades. Naisbitt (1996, 10) states that, "Asia came of age. And as we move toward the year 2000, Asia will become the dominant region of the world, economically, politically and culturally." There have been great efforts to reveal the causes of the remarkable economic growth of East Asia, especially that of South Korea and Taiwan. These efforts have focused on the roles of the market, the private sector, and the state. The goal of this chapter is to reveal that class and social conditions, which have not yet been examined fully, played an important role in the so-called East Asian "economic miracle." Without a deeper understanding of class and social conditions, we cannot fully comprehend South Korea's and Taiwan's economic miracle.

Even among the East Asian miracle cases, South Korea and Taiwan are particularly impressive in their economic achievement. Figures in Table 1 show the remarkable economic development attained by these two countries during the last few decades. We included basic indicators on the GDP, annual growth rate of GDP, GNP per capita growth rate, export growth, growth of manufactured exports, and changes in the industrial structure and the employment structure.

The Four Asian Tigers: Economic Development and the Global Political Economy

Table 1

Indicators of Economic Growth of South Korea and Taiwan

	South Korea		Taiwan	
	1960s	1990s	1960s	1990s
Average annual growth rate of GDP	8.93% (1960 to 1994)		8.86% (1960 to 1994)	
GDP	$2.36 billion (1961)	$330.8 billion (1993)	$1.75 billion (1961)	$241 billion (1994)
GNP per capita	$82 (1961)	$8,483 (1994)	$151 (1961)	$11,597 (1994)
Export	$18.8 million (1955)	$96,013 million (1994)	$116 million (1955)	$93,049 million (1994)
Manufacturing/its share in total exports	$3 million/ 16% of total exports (1955)	$89,868 million/ 93.6% of total exports (1994)	$13 million/ 10% of total exports (1955)	$89,241 million/ 95.9% of total exports (1994)
GDP by industries (agriculture/ industry/services)	35.8%/19.8%/ 44.56% (1960)	6.9%/43.6%/ 49.5% (1994)	28.5%/26.9%/ 44.6% (1960)	3.6%/37.3%/ 59.2% (1994)
Employment by industries (agriculture/ industry/services)	58.6%/13.3%/ 28.1% (1965)	13.6%/32.8%/ 53.6% (1994)	63.0%/8.7%/ 28.3% (1963)	10.9%/39.2%/ 49.9% (1994)

Sources: Council for Economic Planning and Development (CEPD), 1979, CEPD, 1988, 1993; World Bank, 1983, 1992, 1995; Directorate-General of Budget, Accounting and Statistics (DGBAS), 1995a, 1995b; The Bank of Korea, various years; The Bank of Korea, 1995.

What is more important beyond these changes is the fact that South Korea and Taiwan have achieved upward mobility in the "value-added hierarchy" of the world system. There have been few cases in which rapid industrial expansion has been accompanied by upward mobility in the value-added hierarchy (Arrighi, 1996a, 11). If we consider "the collapse of developmental efforts in the 1980s and the related 'strange death' of the Third World" (Arrighi, 1996b, 7) in general, the success of the Asian Tigers' looks even more impressive.

There has been an outpouring of scholarly research about the causes of these remarkable achievements. Studies from many divergent theoretical perspectives agree that economic growth has been attained, but they disagree about the causes and driving forces of the East Asian economic miracle. The market- and state-centered approaches have provided different explanatory frameworks for East Asian growth, focusing either on the role of the market or the state. The market-centered studies argue that East Asia succeeded because of market dynamics and market-friendly policies (World Bank, 1993, 10). These studies assumed that the most efficient allocation of resources in the growth process was possible because market forces were allowed a free play and other forces such as the state did not interrupt but instead played its role in a market-friendly way. Contrary to the market-centered studies, state-centered studies argue that in the East Asian economic miracle, effective state intervention and the state's industrial policies were decisive. Refuting the free market ideology and "the laissez-faire mythology triumphed by mainstream economists and the popular business press" (Lie, 1991, 68), state-centered studies reveal the comprehensive and decisive role of the state in East Asian growth. However, even though they helped reinstate the proper role played by the state in promoting socioeconomic change, they have not fully explored social or class conditions, which allowed the state to play its developmental role. Such social or class conditions were important for the successful role of the developmental state in South Korea and Taiwan, which has had a very special historical condition.

The state-centered studies have touched upon the issue of social conditions that are important for the developmental state. However, they have not examined systematically the class and social conditions that "allow" and "enable" a developmental state to function effectively in a society, and therefore produce rapid economic development. These conditions are not merely contextual factors, but are critical ones in helping us understand why certain institutions such as the developmental states are established and are able to flourish. This chapter is an effort to provide a more systematic and theoretical understanding about how the social and class conditions affect the development process. In the next section we provide a critique of existing frameworks for understanding East Asian economic development, and we present our alternative framework based on social and class conditions. In the following section, we provide a comparative analysis of South Korea and Taiwan: social and class conditions that enabled the state to be an autonomous institution in the two nations' economic development, and how the state changed as a result of changes in social and class conditions.

II. THEORETICAL DISCUSSIONS OF STATE AUTONOMY AND CLASS CONTEXT IN EAST ASIAN CAPITALIST INDUSTRIALIZATION

In this section, we review the state-centered studies, and argue that (1) their central argument focuses on state autonomy, (2) state autonomy is possible based on state–class relations, (3) state–class relations are reflections of broader social and class conditions (4) and, state–class relations are subject to change when social and class conditions change.

A. STATE-CENTERED STUDIES OF EAST ASIAN GROWTH

Criticizing the market-centered approach (World Bank, 1993; Kuo, Shirley W. Y. *et al.*, 1981; Balassa, Bela, 1988; Mason, Edward S. *et al.*, 1980), the state-centered studies or "statist" studies argue that effective state intervention, states' policies such as targeted industrial policies, and setting concrete performance standards have been decisive in economic development. Thus, the state did not merely follow the market, but it led the market, especially through "industry-specific policies" (Wade, 1990b, 233–234).[1]

According to the state-centered studies, the state encourages economic growth by controlling financial institutions and capital mobility, intervening in industrial structures and prices, and overseeing the interface with the international economy. In South Korea, for example, the government made most pivotal investment decisions rather than the market.

Contrary to getting basics right (Page, 1994, 624; World Bank, 1993, 10–11), the state-centered approach asserts that getting them wrong and distorting them in favor of economic growth contributed to rapid economic development (Amsden, 1989; Wade, 1990a).[2] Even export-oriented industrialization (EOI) was made possible by interventionist policies. In this respect, the World Bank's recommendation such as "forget interventions and focus on the fundamentals" may not be sufficient for economic growth in developing countries. Wade (1990a) provides a strong counterargument to the neoliberal economists' assertion that Taiwan's economic development is a prime example of market principles at work. He provides us with a clear argument that the role of the state in Taiwan's development has been to govern the market, rather than follow it (Wade, 1990b, 297). He says that if we look deeply into Hong Kong, which looks like a laissez-faire economy, it works "very differently from the textbook picture of a free market economy or from economies of the Anglo-American kind" and so could be interpreted as even "a variant of the guided market economy" (Wade, 1990b, 258–260). According to Amsden (1989), focusing on the South Korean case, one cannot claim that the effect of government intervention in East Asia is merely residual. She argues that the recommendation of the World Bank, which is that other developing countries should adopt the Bank's own market-friendly policies rather than East Asia's actual policies, lacks coherence. Amsden also indicates in her analysis of Taiwan that "the government of Taiwan has intervened far more in the Taiwan economy than liberal economists who champion export-led growth acknowledge" (Amsden, 1985, 90).

---

[1]Wade (1990a) refers to this approach as "guided market theory," in that the state in South Korea and Taiwan guided the market, they did not merely follow or represent its demand.

[2]Here "basics" or fundamentals mean such economic policies as macroeconomic stability, high investments in human capital, stable and secure financial systems, limited price distortions, openness to foreign technology, export-push trade policy, and minimal state intervention, among which the key is no-distortion and promotion of market functioning.

However, some differences also exist among the state-centered studies. Chalmers Johnson (1987), a key proponent of state-centered studies, has emphasized the state's role in establishing the market itself and promoting it. Johnson argues that in any model of the capitalist developmental state, the commitments of political elites to "market-conforming" methods of intervention in the economy is an indispensable element. Amsden (1989) goes a step further and argues that the state taking the initiatives in economic growth is a common factor that helps explain "late industrialization" in East Asia, which is fundamentally different from the laissez-faire industrialization of Britain and the nineteenth-century pattern shared by the United States and Germany. The South Korean case refutes the economic orthodoxy that assumes a unilinear vision of development and prescribes the free market as a key to growth, and therefore a new approach is needed for a full understanding because "late industrialization is a new paradigm in terms of the operation of the market mechanism and the role of the state" (Amsden, 1990, 31). What is central in this new paradigm is the interventionist state, which coordinates socioeconomic resources toward growth, sets performance goals for high-priority sectors, and controls the oppositions to growth (Johnson, 1987, 151).

According to these studies, the state can maximize its developmental role on the basis of its autonomy and independence from pressures of social groups and classes. Peter Evans makes this clearer by stating that in the "triple alliance" of dependent development in East Asia the state is the dominant partner and "the relative autonomy of the state apparatus and the effectiveness of state intervention are well beyond what can be observed in Latin America" (Evans, 1987, 221).

B. State Autonomy and Social Conditions

In East Asia, the autonomy of the state and its interventionist role have been important, especially in South Korea and Taiwan. State-centered studies, which are based on the theory of state autonomy, came closer to the reality of East Asian growth than the neoliberal market-centered studies.[3] However, they did not consider fully social conditions in which state autonomy could be possible. For statist scholars, the state is viewed as an independent actor, not as dependent actor of socioeconomic forces (Kohli and Shue, 1994, 302). Therefore, to them, the state does not merely reflect the dynamics of economy or civil society, and it is regarded as a force in its own right. We agree with these arguments, since state theorists rightly pointed out that the state has always been a critical and direct agent of socioeconomic change (Evans et al., 1985, 2), thus its role cannot be reduced to social or

---

[3]Especially, South Korea and Taiwan are the most typical cases in terms of wide state intervention among Asian countries, compared to laissez-faire Hong Kong (and, to a lesser degree, Singapore) and resource-rich countries of Southeast Asia (Perkins, 1994).

class conditions. However, we argue here that the state cannot be properly understood without considering the social or class conditions of a particular society. It should be emphasized that "societies affect as much as, or possibly more than, states affect societies" (Migdal *et al.*, 1994, 2).

There could be several reasons why social conditions were not fully examined by the state-centered studies. First, they approached state autonomy only as a function of certain institutional characteristics such as bureaucratic structure, and failed to locate it in its proper social or class context. State autonomy can be divided into two aspects. The first is the autonomy to coordinate class relations toward development. The second is autonomy to coordinate policy instruments toward development. Statists understood state autonomy primarily in the second sense. Therefore, they were unable to capture the social conditions, which made state autonomy and economic development possible. If it were not for the first, the second condition by itself could not have given rise to growth. The statists should be criticized for seeing only the "behavioral" aspects of state intervention, and neglecting social conditions that allowed such behavior to occur. In other words, state autonomy was made possible not only by its "endogenous property," but also by "exogenous conditions" such as class conditions.

Second, the statists did not see that the state may contribute toward conflictual relations among social groups and classes. In reality, certain state policies have class biases either in their purpose or in their unintended outcomes. Some classes or groups become beneficiaries while others are alienated. Thus, the state cannot be immune from social conflicts that may arise between these groups. The reason why "the state-centered approach is focused on explaining the remarkable achievements of the state" and "tends to ignore the social costs and abuses that also result from development" (Kim, 1997, 11) is that this approach does not see state in such a conflictual context.[4] "In spite of Amsden's success in demolishing the market myth, the reason why she ends up buttressing another—the self-congratulatory self-image propagated by the architects of Korean economic strategy" (Lie, 1991, 68–69)—exists here. Without a proper understanding of such conflicts, statists could fall under the "absolutism" of the state role in promoting growth, and can be criticized for its identification with interests of holders of state power and incumbents in high-level positions of policy decision making. This is similar to the neoliberal market theorists, who fell under the spell of free market absolutism and were criticized for their identification with the interests of transnational corporations.

Third, the statists tend to separate the state from society. They assume that the state is autonomous and independent, and, in some cases, they view the state as an overwhelming entity, which could coerce its will upon society without being under the constraints of society. In our view, this could arrive at another "reifica-

---

[4]About the internal costs and negative aspects of the growth itself, see Kim, 1995; Landsberg, 1979; Bello and Rosenfeld, 1992, 11–14.

tion" fallacy of artificially bifurcating the state from society (Jessop, 1990, 288), without an appropriate understanding of the embedded class relations. Statist studies, which perceive the state as the sole omnipotent actor, could be subject to the same criticism accorded to market-centered studies, which neglected factors other than the market.

In this sense, what is important for the state's autonomous intervention is not only the state autonomy per se, but also social conditions that structurally permitted the state's intervention. Therefore, the study of state autonomy should include a careful examination of these social conditions. In our view, state autonomy is a phenomenon of state–class relations, which is based on particular social or class conditions. Thus, the development studies are incomplete if the social context is excluded in the analysis.[5]

There are several dimensions of social or class conditions, which affect state autonomy. First, there is the potential for resistance by the old ruling class, especially the landlord class. Second, there is the potential for opposition by the popular sector including the working class and peasants. The third is whether a developmental alliance can be formed, and whether industrialization/modernization projects can be carried out as a hegemonic project. The first and second conditions are related to whether "basic" classes will be incorporated into the developmental project. The third condition is related to whether other social groups and classes can be incorporated into the developmental project.

The process of economic development involves not only material changes but also social changes mediated by class conflicts. As mentioned above, capitalist industrialization brings about the growth of the bourgeoisie. Therefore, in the process of economic development, opposition can arise from the traditional landowner class, the working class, and various social groups and classes, whose interests are constantly redefined in the growth process.

To argue that state autonomy should be understood in relation to its social or class conditions implies that if social conditions change, state–class relations and state autonomy could change as a result. For example, as growth proceeds "successfully" with the help of the autonomous interventionist state, social and class conditions change: A weak bourgeoisie, which could not have stood on its own feet, will be able to establish a stable basis of capital accumulation. Moreover, the popular sector and working class who were well-disciplined might become mobilized as an active social group. Ironically, the "successful," not failed, intervention of the autonomous state gives rise to class contradictions and conflicts. This, in turn, puts the state in a new context of state–class relations, which may involve a

---

[5]Here the concept "social" can be understood in the same way as Barrington Moore (1966) used it. The difference is that Moore's main focus was on specifying class configurations favorable and unfavorable to the establishment of modern Western democracy, while our focus is on specifying class configurations favorable to state autonomy and capitalist industrialization.

situation where the state may need to use more coercive methods. These changes in class conditions and state–class relations make previous form of state autonomy no longer tenable.

Evans (1995) changed his argument about state–society relations in his recent work to emphasize the interconnectedness of state and society rather than independence from society and class. He stresses the internal organization of the state, on the one hand, and state–society relations, on the other hand, as being the basis of the developmental state. For Evans, internal coherence of effective bureaucracy is discussed in the former, and embeddedness in society is discussed in the latter. "[C]onnectedness complements autonomy and that it is the balanced combination of the two that makes for efficacy. Simplistic notions of the virtues of insulating state from society must be rejected. Some degree of 'insulation' is inherent in creating a cohesive collectivity, but real effectiveness requires combining internal loyalties with external ties" (Evans, 1995, 72). Evans argues that state autonomy for developmental efficiency is based not just on the state's insulation or independence from society, but on the capability of the state in coordinating various social groups' interests and in being embedded in society. Although Evans suggests that his new analysis of the state role is an extension of state autonomy theory, the separation of state from society and embeddedness in it are different. If Evans argued "dis"embeddedness from society before, he changed to argue embeddedness in society. Regardless of whether this change would be considered a qualitatively different argument or an important extension of the earlier arguments, it is important to note that the statists now acknowledge the importance of the state's capacity to work with other centers of power, rather than the state's capacity to force its will on society or to separate itself from society.

In sum, we argue that state autonomy should be examined in its social and class contexts. We argue that in South Korea and Taiwan in particular, the state was an effective developmental state due to the unique social and class relations of these societies.

We examine the nature of their social and class relations in detail in the following section.

C. A Conservative Anticommunist Society and Social Conditions of State Autonomy

The establishment and reproduction of social conditions for state autonomy in South Korea and Taiwan cannot be fully understood without considering the effects of global and local geopolitical issues. In South Korea and Taiwan, the interactional influences of the Cold War and civil war have created a powerful social basis for a conservative anticommunist society, and for a developmental state with unchecked political power for intervening in the economy. In both nations, the anticommunist ideology of the global geopolitical context of the Cold War was internalized and intensified through the respective civil wars, that is, the Korean War in the Korean peninsula between the Communist North Korea (Democratic People's Republic of Korea) and South Korea (Republic of Korea), and the civil war between the Chinese Communist Party (CCP) and the Kuo-Min-Tang (KMT) in China. The anticommunist ideology was thus voluntarily accepted by the populace as well as the state, and provided a social condition in which labor discipline and political repression were possible in the name of "the fight against Communism." In the course of this fight, the ideology of anticommunism not only was to fight and defend against the communist, but also to win "economically." Once the ideologies of anticommunism and economic growth were brought together, the developmental state was able to pursue economic development plans as well as other economic/industrial policies without any social resistance. Anyone who was perceived to be against economic growth was also perceived to be a traitor who was willing to sell his/her country to the Communist adversary.

With the broader geopolitical context in mind, we explore the nature of the state, and in particular, the state–class relations. The tremendous autonomy enjoyed by these two states can only be understood in the context of the Cold War and its internalization in the respective societies. This chapter examines the social class conditions for the developmental state and economic development. The process of economic development is subdivided into four phases based on the specific state–class relations as follows: the formative phase, the deepening phase, the weakening phase, and the transformative phase. A summary of the changes in the conservative anticommunist society of South Korea and Taiwan are presented in Table 2. The first two phases deal with how the state and class conditions were established, and the last two phases focus on how the state–class relations change as a result of changes in the broader social/political/geopolitical contexts.

III. STATE AND CLASS IN THE CONSERVATIVE ANTICOMMUNIST SOCIETY

A. Establishment of the Conservative Anticommunist Society and Change of Class Conditions (1945–Early 1960s)

In this section we discuss how class foundations for state autonomy were established through the breakdown of the landlord class and repression of opposition movements. This period began from liberation from Japanese colonial rule in 1945 until the early 1960s when the export-oriented industrialization began in South Korea and Taiwan. During this period, South Korea and Taiwan were transformed

Table 2

Changes in the Conservative Anticommunist Society

	Formative stage	Deepening	Rising tensions	Crisis	Rearrangement
Time period	Independence to the early 1960s	From the early 1960s (start of the first EOI)	Early 1970s (secondary EOI supplementary by ISI)	Late 1970s	The emergence of "soft dictatorship" in 1988, lifting of martial law in 1988
Character of state autonomy		Hegemonic	Repressive		
Changes in class and social configuration	Land reform and weakening of the landlord class; reversal and imbalance of class relations in favor of ruling bloc; emergence of a conservative society.	Formation of a new developmental alliance and hegemonization of the modernization project; change of negative anticommunist community to a positive progrowth community.	Economic mobilization of the working class; intensification of industrial disputes; development of "Minjung" and "Tangwai" movements; manifestation of mainlander–KMT dominance; difference in trade union policy; defection of urban petty bourgeoisie.	Popularization of opposition (e.g., defeat of KMT in local election) and "hegemonization" of the oppositional alliance; difference in political society; initial enforcement of economic liberalization, prior to political reforms; strengthening of big bourgeoisie; defection of the new middle class.	Rearrangement of state–class relations from above; inclusion of big bourgeoisie in a symbiotic relationship with the state; recomposition within the power bloc; limited inclusion of the working class; political reform under the initiative of the ruling bloc (legalization of opposition parties; dismantling of lifelong National Assembly by courts; amendment of constitution in 1992 in South Korea and 1994 in Taiwan).
Catalyst incidents	The Korean War, 1950–1953, and armistice; civil war and defeat of KMT (1949).	Emergence of comprehensive export–subsidy policies ("19 Point Economic Financial Reform," install of Free Export Zone etc.)	Chung-Li incident in 1977; development of "Tangwai" movement; the emergence of the Yushin system in 1972 and the assassination of President Park in 1979.	Formosa Incident; Chun Doo-Whan regime in 1980 in South Korea; Great Democracy Movement in 1987 and division of the oppositional alliance; defeat in the presidential election in Dec. 1987; lifting of the martial law.	Political liberalization (29th June Declaration in 1987, lift of martial law) and the birth of civilian conservative governments (Kim Young Sam in 1993 in South Korea, Lee Dung-Hwi in 1996 in Taiwan).

into a conservative anticommunist society due to the combined influences of the Cold War and the civil war.

During this period, intense class conflicts over the direction of a new nation-state took place, and they escalated into civil wars: the Korean War in the Korean peninsula, and a war between the communists and the Kuo Min Tang (KMT) armies in China. However, these conflicts did not bring a unified nation–state and instead, two separate regimes emerged: the Republic of Korea (ROK) and the Democratic People's Republic of Korea (DPRK) in the Korean peninsula, and the People's Republic of China (PRC) and the Republic of China (ROC) in China. During violent conflicts accompanying the civil war, oppositional figures and groups were destroyed, which became an important precondition for the establishment of anticommunist societies. Moreover, the regional relocation of the leading movement figures occurred. In South Korea, many leftist leaders moved to North Korea and many right-wing figures moved to South Korea. As a result of combined efforts of the American Occupation Force and the South Korean government, the working class movement and popular opposition movements were nearly abolished and only progovernmental right-wing organizations were allowed to exist in South Korea.

In China, when the "February 27 Incident" broke out in 1947, KMT brutally suppressed the opposition movements in Taiwan and more than a thousand leading figures and people were allegedly killed, injured, or put in jail, or disappeared. Those who moved from mainland China to Taiwan were ardent supporters of the KMT. "Psychologically and sociologically, this withdrawal had a purifying and selective faction in that mostly particularly loyal members or adherents of the Party followed Chiang Kai-Shek to Taiwan into a situation which, at first, was nationally and internationally regarded as not very promising" (Kindermann, 1987, 384). About 2 million mainlanders left China for Taiwan. At the time the population of Taiwan was just six million (Long, 1991, 55). This relocation of population along the ideological line converted Taiwan into a more homogenized right-wing society. Another symbolic incident of relocation was that, among prisoners of war (POWs), the 14,343 defectors who did not want to return to the mainland went to Taiwan with the help of the UN Command. "When they arrived in Taiwan, they petitioned President Chiang in a letter written in blood pledging to fight the Communists to the bitter end under his leadership.[6] In addition, the KMT announced "The Temporary Provisions Effective during the Period of Mobilization for the Suppression of the Communist Rebellion" in 1948, which gave the president tremendous power. This solidified the foothold of the conservative, right-wing faction in Taiwan. The KMT also called off the regular election of the National Assembly, the Legislative Yuan and Control Yuan, giving

[6]This is the reason why "1. 23 Freedom Day" was established. Compilation Committee, 1981, 312.

the mainlander representatives life-long terms. Through these measures, the KMT established a system for absolute control of the Taiwanese (Kim, 1993, 137).

This rearrangement of political factions, removal of opposition forces, and legal institutionalization of political repression integrated South Korea and Taiwan into the U.S.-centered Cold War order. The external logic of Cold War politics was transformed into an internal political and social rule, and thus, the anticommunist society was born. Because the role of the United States was decisive for the existence and survival itself of the South Korean and Taiwanese regimes and their right-wing supporters, the voluntary accommodation to the U.S. hegemonic order took place.[7] Anticommunism became a deeply rooted domestic political ideology.

In the early months of the Korean war, the whole peninsula north of the Nakdong River was under the control of North Korean army. The intervention of UN forces with the U.S. army played a decisive role in preventing South Korea from falling under the control of the communists. The situation was not very different in Taiwan. It was the U.S. pressure that made the Chinese Communist Party give up the attempt to occupy Taiwan after the retreat of KMT to Taiwan.

It should also be noted that the United States was perceived as a "liberator" from Japanese colonial rule in many parts of Asia, including South Korea and Taiwan. Thus, there was a high propensity, especially by the right-wing, to identify with the United States. The internalization of the Cold War in South Korea enabled the strategic intent of the United States to be realized without much resistance. Such change of social and political conditions in favor of the ruling bloc and the hegemonic integration of South Korea and Taiwan into the U.S.-centered Cold War order allowed the formation of a very conservative right-wing society. Since the early 1960s this new social reality has provided a favorable condition for the dominance of the state over society, and for capitalist development.

The establishment of a conservative right-wing society and a vacuum of social movements enabled the "overdeveloped state" (Alavi, 1972) during the colonial period to reproduce itself in the postcolonial period. "The Korean War transformed the South Korean state from an extremely unstable and fragile anticommunist state into a powerful bureaucratic one ruled by authoritarian regime" (Choi, 1993, 22). KMT also "benefited enormously from their inheritance of Japanese state monopolies, and the whole interventionist approach taken by the Japanese to the development of an occupied territory was not lost to" (Amsden, 1985, 79) KMT. In addition, the two nations developed "absurdly swollen military machines" (Cumings, 1984, 69) after the Korean War and the Chinese civil war. In South Korea there were only 75,000 soldiers before the war, but there were more than 600,000 after the war. In Taiwan, the number of soldiers reached as much as

---

[7]Kang (1996) is arguing that without the intervention of U.S. troops during the conflicts after the Independence and the Korean War, the Korean peninsula would have been converted into a unified socialist regime.

600,000 in 1959 and the personnel who were in information agencies amounted to 120,000, or 2.14% of the total adult population (Kim, 1993, 130). Therefore, an already asymmetrical state–society relationship was intensified, and greatly enhanced the institutional basis for state autonomy.

On the other hand, the landlord class was severely curtailed. The confrontation between socialist North Korea and capitalist South Korea pushed South Korea to carry out relatively progressive land reforms, thus weakening the landlord class. This was a major achievement considering the fact that the majority of the assemblypersons had landlord backgrounds. Behind the passing of the land reform law were peasants, who were encouraged by the radical land reform in North Korea, and the experience of a revolutionary land redistribution during the Korean war. On Taiwan, the land reform was also precipitated by a radical version of it in the Chinese Communist Party, and took on a rather progressive character. On the mainland, the KMT had been largely predatory, based on rent-seeking (Evans, 1987, 54). Realizing its own defeat, KMT enforced a series of reform measures with the purpose to reconstruct Taiwan as a base for the eventual recovery of the mainland. These measures included not only registration of members of the KMT, strict application of discipline, consolidation of the central leadership for its renovation, but also economic reforms, including the land reform. This process took the form of "the confiscation with compensation, and distribution with compensation" (Kindermann, 1987, 385–386). Even though the two land reforms were in many aspects incomplete, they were progressive in removing the material bases of the landlord class.[8] Taiwan's land reform by KMT was stimulated by the self-perception that corruption and failure of various reforms on the mainland had resulted in their defeat by the communist party (Gregor *et al.*, 1981, 25). If we categorize Taiwan's land reform as a "preventive reform," we could define that in South Korea as a "competitive reform." The enforcement of the land reform, the disintegration of the material base of the landlord class, and the removal of the opposition potential of the former landlord class against the capitalist modernization were the key factors that made East Asian societies different from most Latin American societies. Because the landed oligarchies can function as powerful opponents against economic growth, removal of the landlord class gave an important social condition for capitalist industrialization and state autonomy. Here we can see the dual impacts of the Cold War: on the one hand, it helped destroy the opposition movements, while on the other hand, it contributed to land reforms, which destroyed the landlord class. Therefore, the internalization of the external Cold War

---

[8]There is much difference of view over the issue of "progressiveness" of land reforms in these two countries. We think that land reforms were incomplete in many aspects such as amount of distributed lands and mode of enforcement and so on. However, they have achieved much progress in terms of disintegration of landlords as a class and weakening of its potential opposition force against industrialization. In spite of this similarity, South Korea was different than Taiwan in that the tenant system was recovered because the government failed to enact supplementary laws.

logic gave rise to the conservative anticommunist society without the landlord class, providing the social conditions for capitalist industrialization in the early 1960s under the state's initiative.

B. The Deepening of the Conservative Anticommunist Society and Unlimited State Autonomy (1960s)

In the 1960s, modernization became a hegemonic project, and a developmental alliance was formed to this end.

The modernization project became an all-consuming goal of the state and society, and a dominant developmental alliance was established. The conservative anticommunist society of the 1950s transformed into a growth-oriented anticommunist society. The ideologies of economic growth and anticommunism were brought together as a coherent whole. South Korea and Taiwan no longer merely had an adversary from which they needed to defend themselves militarily, but also developed a much more proactive strategy to deal with their communist enemies— i.e., economic might to fight communism.

The promotion of an industrialization policy as a part of an anticommunist strategy was applied first to Japan. The United States tried to help Japan recover and upgrade its economy in order to turn it into a model of the United States policy of containment of communist power in Asia. The U.S. wanted South Korea and Taiwan to also join this growth train and to emerge as self-reliant economies, not dependent on foreign aid. One of Walter W. Rostow's first projects, when he joined the Kennedy Administration in 1961 was "to get South Korea and Taiwan moving toward export-led policies and to reintegrate them with the boom in the Japanese economy" (Arrighi, 1996a, 18). Under this strategic consideration, South Korea and Taiwan were given privileged access to "the price competition market"[9] in the U.S., access to the supplies and markets in the U.S.-centered world economy, including easier access to international financial market and protection at home from international competition. These privileges were crucial for the initial stage of export-oriented industrialization. In an effort to contain communism, the United States accorded Most Favored Nations (MFN) status to Japan, Taiwan, and South Korea, and with MFN these East Asian countries could achieve a rapid economic growth.[10] These privileges were crucial during the initial stage of export-oriented industrialization.

---

[9]Kwang-Yeong Shin is dividing the market in the U.S. into a "quality-competition" and a "price-competition" one. The latter implies a market dealing in low price goods.

[10]Arrighi (1996a, 31) is referring to this situation as "the contradiction of the U.S.-centered Cold War world order."

Export-oriented industrialization (EOI) strategy was implemented and began to show success by the late 1960s. In South Korea, the military government, which took power through a coup, became a powerful implementor of this growth strategy, just like the KMT in Taiwan. The previous import-substitution industrialization (ISI) strategy was abandoned in favor of EOI and the state enforced many reform policies for export promotion, including export subsidy, special credit for exports, tax reduction for export enterprises, currency devaluation, an interest rate increase, and other export subsidies. In Taiwan, the single exchange rate system was adopted, and the overvalued exchange rate was normalized. Several laws, including the Provisions for Foreigners' Investment (1959), Technology Joint Promotion Law (1962), Provisions for Export Zone (1965), and others were promulgated during this period. In South Korea, the growth strategy began to yield successful results by the late 1960s: the average annual growth rate of GNP from 1962 to 1971 was 9.2%, and the average annual growth rates of manufacturing and export were 17.5% and 38.1%, respectively (Bank of Korea, various years). In Taiwan, the average annual growth rate of GNP was 11.1% during this period, and between 1953 and 1963, average annual growth rates of exports and manufacturing were 29.7% and 19.4%, respectively (CEPD, 1979; 1993).[11]

Several important social and class conditions formed the foundation for this transformation. First, the class conditions that were laid in the 1950s provided a sound social basis. The weakening of the old landlord class, and the repression of the working class and opposition movements removed potential forces against the state. These changes contributed to the establishment of a new developmental alliance.

Second, the internalization of Cold War logic contributed to the hegemonization of the modernization project. Because South Korea and Taiwan voluntarily incorporated into the U.S.-centered world order, they could be faithful followers of the new Third World policy of the United States. During this period, the Kennedy administration changed its policy on communism, from providing military support to the anticommunist regimes to providing foreign aid in order to promote industrialization and enhance the economic self-reliance of the anticommunist regimes. In the 1950s, the U.S. policy focused only on defending South Korea and Taiwan against communist attacks through direct military and economic aid. In the 1960s, the U.S. policy changed into one that promoted the economies of South Korea and Taiwan so that they could become self-reliant and less dependent on U.S. military and economic aid.

A new developmental alliance was formed in the early 1960s. This alliance was composed of an incipient capitalist class, bureaucrats, conservative politicians, and the military. Class base of this alliance came from peasants, urban petty-bourgeoisie—that is, urban middle and lower classes and others. During the 1960s,

---

[11]In this period, Taiwan enjoyed an earlier and smoother industrial start, and had a higher per capita income than South Korea (Winkler and Greenhalgh, 1988, 18).

the class base of the developmental alliance was relatively stable. This alliance excluded labor.

Labor discipline and acquiescence was easily maintained in the 1960s, since labor did not pose a threat to the state. For example, labor disputes in the 1960s in South Korea numbered only 70 in 1963, 7 in 1964, 16 in 1968, 7 in 1969, and 4 in 1970 (Deyo, 1989, 60). These relatively small numbers of labor disputes imply that the working class was not mobilized as an opposing force against the hegemonic modernization project. In Taiwan, semi-wartime labor laws that had been established on the mainland continued. Labor disputes numbered as low as 30 in 1961, 64 in 1962, 7 in 1964, 5 in 1967, 2 in 1969, and 31 in 1970 (Deyo, 1989, 58). As for the causes of labor disputes, dismissal was 56%, delayed payment of wages was 10.9%, and demands for wage increases were 8.1%. These figures show that laborers were not yet mobilized and that their demands were more reactive than proactive. These conditions continued during the 1960s, since the conservative anticommunist society remained intact.

These class conditions helped establish a particular state–class relationship in favor of the state. As a result, the developmental state could enjoy a great deal of autonomy in economic policy decision making, including selection of monetary and financial policies, industrial targeting, support for specific industries, and so on. In South Korea, the decision-making apparatus headed by the president could mobilize whatever institution or policy instrument it needed. Under such conditions, the comprehensive developmental state could reorganize South Korean society into "Korea, Inc.," or "General Headquarters" (GHQ) style (Song, 1994, 140). Similar situations can also be found in Taiwan. We can call this autonomy of the state "hegemonic autonomy." The 1960s can be characterized by a hegemonic developmental alliance and project, and comprehensive state intervention for pro-business capitalist industrialization.

C. THE RISING TENSIONS WITHIN THE CONSERVATIVE ANTICOMMUNIST SOCIETY AND REPRESSIVE STATE AUTONOMY (1970s)

In the 1970s, the class conditions that provided the basis for state autonomy began to erode, and the conservative anticommunist societies began to show signs of tensions and conflict. As a result, state–class relations changed as well.

Ironically, the 1970s witnessed robust economic development and a deepening of the industrialization process, coupled with increased political repression. South Korea averaged 8.8% growth in GNP, 15.5% growth in mining and manufacturing industries, and 36.8% growth in exports (The Bank of Korea, various years). The rate of dependence on exports reached 90% and the foreign debt reached nearly $359 billion in the late 1970s, arousing concerns about economic dependence and debt crisis.[12] Although the same growth rates were slightly lower than those in the 1960s, Taiwan continued to be one of the most rapidly growing economies in the world. Both South Korea and Taiwan attempted to upgrade their industrial structure from light to heavy and chemical industries during this period. In South Korea, such industrial deepening met with difficulties in the second half of the 1970s. During the same period, Taiwan attained an 8.4% average annual growth of GNP, 12.4% in industry growth, and 23.9% growth in exports between 1974 and 1979 (CEPD, 1979, 1993).

Regardless of such difficulties and two oil crises in the 1970s, both the South Korean and Taiwanese economies continued to outperform their counterparts in the Third World. However, in spite of such economic success, neither South Korea nor Taiwan experienced any measurable improvements in the political arena. In fact, in South Korea, political repression escalated into the pronouncement of the Yushin Constitution in October 1972, which signaled a return of the strong military developmental authoritarian regime. This measure was the government's response to the growing social pressures from workers and citizens for more political openness. Taiwan also experienced a change toward more institutional repression, tightening the government's control of the popular sector. Thus, we name the state autonomy in the 1970s as repressive state autonomy.[13]

What gave rise to such an authoritarian state apparatus in the 1970s? In other words, why was the state confronted with acute social pressures for political openness and why did it respond with an iron fist? First, the compressed late industrialization gave rise to more intense conflict in society. The process of late industrialization relocated scarce resources into a small number of targeted areas, which resulted in extreme inequality in favor of the capitalists in a very short time. This was the cause for a high degree of alienation felt by the popular sector, which led to acute social discontent and conflict.

Second, in the process of compressed late industrialization, the working class increased in absolute and relative numbers in a very short time, and labor movements gradually gained momentum. In 1960, the number of workers in South Korea and Taiwan was 1,046,000 (13.9% of the total active working population) and 695,300 (23.4%), respectively. These numbers increased in 1975 to 3,929,900 (29.4%) in South Korea, and 2,159,000 (38.8%) in Taiwan, and in 1980 up to

---

[12]The whole amount of import and export/ GDP*100.

[13]As for the level of repressiveness, different views were suggested. Koo, Hagen (1989) said that Taiwan's regime was "soft authoritarianism" and less repressive than South Korea's. Deyo (1989) also argues that labor control in Taiwan was more hegemonic, moderated, and corporate. Contrary to these views, Jun Kim (1993), who argued that the Taiwanese political regime has been more repressive and exclusive, analyzed characteristics of industrialization, the role of the state in it, the formative working class, the political system, labor policy, and relations between labor and capital.

4,498,800 (33.1%) in South Korea and 3,302,900 (43.6%) in Taiwan (Kang, 1990, 56, 262). The working class discovered its class interest and began to demand its rights. It was no longer the acquiescent group of the 1960s.

During this period, labor movements focused on economic issues such as wages rather than on political issues such as withdrawal of the military from politics. In South Korea, the government continued to enforce policies to suppress expansion of trade unions. In opposition to such policies, labor began to organize democratic trade unions. However, in Taiwan, the government's policy was the opposite of South Korea's: the Taiwanese government encouraged trade unions to organize and attempted to control the working class through the unions. Thus, the labor movement in Taiwan focused on issues, such as enhancement of working conditions, and wage increases.

Compared to the 1960s when workers were incorporated into the development ideology, in the 1970s workers began to voice their own interests. In both countries, a group of workers with class consciousness began to emerge, and several industrial sectors saw the growth of antigovernment movements. Relatively speaking, labor movements in Taiwan were better incorporated into mainstream movements patronized by the government than they were in South Korea, and they were less militant than their South Korean counterparts. Nevertheless, labor movements in both countries became more active in the 1970s than they were in the 1960s.

In response to the changes taking place among workers and society in general, opposition movements began to crystallize their demands, and oppositional alliance began to form, although they were still weak (Cho, 1993, 112–118). In South Korea, in spite of the Yushin Constitution, social movements to restore the democratic Constitution spread. The "campaign for one million petitions for the Constitutional Amendment" expanded. The Park regime announced a series of "Emergency Presidential Decrees" to repress the opposition from further expansion. In April 1975, the fourth decree was announced to arrest students involved in "National Democratic Alliance of the Youth and Students," and in May 1975 the ninth emergency decree was announced to arrest anyone who was engaged in antigovernment activities or who was even only verbally critical of the government. From 1975 until 1979, when Park was assassinated, South Korean society experienced a serious setback in democracy. Despite the government's attempts to repress antigovernment movements, the anti-Yushin sentiment was beginning to spread to the general public. Progressive Christian leaders, student activists, and labor organizers became more active and mobilized against the government.

Although the intensity of the opposition movement was relatively low in Taiwan compared to South Korea, the opposition movement began to spread and develop in Taiwan as well. The establishment of *University Journal* in the early 1970s and the publication of *Summer Stream* in 1975 were symptomatic of the spread of the opposition movement in Taiwan. In universities, antigovernment activism spread and began to demand democratization. Although political appeasement policies were undertaken around the death of Chiang Kai-shek in 1975 and the succession to the presidency by his son, Chiang Ching-kuo, including the release of political prisoners, the opposition movement escalated. Newspapers and other media also became more critical of the government.

During this period, the "nonparty (tangwai)" or those outside the party symbolized the opposition's expansion. In the regional election in 1977, the nonparty began to appear as the union of independent candidates, including famous persons such as Whang Shingae and Kang Ryongsang.[14] *The 1980s* and *Formosa* were newly published in 1979, which represented the opposition's political views. The Formosa group opened regional offices throughout Taiwan. In the quadrennial election of local officials in the fall of 1977, Hsu Hsin-liang, who openly opposed KMT, was elected by majority support. This, in turn, precipitated a massive opposition movement against the authoritarian KMT rule. The "Chung-li incident" in November 1977 marked the first massive outbreak of antigovernment opposition in 30 years. "After Chung-li, society began aggressively to press its interests against the state" (Gold, 1986, 130). "The incident broke many of the taboos that had kept political life in Taiwan within strict bounds" (Long, 1991, 70). Although the KMT treated the leaders of the Chung-li Incident brutally, the newspapers continued to report opposition activities, and these reports fed the opposition movements.

As opposition spread to various sections of society by the late 1970s, the oppositional alliance began to take shape, which was based on the horizontal, albeit weak, coalition of various regional and sectoral movements. In South Korea this alliance took the form of the "Minjung" movement. The Minjung movement was based on a loose horizontal oppositional alliance of students, workers with political consciousness, the oppressed general populace, church activists, and intellectuals.

A unique issue in Taiwan's opposition movement was the mainlander-KMT dominance over the Taiwanese. In other words, along with class or political differences, subethnic discrimination was at the basis of the Taiwanese opposition. Within the opposition camp, a split between those demanding reunification with the mainland, and those demanding Taiwan's independence began to appear. While the opposition was united against dictatorship in South Korea, the opposition in Taiwan was divided over the subethnic conflict along with class conflict. In the late 1970s, this division was manifested with, for example, the young Taiwanese writers opening "xiang-tu" or the nativist school, which emphasized Taiwanese cultural identity (Long, 1991, 69).

These changes in social and class conditions, which included the deepening of structural contradictions, activation of the working class movement, and the emergence of the oppositional alliance, precipitated a disintegration of the developmental

---

[14]The "nonparty" originally meant candidates who were not affiliated with the KMT, but the meaning expanded to include independent candidates who had an oppositional orientation.

alliance. During this period, a gradual increase in the number and influence of opposition leaders and opposition movements changed the balance of class relations in favor of the opposition. In the 1960s, the developmental alliance was dominant and there was no oppositional alliance to speak of. In the 1970s, the developmental alliance began to disintegrate and the oppositional alliance was formed. As a result, the relationship between the developmental and oppositional alliances began to change, and eroded the state's dominant position over society as well.

The growth of the opposition and the activation of the popular sector made it difficult for the state to be hegemonic, and as a result, state autonomy was possible only through coercion and repression. This was manifested clearly in the changes in labor policies. In the 1960s, the labor law was not in need of amendments due to the inactivity of the labor movement. However, the situation changed in the 1970s. In South Korea, "Temporary Special Law on Trade Unions and Arbitration of Labor Disputes in Foreign Investment Companies" was enacted in 1970, and the labor law was revised in 1973, which resulted in major setbacks in labor rights.

While the South Korean government tried to control trade unions with increased political repression, the Taiwanese government tried to coopt the institutionalized trade unions. Taiwan's labor policy was basically oriented toward encouragement of the formation of trade unions, some control of trade union activities, and co-optation of workers. As a result, in South Korea, the labor law was revised in favor of entrepreneurs, while in Taiwan, the labor law was preserved without any significant amendments.[15] As rapid industrialization progressed and the discontent of workers increased, the KMT attempted to strengthen its control on trade unions, while it continued to encourage the organization of trade unions (Lee, 1988). There is a difference between South Korea and Taiwan in that the former controlled trade unions through repression, while the latter did it through co-optation.[16]

These changes correspond to the internal disintegration of the developmental alliance. As the heavy and chemical industrialization proceeded, class relations changed significantly. First, the relation between the state and the bourgeoisie changed. In South Korea, the 1970s was a decade of growing symbiosis between the state and the *chaebol*. The state was much more in need of the *chaebol*'s support in the 1970s compared to the 1960s, because it was confronted with greater opposition from the popular sector. The tight alliance between the state and the big *chaebol* helped consolidate a conservative coalition, solidifying the support of the *chaebol* for the state (Kim, 1997). This narrow alliance formed between the state and big *chaebol* (not the bourgeoisie in general) meant the marginalization of even the mid-

---

[15]This was revised only partially in 1975.

[16]For more detail of the difference of labor policy and the consequential labor movement, see Shin (1990).

dle and small bourgeoisie, which resulted in many of them defecting from the developmental alliance. "The heavy and chemical industrialization and the president's Emergency Decree show the changing nature of the state-business relationship: the alliance was no longer between the state and large businesses, but more specifically between the state and a few *chaebol* chosen by Park" (Kim, 1997, 165).

In addition, the urban petty bourgeoisie began to withdraw their support from the Park regime, which implied an internal disintegration of the popular basis for the developmental state. The urban petty bourgeoisie, which is considered to be about 13.5% of the entire population, received few economic benefits, and thus, began to voice their discontent in parliamentary elections. In the 1978 election, support for the government party, the Democratic Republican Party, was only 31.7%, while the major opposition party received 32.8% of the votes (United Communication, 1988). Popular uprisings in Masan and Pusan in late 1979 represented the defection of the middle and small bourgeoisie and the urban petty bourgeoisie, which had been alienated from the state-big *chaebol* collusion. Their discontent was expressed against economic policies, especially the economic stabilization policy.[17]

However, in spite of such defections, the developmental state did not experience a radical breakdown, as did Nicaragua, Iran, and Vietnam. The reason was the continued support of peasants and of the newly expanding middle class. The South Korean government attempted to coopt the rural sector through policies, such as the "Dual Rice Price System" and the "New Village Movement." "Even though the magnitude of actual benefits to the rural sector is a matter of debate, pro-rural political symbolism consolidated a base of rural support" (Haggard and Moon, 1993, 79). In addition, the new middle class, which was the main beneficiary of the state's economic policies, continued to provide its support for the government's economic policies. The middle class in South Korea and Taiwan comprised 3.4% and 2.5%, respectively, of total population in the early 1960s but increased to 4.3% and 6.2% in 1975, and 6.3% and 9.6% in 1980 (Kang, 1990, 56, 162). Increase in social support bases helped the developmental authoritarian state to maintain its prowess in spite of defections of other groups and classes.

The difference between the South Korean and Taiwanese governments in response to the changes in the anticommunist society was that the former became more authoritarian without any inclusive measures, while the latter enforced some measures to mitigate discontents of people. They included recruiting native Taiwanese elites into government service and other important positions, some opening for criticism within the party, especially within intellectual circles, and absorption of political demands through supplementary election of main governmental agencies (Kim, 1995, 140–141). These changes in Taiwan provided a foundation for a relatively less conflictual democratization in the 1980s.

---

[17]About the conflict over the accommodation of the macroeconomic policy in the state bureaucrats, see Haggard, 1994, 64–69; Haggard and Moon, 1993, 81.

In sum, ironically, industrialization activated the opposition, which brought changes in state–class relations. These changes necessitated a transformation of the functioning of state autonomy. Confronted with increasing conflict in the developmental alliance, the hegemonic state autonomy was forced to change to a repressive one based primarily on coercion.[18]

D. Crisis in the Conservative Anticommunist Society and Transformation of State–Class Relations

In the 1980s, the conflict within the conservative anticommunist society developed into a full-blown crisis. This broadened the societal base for democratization, and changed the state–class relationship irrevocably. This section will show that in South Korea, state–class relations were rearranged in a conservative way, because the oppositional alliance failed to overturn the authoritarian developmental regime. Even though the oppositional alliance threatened to break down the developmental state, it could not succeed in dismantling the repressive state structure and dominant agencies, and as a result, democratization proceeded in a top-down manner under the initiative of the former ruling bloc.[19]

In the 1980s, political upheaval was more dramatic and widespread than in the 1970s. Faced with massive political upheaval, the authoritarian developmental state was forced to change its developmental strategy that was supportive of big businesses at the expense of all other popular sectors.

In retrospect, the "transformative" phase of democratization began with economic and political liberalization, which was enacted to overcome the economic and political crisis of the developmental authoritarian regime. Economic liberalization included opening the internal market including the primary and the tertiary ones, and inviting foreign capital for investments. It also included privatization of state-owned enterprises such as banks.

The following factors forced the South Korean government to adopt economic liberalization policies. First, big business grew thanks to the heavy and chemical industrialization of the 1970s and became the dominant economic class, which demanded autonomy from heavy-handed state intervention. Second, the concentration of economic decision making in the hands of a few state elites in-

---

[18]The assassination of President Park in 1979 showed that the unlimited exercise of the state power or state autonomy could not maintain itself by coercion. That incident signified the breakdown of the dictatorship resisting a change of the mode of functioning of state power (and state autonomy as a part of it), which was forced by the change in state–class relations.

[19]One reason why this occurred is that the democratic transition proceeded without an economic crisis. This economic situation enhanced the capacity of the former ruling bloc to mobilize resources and control decisions related to the transition. Haggard and Kaufman, 1995, Ch. 4.

creasingly became a target. Third, the United States and other advanced industrialized countries demanded a greater opening of the domestic markets of South Korea and Taiwan, as these economies grew and inundated the former markets with relatively cheap goods.

During the early 1980s, Taiwan continued to grow, with 7.1% growth in GNP, 7.4% growth in manufacturing, and 15.8% growth in exports (CEPD, 1979, 1993). In 1986, Taiwan had a trade surplus of $16 billion (Ibid.). In the early 1980s, South Korea's economy grew an average of 10.3% in GNP, 11.8% in mining and manufacturing, and 20.3% in exports (The Bank of Korea, various years). South Korea's economy benefited from the so-called "Three Low Period" during the mid- to late-1980s, in which low crude oil prices, low interest rates, and Japan's rising yen against the U.S. dollar brought a booming export business to South Korea. As a result, South Korea was able to avert a debt crisis.

South Korea and Taiwan were similar in that economic liberalization preceded political liberalization. The developmental authoritarian state experienced a dynamic change in its political order after economic liberalization. The "transformative" period of the conservative anticommunist society, which began with the economic liberalization policy in the early 1980s, can be divided into two subphases: before and after political liberalization. The first phase (1980–1987) covered the period until the so-called "Great Democracy Struggle" and the June 29th Declaration in 1987 in South Korea, and the lifting of martial law in Taiwan in 1987. During this period, democratic struggles intensified with demands for democratic change in the developmental authoritarian state, including a direct presidential election, the lifting of the martial law, and change of pro-bourgeoisie developmental policies toward greater economic equality. As democratic struggles intensified, the conservative developmental alliance and its project faced a major crisis and started to disintegrate. In the second phase (1987–present), political conflicts as well as collusion among political forces occurred in a politically liberalized context, and state–class relationships were rearranged along the conservative top-down path of democratization.

In the first phase, opposition to the developmental authoritarian regime, including the developmental alliance and its project, became more intense and spread to various areas. Even though the conservative anticommunist society's disintegration began to take place in the 1970s, the developmental authoritarian state was able to prolong its life with increased political repression. However, in the 1980s, the authoritarian developmental state reached its limit when it could no longer sustain itself with repression. Change was inevitable.

The Chun Doo Hwan regime marked even harsher and widespread political repression than the Park regime. First, wider political exclusion was imposed. Many opposition party figures were excluded from the formal political arena in the name of "purification" of "corrupt" politics (including influential potential political competitors such as Kim Dae-Jung and Kim Young Sam), which resulted in fueling antigovernment demonstrations on the streets. In addition, the Chun regime took comprehensive measures to repress the opposition organizations that sprouted during the Park regime. Such repressive measures were able to only temporarily silence the opposition, and the opposition movement spread into wider areas compared with the 1970s. During the first half of the Chun regime, the Minjung movement changed into a more organized and popular opposition movement with broader popular support. During this phase, the reactive oppositional alliance vis-à-vis the developmental alliance transformed into a more proactive one. In response, the state adopted an "appeasement policy" (Cho, 1994a) to lessen the level of crisis in late 1983. Originally, the appeasement policy was aimed at weakening the increasingly expanding opposition and dividing the oppositional camps. However, the result was the opposite: opposition movements expanded into various social areas, and in 1987 reached their peak.[20] The 1985 parliamentary election marked a turning point for the opposition: it entered the formal political arena. The "Great Democracy Struggle" of June 1987 was the culmination of the democratic opposition during the 1980s. During the peak of demonstrations, several million participated for as long as 20 days. The opposition demanded the retreat of the military. Even the middle class, which had not actively supported the opposition, rushed into streets filled with tear gas. The military gave in to this massive democratic struggle and accepted some of the people's demands in the form of the "June 29th Declaration." The declaration included a direct presidential election, freedom for political activities, remission and reinstatement of expelled political figures, and so on (Cho, 1996).

In the 1980s, social movements in Taiwan expanded their popular and organizational bases, and spread to nearly all social arenas. These included the labor movement, the consumer movement led by urban intellectuals and professionals, the environmental movement including antipollution protests from local victim groups, the conservation movement, the women's movement, the aborigines' human rights movement led by the educated and politically conscious aborigine youth, a student movement, and church protests (Hsiao, 1994, 208; Tien, 1988, 23–28; Bello and Rosenfeld, 1992). These various social movements exerted substantial pressure for democratization, and the authoritarian KMT regime was forced to adopt political liberalization measures.

Like South Korea, the student movement in Taiwan played an important role in the opposition. It was particularly important in motivating other movements to become politically active by directly criticizing the KMT's rule, and thus, securing political room for the opposition. Tight control of universities by the KMT also weakened in the 1980s. For example, a student who was not affiliated with the

---

[20]For the development of the farmers' movement, the urban poor people's movement, the environmental movement, the women's movement, the labor movement, and related political change, see Hart-Lansberg, 1993, Ch. 11 and 12.

KMT was elected as a president of the "General Association of Students." Also in South Korea, a new oppositional student association was formed, which displaced "the Student Defense Corps," established in 1983 by the government. This event signified a weakening of the social control system of the state, and a relative strengthening of the opposition movement.

Development of the opposition movement in the 1980s started with the popular opposition against the suppression of the Formosa group—i.e., the "Formosa Incident." During the incident, a massive clash between the police and the public took place, and the KMT government arrested many opposition leaders. This incident became a catalyst for the development of the opposition. It grew in the 1980s with the popularization of nonparty movements. In the regional election in 1981, many democratic candidates ran, using a common theme. In 1984, the "Public Policy Studies Association of Non-Party Candidates" was founded as a permanent establishment, and formed the foundation for the Democratic Progressive Party (DPP) (Long, 1991, 194–198). The election results showed that independent candidates received 17% of the vote in 1975, but that number increased to 27% in 1980, and 33% in 1986. These numbers indicate the increasing number of people defecting from the KMT, and their strong desire for democracy.[21] In local level elections, non-KMT candidates received 28.5% of the vote (Chao, 1987, 318). Even though the nonparty movement stayed moderately progressive (Sutter, 1988, 45–60), development of that movement signified that the KMT had no option but to adopt political liberalization measures.

The oppositional alliance, which had existed only as a loose horizontal network in the 1970s, developed into a more organized form during the 1980s. The oppositional alliance began to engage in strategic maneuvers (Cheng and Kim, 1994, 127–128) in order to force a serious transformation within the developmental regime.

Deepening of the oppositional alliance was helped by defection of the middle class from the developmental alliance. Even though the middle class was not a single homogeneous class and its role in democratization was fluid and variable, it (especially, the intellectuals) was a strong driving force for democratization (Koo, 1991, 490–505), at least during the first half of the 1980s.

Moreover, in the late 1970s the urban petty bourgeoisie began to defect from the developmental alliance. This greatly enhanced the social basis of the democratic transition. Extensive involvement by clerks, white collar workers, and urban-based small merchants exemplified important changes in class conditions. Peasants, most of whom were still supportive of the government party, also began to express some discontent with the government's policy of opening the domestic market to foreign agricultural imports. Such changes in the agricultural policy influenced the peasants'

---

[21]In the triennial supplementary elections held in December 1983, the total vote of the "Tangwai" fell to 22%, mainly because of the internal division of the nonparty movement. Gold, 1986, 118.

political attitude toward the government. During this time, tension arose between peasants on the one side, and the bourgeoisie and the urban middle class on the other, over the opening of the agricultural market. The opening of the domestic agricultural market symbolized a change in the developmental state's policy in favor of the latter. The discontent of the peasants escalated and became a source of pressure for democratic change.

Expansion of the opposition, and the formation and intensification of the oppositional alliance, made changes inevitable in the authoritarian developmental regime, especially in state–class relations. Most importantly, state autonomy as an expression of state–class relations (which was based on labor discipline and people's acquiescence, and on the broader social context of a conservative anticommunist society) had to change, since the anticommunist society changed, and the workers and the public were no longer acquiescent.

The second phase (1987–present) is a period in which competition and conflict over the direction of the developmental state in a new political context proceeded after the political liberalization from above. The new political context refers to the situation after the democratic movements and the June 29th Declaration in 1987 in South Korea, and after martial law in Taiwan in 1988. In December 1987, Roh Tae-Woo, who was an ex-military general, was elected as South Korean president according to a new Constitution. The new Constitution was a direct outcome of the democratic movement. President Roh founded a new government party through the merger of three parties in 1990, which included the Democratic Justice Party (the government party), and two other opposition parties—the Unification Democratic Party headed by Kim Young Sam and the Democratic Republican Party headed by Kim Jong-Pil.[22] Kim Young Sam was elected president in 1992. This change implied that the transformation of the developmental state and state–class relations were led by the developmental ruling bloc and not the oppositional alliance.[23]

In Taiwan, the lifting of martial law in 1987 meant the beginning of political reforms initiated by the KMT. More room was made for legalized political and social opposition. Opposition parties such as DPP that were legally prohibited from organizing in the past became institutionalized. Political reforms, which began in the mid-1980s, were as follows: the founding of parties was allowed in January 1989; the dismantling of the so-called "life-long National Assembly" by court decision in June 1990; the official declaration of the end of the "Period of Mobilization for the Suppression of the Communist Rebellion"; repeal of the "Temporary Provisions," effective in May 1991; the national election for all of the seats in the National Assembly in December 1991 and the Legislative Yuan in December

---

[22]This could be seen as a compromise among many that occurs as a result of a union among hardliners and moderates in the ruling bloc, and radicals and reformers in the opposition bloc as Przeworski (1991, 66–88) analyzed. For South Korean cases related to this compromise, see Cho, 1994a.

[23]This change means a transformation from a military regime to a "low-intensity democracy" in order to lower the crisis and opposition militancy. Graf, 1995, 154.

1992; amendment of the Constitution in May 1992 and July 1994; and finally, a new election of the president by the people's direct vote. In the presidential election in 1996, Lee Dungwhi, who represented the former developmental ruling bloc, was reelected. This meant that the crisis of the developmental regime did not lead to a complete breakdown of the former regime. Quite the contrary; the ruling bloc reorganized itself and rearranged the former state–class relationship in a way that favored itself.

This chapter argues that state autonomy is based on particular state–class relationships, and based on broader social or class conditions, and thus, the state–class relationship and mode of state intervention will change as social conditions change.[24] However, the important issue is how that change occurs, whether it is realized from the top down in a conservative way under the initiative of the previous developmental alliance or from bottom up in a radical way under the initiative of the oppositional alliance. These two modes represent the qualitative character of the transformation. The aforementioned process of political change shows that so far South Korea's and Taiwan's experiences belong to the former form of transition. Even though the conservative anticommunist society and its developmental state faced a major crisis, oppositional alliance could not overthrow them during critical periods and thus, was unable to dismantle the authoritarian regime. If the conservative anticommunist societies had been dissolved in a more radical way, the state––class relationship would have changed in very different ways. In the end, the conservative anticommunist societies of South Korea and Taiwan and their developmental states were transformed in the top-down way and experienced a controlled transition in the economy as well as in the political arena. In this sense, they can be defined as the conservative rearrangement of the state–class relationship.

How have the state–class relationship and the anticommunist right-wing society changed in the process of the conservative transformation of the authoritarian developmental regimes? Class conditions, which changed due to the growth of the opposition movement, the mobilization of the popular sector, and the growth of the bourgeoisie, brought about changes in the state–class relationship and in state autonomy. Unlike the 1960s, when class conditions included the absence of a landlord class and a weak bourgeoisie, new class conditions in the 1980s included a strong bourgeoisie and a militant working class. These changes, in turn, forced changes in the state–class relationship.

First, important changes took place between the state and the bourgeoisie. Because the bourgeoisie had a secure economic basis, it began to demand more independence from the tight reign of the developmental state. It began to extend its economic power to social and political arenas. The state, which in the past enjoyed unlimited autonomy over economic policy, had to be more accommodating of the

---

[24]If we focus on the phenomenal autonomy the state enjoys, this change is from a comprehensive to the limited developmental state. Kim, Eun Mee, 1993.

bourgeoisie, and the latter was invited to partake in policy decisions. If the past state–bourgeoisie relationship can be defined as the hierarchical symbiosis of a senior–junior relationship, it could now be defined as collaborative symbiosis, reflecting the strengthened position of the capitalist class, especially the big businesses. In South Korea, the collusion between the state and big businesses is stronger than in Taiwan, because the state favored big business exclusively at the expense of small- and medium-sized enterprises.

The internal constitution of the developmental ruling bloc also changed into a postdevelopmental conservative alliance, as the top-down conservative democratic transition took place. The former developmental ruling bloc, which was composed of big business, bureaucrats, conservative politicians, and the military, changed into a new postmilitary ruling bloc, in which the military was no longer at the fore. In Taiwan, the former ruling bloc, which was composed of mainland political elites, big business, and bureaucrats, changed to a new conservative ruling bloc, which was composed of second-generation mainlander elites, native Taiwanese economic and political elites, big business, and bureaucrats. As for membership of government party elites, the emergence of the conservative civilian governments of Kim Young Sam in South Korea in 1993 and of Lee Dungwhi in Taiwan in 1996 show that there was only partial removal of former authoritarian members. In both South Korea and Taiwan, the above transformation occurred with the moderates in charge. And thus, political reforms were also moderate and limited.

These political reforms were not very inclusive of the working class. Responding to the growth in the labor movement, the governments tried to coopt some segments within the working class, and to weaken the intensity of the labor movement by introducing a limited corporatist labor policy. In South Korea, the previously progovernment labor organization—The Federation of Korean Trade Unions (FKTU)—tried to show some autonomy in order to prevent a breakdown due to the growth of the democratic labor movement. The government encouraged this metamorphosis.[25] The government also tried to repress a more militant democratic labor movement headed by the Korean Confederation of Trade Unions (KCTU) by legalizing a moderate labor movement and by denying legalization of radical labor groups. This can be called a rudimentary corporatist policy.

While the civilian government in South Korea, for the first time, tried to introduce corporatist state–labor relations, the Taiwanese government tried to further develop the corporatist method (Deyo, 1989). Changes that occurred in the post-martial law period include giving more room to the opposition and industrial conflicts such as strikes, and coopting workers with economic incentives. In addition, the KMT government rescinded the "Temporary Provisions over Labor Disputes

---

[25]Social movements have driven the democratic transition, which in turn gives rise to a new condition in which they differentiate themselves. Among the phenomena related to this, there is a differentiation of "new social movements" and a new attempt by the former government-patronized movement to win an autonomous social basis of support (Cho, 1996).

Effective during the Period of Mobilization for the Suppression of the Communist Rebellion" in 1988, partially removing the institutionalized control over collective actions. In other words, policies about labor conflicts changed from prohibition of collective action to partial allowance of collective action. The KMT tried to maintain peaceful industrial relations by extending its earlier corporatist method and reducing its tight control over collective action.

Conservative democratic transition proceeded on two fronts: rearranging the relations among actors within the ruling bloc on the one hand, while continuing to exclude the working class and popular sector and coopting only the conservatives within those groups on the other hand. These processes were contradictory to each other and produced tension and conflict.

In sum, during the fourth period (from the early 1980s to the present) conservative anticommunist society and the authoritarian developmental state faced major challenges due to the remarkable growth of the opposition and the oppositional alliance. However, the opposition movements failed to capture state power, and therefore, a conservative democratic transition from the top took place and, state—class relations were also rearranged in that context. In the 1970s, the authoritarian developmental regime and its developmental project became increasingly repressive and maintained itself through coercion. Because of a serious rupture and its crisis in state—class relations, transformation of the regime became inevitable. However, since a conservative path of transformation became dominant due to the defeat of the oppositional alliance, the transformation in state—class relations in the 1980s took place in a conservative way, resulting in a limited rearrangement. This limited transformation proceeded in the following manner: (1) inclusion of big business into a collaborative symbiosis relationship with the state; (2) rearrangement of the internal relationship within the developmental ruling bloc; and (3) limited inclusion of the working class. This limited conservative democratic transformation continues to evolve and change. Changes in state—society relations clearly show that state autonomy, which state-centered studies assumed as an inherent property of the state, is possible only in certain social conditions and is inevitably forced to change when social conditions change.

IV. CONCLUSION

This chapter examines the class and social conditions of state autonomy, which has not been fully examined by the developmental state theory of East Asian growth. We argue that state autonomy, which is a key concept of state-centered studies, is based on broader class and social conditions. In addition, we emphasize that state—class relations change as a result of changes in class and social conditions.

We divided the contemporary history of South Korea and Taiwan into four phases, and defined the particular class and social configuration in South Korea and

Taiwan as a conservative anticommunist society. During each phase, we examined how those conservative anticommunist societies changed and how that change influenced state–class relations and state autonomy.

During the formative phase of a conservative anticommunist society—i.e., the period from the independence from the Japanese colonial rule in 1945 to the time just prior to the start of EOI in the early 1960s—land reform was conducted, and as a result the landlord class's material base was severely weakened. Through the civil wars in Korea and China, opposition movements were dismantled, which resulted in a change in class relations in favor of the ruling bloc. This contributed to the establishment of an anticommunist right-wing society, and provided the social basis for state autonomy. During the second phase, which was named the deepening phase of the conservative anticommunist society, we witnessed the formation of a new developmental alliance and we saw that the modernization project became a hegemonic one based on the class conditions laid during the previous phase. This signified a change from a conservative anticommunist society to a more growth-oriented society.

During the third phase, which occurred from the early 1970s to the early 1980s, an internal fissure began to appear as a consequence of expansion of the contradiction of the industrialization and increasing mobilization of the popular sector and the opposition. The rupture of the conservative anticommunist society affected class conditions. The state began to rely more heavily on coercion than consensus. The state had become an authoritarian developmental state. In the 1980s, the conservative anticommunist society and past state–class relations faced a serious crisis and were forced to transform. We called this period a transformative phase of the conservative anticommunist society. During the first half of this phase (before political openings in 1987), democratic struggles intensified and the oppositional alliance pressed for a dismantling of the authoritarian developmental state. However, the oppositional alliance failed to force the regime to break down, and as a result, the former ruling bloc was able to take the initiative in rearranging the conservative anticommunist society and state–class relations. During the latter half of this phase after 1987, state–class relations were rearranged in a conservative manner, since the democratic transition was controlled from the top.

For the first two phases, we argue that certain class conditions—i. e., breakdown of the landlord class, weakening of opposition movements, and hegemonization of modernization project and developmental alliance—enabled the state to autonomously carry out its policies. In our discussion of the latter two phases, we analyze how class conditions—e. g., mobilization of the working class and the popular sector, internal disintegration of the developmental alliance, and growth of the oppositional alliance—forced the state and state–class relationship to change.

We conclude that state autonomy, which the state-centered studies assume is an inherent property of the state, is actually a function of particular social and class conditions, and that economic development can be understood fully only when we take into consideration class and social conditions.

REFERENCES

Abegglen, J. C. (1994). "Sea Change: Pacific Asia as the New World Industrial Center." New York: The Free Press.

Alavi, H. (1972). The state in post-colonial societies: Pakistan and Bangladesh." *New Left Review* **74**.

Amsden, A. (1985). The state and Taiwan's Economic Development, *in* "Bringing the State Back In" (Evans, Peter B., Dietrich Rueschemeyer and Theda Skocpol, Eds). Cambridge: Cambridge University Press.

Amsden, A. (1989). "Asia's next Giant: South Korea and Late Industrialization." New York: Oxford University Press.

Amsden A. (1990). Third World industrialization: "Global fordism" or a new model? *New Left Review* **182**.

Arrighi, G. (1996a). The rise of East Asia: World systemic and regional aspects. *International Journal of Sociology and Social Policy* **16**, 7.

Arrighi, G. (1996b). "Global Restructuring and the 'Strange Death' of the Third World." Paper presented at the Annual Colloquium Series hosted by Center for Social Theory and Comparative History, May 20.

Balassa, B. (1988). The lessons of East Asian development: An overview. *Economic Development and Cultural Change* **36**, 3.

The Bank of Korea, various years, *Economic Statistics Yearbook.*

The Bank of Korea. (1995). *Monthly Bulletin,* July.

Bello, W., and Rosenfeld, S. (1992). "Dragons in Distress—Asia's Miracle Economies in Crisis." San Francisco: A Food First Book.

Castells, M. (1992). Four Tigers with a dragon head: A comparative analysis of the state, economy and society in the East Asian Pacific Rim, *in* "States and Development in the Asian Pacific Rim" (R. Appelbaum and J. Henderson, Eds.) London: Sage Publications.

Council for Economic Planning and Development (CEPD), Executive Yuan, ROC, 1979, 1988, 1993. "Taiwan Statistical Data Book." Taipei.

Chao, C.-M. (1987). Political participation in the ROC, *in* "Reform and Revolution in Twentieth Century China" (Shaw, Y., Ed.). Taipei: Institute of International Relations, National Chenchi University.

Cheng, T., and Eun Mee Kim. (1994). Making democracy: Generalizing the South Korean case, "The Politics of Democratization: Generalizing East Asian Experiences" (E. Friedman, Ed.). Boulder: Westview Press.

Cho, H.-Y. (1993). "The Modern Korean Social Movement and Organization" (in Korean). Seoul: Hanul Publishing Company.

Cho, H.-Y. (1994a). A political-sociological study on the transition to democracy in Korea (in Korean). *Currents and Prospects* **21**, Spring, Baeksanseodang.

Cho, H.-Y., and Kim Yeong-Beom. (1994b). "Democratic Transition and Politicization of Progressive Forces—Based on the Comparison of South Korea and Brazil" (in Korean). Korean Association for Industrial Studies, The Change of Korean Society. Seoul: Hanul Publishing Company.

Cho, H.-Y. (1996, April 11–14). The democratic transition and the change of social movements in South Korea. Prepared for the Panel, "The Aftermath of Democratization in South Korea," at the Annual Meeting of the Association for Asian Studies, Honolulu, Hawaii.

Choi, J.-J. (1993). Political cleavage, *in* The State and Society in Contemporary Korea (H. Koo, Ed.). Ithaca: Cornell University Press.

Compilation Committee. (1981). "A Pictorial History of the Republic of China," Vol. 2. Taipei: Modern China Press.

Cumings, B. (1984). The origins and development of the Northeast Asian political economy: Industrial sectors, product cycles, and political consequences, *in* "The Political Economy of the New Asian Industrialism" (F. Deyo, Ed.). Ithaca: Cornell University Press.

Deyo, F. (1987). State and labor in East Asia, *in* "The Political Economy of the New Asian Industrialism" (F. Deyo, Ed). Ithaca: Cornell University Press.

Deyo, F. (1989). "Beneath the Miracle: Labor Subordination in the New Asian Industrialism." Berkeley: University of California Press.

Directorate-General of Budget, Accounting and Statistics (DGBAS). (1995). National Income in Taiwan Area of the Republic of China.

Directorate-General of Budget, Accounting and Statistics (DGBAS). (1988, 1995). Statistical Yearbook of the Republic of China.

Evans, P. B., Rueschemeyer, D., and Skocpol, T., Eds. (1985). "Bringing the State Back In." Cambridge: Cambridge University Press.

Evans, P. (1987). Class, state, and dependence in East Asia, in "The Political Economy of the New Asian Industrialism" (F. Deyo, Ed.). Ithaca: Cornell University Press.

Evans, P. (1995). "Embedded Autonomy: States and Industrial Transformation." Princeton: Princeton University Press.

Gereffi, G. and Wyman, D. L. (1990). "Manufacturing Miracles: Paths of Industrialization in Latin America and East Asia." Princeton: Princeton University Press.

Gold, T. B. (1986). "State and Society in the Taiwan Miracle." Armonk: M. E. Sharpe, Inc.

Graf, W. (1995). The state in the Third World. "Socialist Register 1995." London: The Merlin Press.

Gregor, J. A., Chang, M. H., and Zimmerman, A. B. (1981). "Ideology and Development: Sun Yat-Sen and the Economic History of Taiwan." Berkeley, CA: University of California Press.

Haggard, S., and Chung-In Moon. (1993). The state, politics, and economic development in postwar South Korea, in "The State and Society in Contemporary Korea" (K. Hagen, Ed.). Ithaca: Cornell University Press.

Haggard, S. (1994). From the heavy industry plan to stabilization: Macroeconomic policy, 1976–1980, in "Macroeconomic Policy and Adjustment in Korea 1970–1990" (S. Haggard et al., Eds.). Harvard Institute for International Development and Korea Development Institute.

Haggard, S., and Kaufman, R. (1995). "The Political Economy of Democratic Transition." Princeton: Princeton University Press.

Hart-Lansberg, M. (1993). "The Rush to Development." New York: Monthly Review Press.

Hsiao, H.-H. M. (1994). Political liberalization and the farmers' movement in Taiwan, in "The Politics of Democratization: Generalizing East Asian Experiences" (E. Friedman, Ed.). Boulder: Westview Press.

Hwang, Y. D. (1991). "The Rise of a New Word Economic Power: Postwar Taiwan." New York: Greenwood Press.

Jessop, B. (1990). "State Theory: Putting Capitalist States in Their Place." University Park, PA: The Pennsylvania State University Press.

Johnson, C. (1982). "MITI and the Japanese Miracle: the Growth of Japanese Industrial Policy, 1925–1975." Stanford: Stanford University Press.

Johnson, C. (1987). Political institutions and economic performance: The government–business relationship in Japan, South Korea, and Taiwan, in "The Political Economy of the New Asian Industrialism" (F. Deyo, Ed.). Ithaca: Cornell University Press.

Kang, H.-K. (1990). "The Spatial Differentiation of Classes in NICs: Focused on the New Middle-Class in South Korea and Taiwan" (in Korean), Ph.D. dissertation, Seoul National University.

Kang, J.-K. (1996, April 20). "The Role of the United States in the Division of Korea and Korean War." Paper presented at the Southern California Korean and Korean American Studies Group Colloquium, University of Southern California.

Kim, D.-H. (1995, March 7). "Korean Economic Development: Miracles and Mirage?", World Summit for Social Development NGO Forum '95, Special Workshop on Economics of Rapid Growth.

Kim, E. M. (1993, May). Contradictions and limits of a developmental state: With illustrations from the South Korean case. *Social Problems* **40**, 2.

Kim, E. M. (1997). "Big Business, Strong State: Collusion and Conflict in South Korean Development, 1960–1990." Albany: State University of New York Press.

Kim, J. (1993). "Labor Politics and Labor Movements in Asian Authoritarian Regimes: a Comparative Study on Korea and Taiwan" (in Korean), Ph.D. dissertation, Department of Sociology, Seoul National University.

Kim, J. (1995). Democratization of Taiwan (in Korean). *Currents and Prospects* **26.**

Kindermann, G.-K. (1987). Agrarian revolution and land reform in divided China, *in* "Reform and Revolution in Twentieth Century China" (Shaw, Y., Ed.). Taipei: Institute of International Relations, National Chenchi University.

Kohli, A., and Shue, V. (1994). State power and social forces: On political contention and accommodation in the Third World, *in* "State Power and Social Forces: Domination and Transformation in the Third World" (S. Migdal, A. Kohli, and V. Shue, Eds.). New York: Cambridge University Press.

Koo, H., (1989). The state, industrial structure and labor politics: Comparison of South Korea and Taiwan. The Korean Sociological Association, Industrial East Asia: Tasks and Challenges, Proceedings of the 5th Asian Regional Conference of Sociology.

Koo, H. (1991, August). Middle classes, democratization, and class formation: The case of South Korea. *Theory and Society* **20.**

Krugman, P. (1994, Nov./Dec.). The myth of Asia's miracle. *Foreign Affairs.*

Kuo, S. W. Y., Ranis, G., and Fei, J. (1981). "The Taiwan Success Story: Rapid Growth with Improved Distribution in the Republic of China, 1952–1979." Boulder: Westview Press.

Landsberg, M. (1979, Winter). Export-led industrialization in the Third World: Manufacturing imperialism. *Review of Radical Political Economics* **11,** 4.

Lee, J. S. (1988). "Labor Relations and the Stages of Economic Development: the Case of the Republic of China." Conference on Labor and Economic Development, Chung-Hwa Institute for Economic Research.

Lie, J. (1991, Oct.–Dec.). Review: Rethinking the "miracle" economic growth and political struggle in South Korea. *Bulletin of Concerned Asian Studies* **23,** 4.

Long, S. (1991). "Taiwan: China's Last Frontier." New York: St. Martin's Press.

Mason, E. S. *et al.* (1980). "Economic and Social Modernization of the Republic of Korea." Cambridge: Harvard University Press.

Migdal, J. S., Kohli, A., and Shue, V. V. (1994). "State Power and Social Forces: Domination and Transformation in the Third World." New York: Cambridge University Press.

Moore, B., Jr. (1966). "Social Origins of Dictatorship and Democracy." Boston: Beacon Press.

Naisbitt, J. (1996). "Megatrends Asia: Eight Asian Megatrends that Are Reshaping our World." New York: Simon and Schuster.

Page, J. M. (1994). The East Asian miracle: An introduction. *World Development* **22,** 4.

Paik, N. (1993, Jan.–Feb.). South Korea: Unification and the democratic challenge. *New Left Review* **197.**

Perkins, D. H. (1994). There are at least three models of East Asian development. *World Development* **22,** 4.

Przworski, •. (1991). "Democracy and Mark: Political and Economic Reforms in Eastern Europe and Latin America." Cambridge: Cambridge University Press.

Shin, K.-Y. (1990). "The Industrialization and Trade Union Movement: Comparative Study of South Korea and Taiwan" (in Korean). *Asian Culture* **6.** Institute of Asian Culture, Hanllym University.

Song, B.-N. (1994). "The Rise of the Korean Economy." Oxford: Oxford University Press.

Sutter, R. G. (1988). "Taiwan: Entering the 21st Century." Lanham: University Press of America.

Tien, H. (1994). Toward peaceful resolution of Mainland-Taiwan conflicts: The promise of democratization, *in* "The Politics of Democratization: Generalizing East Asian Experiences" (E. Friedman, Ed.). Boulder: Westview Press.

Tien, H. (1988). Social change and political development in Taiwan, *in* "Taiwan in a Time of Transition" (Feldman, H., *et al.,* Eds.). New York: Paragon House.

United Communication. (1988). "A Yearbook 1988." Seoul.

Wade, R. (1990a). "Governing the Market: Economic Theory and the Role of Government in East Asian Industrialization." Princeton: Princeton University Press.

Wade, R. (1990b). Industrial policy in East Asia: Does it lead or follow the market? *in* "Manufacturing Miracles: Paths of Industrialization in Latin America and East Asia" (G. Gereffi and D. L. Wyman, Eds.). Princeton: Princeton University Press.

Winkler, E. A., and Greenhalgh, S. (1988). Analytical issues and historical episodes, *in* "Contending Approaches to the Political Economy of Taiwan" (E. Winkler and S. Greenhalgh, Eds.). Armonk: M. E. Sharpe, Inc.

World Bank. (1983, 1992). "World Tables." Baltimore: The Johns Hopkins University Press.

World Bank. (1993). "The East Asian Miracle: Economic Growth and Public Policy." Oxford: Oxford University Press.

World Bank. (1995). "World Data 1995." World Bank Indicators on CD-Rom.

CHAPTER 6

Is Small Beautiful?
The Political Economy
of Taiwan's Small-Scale Industry

Karl Fields
Department of Politics and Government
University of Puget Sound
Tacoma, Washington 98416

I. INTRODUCTION

The island nation of Taiwan has experienced perhaps the most successful instance of peripheral socioeconomic development in the second half of the twentieth century. In 1949, Taiwan had a per capita GNP of $224 (in U.S. dollars) and an inflation rate of more than 3000%, and was oppressively ruled by a transplanted authoritarian regime. But for the nearly five decades since that inauspicious beginning, Taiwan has successfully pursued rapid economic growth with stable prices and full employment. Taiwan's 1995 per capita GNP surpassed $12,000, with an inflation rate below 3%, an unemployment rate below 2%, and remarkable income equity. In March of 1996, its citizens (for the first time ever in a Chinese society) popularly elected their own president—a native Taiwanese.[1]

Accounting for this "developmental miracle" is now a growth industry, with scholars, pundits, and politicians offering a host of varied explanations. Among the factors often credited with contributing to both the socioeconomic "growth with equity" and relative political stability Taiwan is experiencing is its industrial structure of small-scale enterprise.[2]

---

[1] The statistics are from *FCJ*, various issues.
[2] See, for instance, Stites; DeGlopper; Shieh, 1992; Park and Johnston.

The Four Asian Tigers: Economic Development and the Global Political Economy

The sheer ubiquity of small- and medium-sized enterprises (SME) in Taiwan's economy makes them likely candidates in any explanation of Taiwan's successful industrialization. Regardless the indicator used, these SME dominate Taiwan's economy, comprising in recent years more than 98% of all firms, more than 60% of all manufacturing enterprises (more than 99% of commercial enterprises), employing on average 70% of the work force, and most significantly producing nearly half of output value and more than 60% of Taiwan's exports (Meyanathan and Munter, 11–12; Chou, 1067). Gates judges these small, petty-capitalist, family firms—and the wider community institutions enabling them to survive—a "strong factor" in Taiwan's relative prosperity and income equality, leading to capitalist expansion, higher living standards, and "retention within Taiwan's economy of a greater proportion of the wealth its people have created" (Gates, 227).

Others, however, are less praiseworthy of the contributions of Taiwan's small businesses. Scholars and policymakers in Taiwan cite among other liabilities the poor capitalization, inefficient management, backward technology, and marketing dependency of the vast majority of these "mom-and-pop" enterprises.[3] Highly critical of the traditional conservatism and independence of these small family firms, a former minister of economic affairs in Taiwan warned in 1991 that "if the situation goes on as it has in the past, with the Chinese here holding to the mentality of going each his own way, then they will either migrate to distant lands or will find their own destruction at home."[4]

Is then small beautiful? And even if it were, can it still be, in an increasingly competitive and technologically sophisticated global market? Taiwan's rapid industrialization and the pivotal role of SME in this process make Taiwan a useful case for exploring these questions. This chapter concludes that small-scale industry in Taiwan has been an integral part of Taiwan's developmental miracle. However, these SME are only one leg of an industrial "tripod" that also includes upstream large-scale enterprises providing inputs to SME subcontractors and downstream multinational giants serving as marketing channels for SME manufactures.[5]

Moreover, evolving technologies and markets will permit small firms (and economies reliant on small firms) to continue to prosper in certain settings. This is possible only as these firms become and remain flexible and nimble in their production techniques and cooperative in their relationships with other firms, particularly subcontracting networks. To do so, small firms need access to technological inputs, and highly skilled labor and the economic agents comprising subcontracting networks require some level of trust. Both technology and trust, however, are typ-

---

[3]See, for example, Yen; Yen and Yen; Mody.
[4]Former minister of economic affairs Zhao Yaodong, as cited in *EN,* July 15, 1991.
[5]The term "tripod" is borrowed from Gates, 240.

ically in short supply in developing countries and particularly within and among small enterprises in these economies (Doner *et al.*).

Using a "new institutionalist" framework, this chapter argues that regime motivations, market opportunities, and cultural proclivities have converged to create an industrial structure in Taiwan conducive to the adoption of flexible specialization as a pattern of industrial governance. The chapter first introduces the theoretical framework of new institutionalism and the concept of flexible production as a form of industrial governance facilitated by a certain set of sociocultural and political institutions. It next describes Taiwan's industrial structure of multitudinous SME and the less obtrusive upstream and downstream strata of large enterprises and the linkages provided among and between them by dense subcontracting networks.

It then discusses the political, economic, and cultural factors that shaped or enabled the emergence of these variegated small firms linked by temporary subcontracting networks, and it assesses the obstacles these networks face in adopting or enhancing flexible production techniques. The final section analyzes the government's crucial, although not entirely successful, efforts to provide collective goods and enhance cooperation within these networks. It concludes with a brief discussion of the economic and sociopolitical consequences of Taiwan's industrial structure and some areas for future research.

II. NEW INSTITUTIONALISM AND FLEXIBLE SPECIALIZATION

"New Institutionalism" refers to a "collection of challenges" from a variety of social science disciplines to the utilitarian explanation of human behavior (March and Olsen). In the realm of economics, new institutionalists question even the theoretical value of the neoclassical economists' assumed atomized and omniscient economic actors motivated by rational self-interest engaging in frictionless, arms-length transactions. These new institutionalists focus instead on the ways in which institutions—social arrangements ordering human interactions—shape the preferences and behaviors of economic actors and influence how they resolve problems of resource scarcity and information complexity among each other.[6]

Although the owners and operators of small-scale firms in Taiwan undoubtedly pursue rational economic goals, their efforts—and even perceptions of how—to do so have been fundamentally shaped by the institutional environment in which

---

[6]New institutionalist studies have become accepted subfields in a number of academic disciplines including economics ("new institutional economics"), sociology ("new economic sociology" and "organizational sociology"), political science ("political institutionalism" and "positive theory of institutions"), and history ("new economic history"). For reviews and bibliographies of these literatures, see Powell and DiMaggio; Fields.

these entrepreneurs and their family firms are embedded. This environment is si-multaneously and dynamically structured by cultural norms, public policies, and ongoing social and political relations.[7] Although this is true of economic activity in any national setting, "petty capitalism" in an Asian context seems particularly embedded.[8]

In their comparison of industrial organization in Japan, Korea and Taiwan, Orru and colleagues conclude that each of these political economies has created "a context of fiscal, political, as well as social institutions that limit and direct the de-velopment of fit organization forms . . . [and] the important role of the state in economic affairs leads us to believe that institutional and normative factors are par-ticularly important to organizational viability in those nations" (Orru *et al.*, 41). The predominant form of enterprise organization in Taiwan, as this chapter demonstrates, is the small, family-owned and -operated firm linked through vari-ous informal networks to other like firms.

Economies dominated by family-run SME are the rule, not the exception, in both advanced and developing capitalist countries. In developing countries, these small family firms—lacking economies of scale and scope and the financial means to upgrade technological and managerial skills—are typically viewed as a liability in terms of industrial competitiveness and a drag on industrial development. However, dramatic shifts in the international economy and global production technology have focused interest on the potential competitive advantage of so-called "post-Fordist flexible specialization" (Hirst and Zeitlin).

Theorists of the organization of industrial production have argued that the global economy is witnessing a "second industrial divide," where the established "mass production" model of industrial development is now being called into ques-tion as the best form of technological and industrial development. This mass pro-duction model, employing product-specific machines and semiskilled workers to produce standardized goods in sufficient volume to capture economies of scale, emerged at the time of the first industrial divide in the nineteenth century and came to dominate in the twentieth century "Fordist" boom (Piore and Sabel).

These theorists postulate an alternative model or technological paradigm, la-beled "post-Fordist," "flexible specialization," or "craft production."[9] This ideal type or "vision of industrial efficiency" emphasizes the "manufacture of a wide and changing array of customized products using flexible, general-purpose machinery and skilled, adaptable workers" (Hirst and Zeitlin, 2). As product differentiation in-creases in value, flexible small firms with specialized knowledge can be more com-

[7]This "embedded enterprise" framework is developed in detail in Fields.

[8]Gates describes "petty capitalism" in the Taiwan setting as "family-headed businesses" that "de-pend heavily on informal networks of partnership and credit rather than on law and the state's banking system" and "relate to the state as they would to a powerful gang running a local protection racket" (Gates, 225).

[9]This paragraph draws on Hirst and Zeitlin, 1–8.

petitive than large enterprises attempting to master the broad ranges of technology. Moreover, advancing technologies have led to very different economies of scope and scale in many industrial sectors, lowering entry barriers for SME, especially as subcontractors for larger firms (Meyanathan and Munter, 6).

Drawing on the successful implementation of this production strategy in Japanese subcontracting networks and European industrial districts, these theorists argue that flexible specialization is "incompatible with a neo-liberal regime of un-regulated markets and cut-throat competition," depending "for its long term success on an irreducible minimum of trust and cooperation among economic actors, both between managers and workers within the firm and between firms and their external subcontractors" (Hirst and Zeitlin, 7).

Piore and Sabel suggest that one consequence of this potential shift in technological paradigms could be the migration of mass production to less-developed countries as the advanced industrial societies increasingly adopt technologies of flexible production.[10] In contrast, Hirst and Zeitlin contend that "flexible specialization might also be conceived as an alternative development strategy for parts of the Third World itself." They argue that such an approach could draw on "existing forms of small-scale enterprise concentrated in the substantial 'informal' sectors of many developing economies" and the "unavoidable flexibility of pre-existing forms of mass production imposed by the constraints of narrow markets and shortages of appropriate skills and materials." They conclude that the question of which of these two scenarios—or combination thereof—plays itself out in any given setting depends on the "outcome of strategic choices and political struggles" (Hirst and Zeitlin, 5, 6).

Taiwan would appear to provide firm evidence for the latter scenario. Writing in 1991, Amsden reports that "Taiwan's subcontractors are famous for their 'flexible specialization,'" which they achieved, she argues, through paring to a minimum costs associated with fixed capital and inventory, by engaging in single tasks and producing, purchasing and selling in small lots (Amsden, 1991, 1129).

Writing in the same year, Biggs concurs, describing a near ideal-typical flexible production system in Taiwan:

> To reduce costs, and most of all to enhance flexibility in the face of capricious international markets, Taiwan's businessmen specialized to the maximum degree and took up many forms of subcontracting in both supplier and producer activities. Most export producers became linked to tight networks of small independent 'job-shoppers,' each producing small parts of a product that would be finally assembled by the central factory and exported through foreign or local trading companies (Biggs, 193).

Again Biggs emphasizes "smallness," contending the success of Taiwan's flexible production strategy "has depended crucially on the country's industry structure" (Biggs, 192).

[10]Piore and Sabel, 279–280, as cited by Hirst and Zeitlin, 5.

Constant innovation (the "product" of flexible production) requires erst-while competitors and other economic actors in the marketplace to be able to trust and to be willing to cooperate with each other in overcoming the problems of re-source scarcity and information complexity (Doner *et al.*). But although smallness inclines firms in Taiwan to specialize, it does not compel them to cooperate. In fact, short-term market rationale dictates price competition, while deep-seated Chinese cultural norms sharply curtail the boundaries of trust. With some impor-tant exceptions, hierarchical linkages among firms in Taiwan remain short-term and often predatory; horizontal price competition is fierce.

Recognizing the potential benefits of flexible production and the dangers of not realizing these benefits in an economy whose industrial structure largely pre-cludes an alternative mass production approach (Mody), Taiwan's government has sought to encourage flexible specialization and overcome market failures and cul-tural obstacles impeding their adoption. To this end, the state has created institu-tions designed to provide the collective technical and financial goods necessary in Taiwan's disintegrated economy and to enhance (or expand) cooperation and limit competition in the subcontracting system.

The final section of this chapter demonstrates that these efforts have met with mixed results. In Wade's terms, the state's efforts as provider of public goods have been an instance of successful "big followership," whereas its efforts to rationalize the subcontracting network through its "center-satellite program" (CSP) have been largely an exercise in "small leadership" or at best "small followership."[11] Before turning to these sociocultural and political institutions structuring the environment in which Taiwan's SME are embedded, we first describe the structure of and link-ages among these firms.

III. WHAT IS SMALL? THE ORGANIZATIONAL STRUCTURE OF TAIWAN'S SME

With a population of just over 21 million people, Taiwan has nearly one mil-lion registered firms.[12] As in virtually all economies, the overwhelming majority of these are small- and medium-sized enterprises (SME). This section introduces Tai-

---

[11]Wade distinguishes four categories of government intervention in the market: "small follow-ership," helping firms to do what they would have already done; "big followership," assisting firms sig-nificantly to extend the margin of their investments; "small leadership," providing assistance with too little resources or too little influence to make a difference; and "big leadership," providing initiatives large enough to make a real difference to investment and production patterns (Wade, 29).

[12]*AE,* January 1995, 104. Large as this figure is, this total certainly underestimates the actual number of firms operating in Taiwan. Many of the smallest firms evade taxes and other bureaucratic has-sles by not registering with the government (Shieh, 1990, 39). Balancing this oversight, many other reg-istered "firms" are nothing more than licenses, business cards and fake addresses set up as fronts or ventures for purposes of tax evasion, financial schemes, speculation, or even social prestige.

Table 1

Cross-National Comparison of SME in East and Southeast Asia

Country and year	National definition of SME	Percent of total firms	Percent of total workforce	Percent of value added	Percent of total exports
Taiwan 1987	capital < $1.5 mil assets < $4.5 mil	97	70	55	66
Korea 1987	1–1000 employees	98	66	38	34
Hong Kong 1987	1–200 employees	98	62	57	17
Singapore 1987	assets < $3.7 mil	91	46	31	18
Indonesia 1985	5–199 employees	n.a.	n.a.	20.5	52.4
Malaysia 1988	< 199 employees	n.a.	n.a.	36.4	46.5
Philippines 1983	< 199 employees	n.a.	n.a.	21	43.3
Thailand 1990	< 299 employees	n.a.	n.a.	n.a.	50.3

Sources: For Taiwan, Korea, Hong Kong and Singapore, see Regnier, 24; for Indonesia, Malaysia, the Philippines, and Thailand, see Hill, 7.

wan's SME by defining them, describing their role in the overall economy in comparative context, and examining their organizational structure of subcontracting networks and linkages to both upstream suppliers and downstream market outlets.

In his comparative study, Hill notes that the analysis of SME is difficult because there is no straightforward, internationally accepted definition of the category. Moreover, as the average size of firms within a national economy expands, the definition too must change. Hill adopts a working definition of a work force of up to 200 employees, but warns that even within these parameters (as with any definition), the SME sector encompasses a great diversity of firms. These range from well-established, sizable factories with fixed capital and labor costs at the "medium" end of the spectrum to family-based cottage enterprises doing seasonal piece work, employing little or no wage labor. This wide variety of firm type is certainly the case in Taiwan. A final problem of definition involves determining where the "firm" ends and the market begins, given the dense (and usually informal) ties of cross-investment, subcontracting, and other connections typical among small firms (Hill, 3–5).

The official definition of SME in Taiwan has changed over time, reflecting revisions in laws and assistance programs and the growth of Taiwan's economy. Since 1982, the SME category has included manufacturing firms with paid-in capital of less than approximately $1.5 million and total assets of less than $4.5 million, and commercial or other service enterprises with annual turnover of not more than $1.5 million (Wu and Chou, 18). So defined, in 1993 these firms accounted for 34% of aggregate sales ($193.8 billion), 55% of total exports ($46.5 billion), and 69% of total employment (*AE*, January 1995, 104).

Although cross-national comparisons are only partially commensurable, Table 1 compares the status of SME in several East and Southeast Asian economies.

Differences in categorization and year of measurement limit the ability to draw significant comparisons from Table 1. Nonetheless, several useful similarities and differences relevant to Taiwan emerge. Although Taiwan is near or at the top in all four categories measured, there is little difference across the Four Tiger economies in the dominant position of SME in terms of both percentage of total firms and percentage of total workforce (though both are lower in Singapore because of the dominant role of multinationals (MNCs) and large state-owned enterprises (SOE) in a city–state economy).

Only in Taiwan and Hong Kong do the SME account for a majority of their economies' value added. More significantly, SME in Taiwan produce virtually two-thirds of the nation's exports. This is a figure nearly four times the level of Hong Kong and Singapore, nearly twice that of Korea, and substantially more than the other four Southeast Asian economies included in the table. This SME dominance of Taiwan's export production is even more impressive when one considers the volume of Taiwan's exports. In 1992, more than $46 billion worth of Taiwan's total of over $80 billion in exports was produced by nearly one million SME (*AE,* January 1995, 104).

Chou notes that by 1985, Taiwan's manufacturing sector accounted for 43% of the overall economy and that the percentage of manufactures in total exports has risen from 8% in 1953 to nearly 94% in 1985. In that year, SME produced 65% of Taiwan's manufactured exports and 71% of total SME production was exported. Thus, not only do SME export extensively, their production is also export intensive. Chou concludes that this makes Taiwan unique among other industrialized countries that typically rely on large enterprises for export production (Chou, 1067).

In order to understand why SME and not larger firms dominate Taiwan's export market, it is necessary to examine the division of labor within Taiwan's industrial sector and the role of small-scale industry in that division of labor. In short, small- and medium-sized firms in Taiwan occupy a crucial intermediate role between large-scale public, quasi-public, and private enterprises in the upstream sector and equally large multinational trading and marketing concerns in the downstream sector. The former provide raw materials and intermediate inputs to the small-scale assemblers and subcontracting networks and the latter provide marketing outlets. Because they are able to capture the scale economies of mass production on the one hand and mass marketing on the other, both the upstream and downstream legs of this industrial tripod provide financial credit and technical assistance to the smaller firms. We examine each of these legs in turn, focusing primarily on the subcontracting networks and their upstream and downstream linkages.

During the 1950s and even the early 1960s, most SME in Taiwan engaged in commerce and other service activities. Small-scale manufacturing enterprises were largely concerned with catering to the demands of rural populations. Over the course of the 1960s, exports began to surge in many sectors of Taiwan's economy, providing the opportunity for the rapid rise of labor-intensive, export-oriented SME in the 1960s and 1970s (Park and Johnston, 187–192). These SME operated small, labor-intensive plants making standardized light-industry products that competed on the basis of price (Wade, 70).

Two oil crises in the 1970s and an extended recession in the West in the early 1980s shrunk Taiwan's market and squeezed the SME particularly hard. In addition, these family-owned firms were already plagued at home by a host of challenges. These included tight credit, increasingly strict environmental standards, rising labor, land, and raw material costs, appreciating currency, outdated technology, poor management skills, and a short-sighted strategy of "copycat" binge production of trendy products for quick profits.

With the factors underlying their comparative advantage rapidly eroding, Taiwan's SME faced two options (short of extinction). The easier, and more popular choice for these "industrial nomads" (Shieh, 1990, 99) was to shift their labor-intensive production offshore in search of cheaper factor inputs (chiefly labor). Facilitated by the government's lifting of restrictions on capital outflows in 1987, more than 11,000 firms, most of them relatively small, invested nearly $20 billion in Southeast Asia and China through 1992 (*FEER,* March 18, 1993).

The second, but more risky and difficult option, was for these firms to remain at home, upgrade and automate production, improve efficiency, and compete not on price, but on quality and profit from value added. Although increases in firm-level expenditures in research and development over the 1980s have not been that significant (Tsay), by the end of the 1980s, many small firms had "sprung up in higher technology sectors, such as computers, integrated circuit designs, machine tools, high-quality sports goods, and expensive toys, where product differentiation and performance matter more and price matters a little less" (Wade, 70).

These SME options of both exit and upgrade were facilitated by large-scale enterprise as upstream suppliers of raw materials, and in many cases technology and finance. Noting three categories of big businesses—state-owned (and party-owned) enterprises, transnational corporations, and large private domestic firms—Amsden argues these big firms dominated the economy from the 1950s through the 1970s. She notes that the share of value added by firms with 500 or more employees for that period was actually greater in Taiwan than in South Korea and other comparable late-developing countries (Amsden, 1991, 1122). Taiwan's upstream petrochemical, plastics, steel, and textile industries are all dominated by large state- and party-owned enterprises such as China Petroleum and China Steel, and private conglomerates such as Formosa Plastics (Wade; Fields).

In addition to raw materials, a 1988 survey of the knitwear industry found that 45% of contractors gave technical advice to subcontracted workshops and 43% provided loans (Shieh, 1990, 74). Often to the chagrin of their former employers, much of this vertical technology transfer occurs through "spin-offs," as midlevel managers and other skilled employees leave the firm to start their own companies, often bringing customers and subcontractors with them from the former firm (Silin; Shieh, 1990).

Concerning loans, Taiwan's banks direct the lion's share of their funds to large public and private firms who then lend money for equipment and working capital to smaller downstream customers, subcontractors, and suppliers at higher rates through trade credit and other forms of loans on the informal curb market (Biggs, 194). A 1983 survey conducted by the Central Bank of China found that private firms with assets of less than NT$1 million (approximately US$30,000) received 90% of their loans from the curb market. Those with assets of up to NT$5 million received 69% of domestic borrowings from the informal market and those between NT$40 million (the asset ceiling for inclusion in the SME category) and NT$100 million still received 40% of funds from the curb market (Shea, 701).

Tang notes that this informal market takes many forms (tolerated by the government to varying degrees) including: (1) trade credit in the form of supplier credit and loans from upstream firms to downstream contractors; (2) internal sources (Tang estimates this comprises 60 to 65% of total investment funds for SME), which include personal and family savings and rotating credit associations or *biaohui;*[13] (3) underground bankers; (4) employee deposit schemes; (5) leasing companies, which are particularly important for SME purchase of heavy equipment and machinery; and (6) postdated checks (Tang, 845–855). All but the internal sources are linked at least to some degree to larger firms.

The result of these financial, technical and production linkages is a "dualistic" and "densely interconnected" domestic industrial structure in which "the export success of the smaller, direct exporting firms cannot be understood independently of the productive performance of the big firms" (Wade, 70). Amsden concurs, arguing that without these large-scale and domestic sources of upstream inputs, Taiwan's flexible production system of subcontracting based on small-lot purchases would not be feasible (Amsden, 1991).

The same can be said about the downstream or marketing end of this "commodity chain."[14] Wu and Chou argue that Taiwan's SME are able to operate efficiently because they do so in industries that do not require significant economies of scale, whereas scale economies in international marketing occur in every industry. Most SME in Taiwan specialize in some manufacturing or assembly niche and leave the marketing to Japanese general trading companies, Western mass buyers, and local conglomerates handling their own trade. They note that even so-called "export" trading companies from Taiwan typically offer only communication and

---

[13]These revolving credit associations are ubiquitous in Taiwan and virtually all other Asian societies and communities. Tang cites a 1980 survey that found that 85% of households in Taiwan participated in *hui* and a 1992 survey finding that 95% of businesspeople in Taiwan participated (Tang, 849). They are probably the most significant source of raising funds to start a small business. For an explanation of their functioning in Taiwan and a bibliography of relevant studies, see Fields, 161.

[14]The term "commodity chain" is taken from Gereffi.

paper work services, not actual marketing (Wu and Chou, 22–23). Foreign trading companies (chiefly Japanese *sogo shosha*) and transnational OEM (original export manufacturer) purchasers are estimated to handle between 50 and 60% of Taiwan's export trade (Fields, 221–222).

The specialization of Taiwan's SME has left them highly dependent and closely linked to both upstream suppliers and downstream marketing concerns (Chou, 1082). The nature and variety of these dense interconnections are key to understanding both the opportunities for and obstacles to the emergence of flexible production patterns in Taiwan. Some of these linkages comprise relatively stable ties (most often agglomerative) between member firms of Taiwan's private business groups or "related enterprises" (*quanxi qiye*). As de facto extensions of family firms legally separated for tax and inheritance motives, these intragroup firms have important managerial and financial connections, but engage in surprisingly little vertical or horizontal integration.[15]

Vertical ties within the production chain are typically highly disintegrated and temporary. These linkages between upstream suppliers and downstream traders and within the SME subcontracting networks typically range from spot market, noniterative transactions to a "temporary spider web" of trading companies, factories, and family workshops assembled for the duration of a particular job (Shieh, 1990; *AB,* January 1991). Significantly, the 1988 knitwear survey cited earlier found that unlike the relatively dense nature of vertical technical and lending linkages, only 1% of those polled actually invested in subcontracted workshops and only 1% received investments from these subcontractors (Shieh, 1990, 74).

Whitley refers to these subcontracting networks among Chinese family firms as "molecular" systems of coordination; highly flexible and capable of rapid change, but short-lived and centrifugal. He contends that relational contracting is just as prevalent in Taiwan as in Japan, but that whereas these quasi-market relationships in Japan are long-term and based on trust, in Taiwan they are short-term and based on distrust (Whitley, 1990, 59; see also Gold, 86). Amsden, in contrasting Taiwan's subcontracting system with those of Japan and Korea, notes that rather than layers of subcontractors clustered around one big firm, subcontracting in Taiwan has a "more highly developed division of labor," with even primary contractors responsible for limited numbers of production stages and firms less vertically integrated (Amsden, 1991, 1129).[16]

---

[15]There is a growing body of literature on business groups in Taiwan and in East Asia and a well-established literature on the Chinese family firm. For bibliographies, see Hamilton, ed.; Fields.

[16]Taiwan's industry was not always characterized by vertical disintegration. In fact, in her 1974 field research on the machine tool industry in Taiwan, Amsden described the industry as having a "low degree of specialization and a high degree of vertical integration" and no evidence of the use of subcontractors (1977, 222). Writing of the same industry in 1981, Amsden notes a dramatically expanded division of labor, with "a well-articulated system of subcontracting and satellite shops," which she compares favorably to those of Japan. Amsden attributes this transition to changes in the "size," "type" and "rate of growth" of the machine tools market (1985, 277).

Although distinct from Japanese subcontracting patterns, there is evidence of some technology-driven convergence with the Japanese model. Smitka notes up until the early 1960s, Japan's automobile assemblers could rely on spot markets to secure from parts suppliers the relatively simple components they required. But increasingly technical specialization with its accompanying sunk costs compelled the assemblers to seek longer-term, more dependable ties with suppliers (Smitka, 160–166).

Similarly, Biggs notes for Taiwan that subcontracting linkages are particularly strong in those industries manufacturing products of high complexity. This he attributes to the need for loyalty and dependability because of the greater fixed costs in physical and human capital. He cites specifically the highly competitive machine tool industry in the central Taiwan city of Taichung with its "tight networks of highly skilled subcontractors."[17] Because of the demand for high-quality and reliable machine tool suppliers and contractors in this region, the larger contractors made both loan and equity investments in their smaller subcontractors to ensure loyalty and dependability (Biggs, 194).

IV. ENABLING FACTORS AND OBSTACLES TO FLEXIBLE PRODUCTION

Taiwan's industrial structure, with its prominent role for variegated and disintegrated smaller firms linked by temporary subcontracting networks, is a consequence of political motivations (regime ideology and strategy), market impulses, and cultural proclivities. These factors and their institutional consequences have conspired not only to enable the current system of industrial governance, but also to hinder any transition to an alternative system.

The primary goal of the Nationalist Chinese (KMT) regime since its defeat on the Mainland and relocation to Taiwan in 1949 has been to strengthen Taiwan militarily and politically by fostering economic development under conditions of price stability and relative social equity. Bolstered by Sun Yat-sen's quasi-socialist ideology of "People's Livelihood" (*minsheng zhuyi*), the Nationalist regime has consciously and assiduously limited the concentration of private capital (Fields; Gold).

This ideological motive was reinforced by the ethnic-based division of labor that put virtually all political power in the hands of the minority Mainlanders and left the private sector open to the local Taiwanese majority. While this mitigated Taiwanese opposition to political subjugation by providing the Taiwanese with economic outlets, it also raised concerns among the political leaders that this economic power could be translated into political power. Learning from its defeat on the Mainland, and as an exogenous minority regime, the Nationalist state has sought legitimacy not from a landed aristocracy nor from a coterie of privileged

---

[17]Note Amsden's concurrence in footnote 16.

capitalists, but from the multitude of small producers and smallholders its "growth with equity" policies have fostered.

Under these conditions, and reinforced by the recommendations of American-trained neoclassical economic advisors, many policymakers have felt the state cannot afford politically or economically to use explicit discretionary compliance mechanisms that favor a few firms at the expense of the majority of others. Unlike South Korea and Japan, state incentives to manufacture and export were granted across the board, and were not limited to a handful of premier firms. Tax laws, labor laws, and other state policies in fact provide strong incentives to limit firm size (Fields; Biggs and Levy).

These political circumstances have allowed the "fittest" to survive and thrive in an intensely competitive domestic market and export regime open to literally all (small) comers and subject to the vicissitudes of the international economy. These internal and external market forces have made feasible and in many cases have fostered Taiwan's flexible subcontracting system.

Shieh argues Taiwan's subcontracting system is a direct consequence of its export-oriented industrialization (EOI) strategy under conditions of dependent capitalism. Taiwan's niche in this system has been to supply simple, labor-intensive products with readily divisible production steps (Shieh, 1990, 113). While international demand for these products has been voracious, it is modulated by quotas, seasonal fluctuations, and mercurial shifts in consumer trends and tastes. The molecular subcontracting production system has been shaped by this international demand and has in turn allowed Taiwan's entrepreneurs to respond to its whimsical nature flexibly, cheaply, and efficiently.

In addition, Taiwan's flexible response was made possible by the transactional efficiency of its domestic market. Able to draw on a pool of educated labor and experienced merchants initially absent in places such as Korea (Levy, 1988; 1991), Taiwan's SME have proliferated and many have prospered because of the relative ease with which they can enter into subcontracting relations with other small firms and link up with foreign or domestic trading firms.

This allows entrepreneurs to start up production at a relatively small scale and with little up-front investment in either equipment or market information (Levy and Kuo). These large numbers of both participants and transactions have enhanced the market's transactional efficiency and have reduced the cost of these transactions.[18] Declining transaction costs have steered entrepreneurs away from hierarchies and toward greater use of the market (Williamson), resulting in Taiwan's "extreme form of subcontracting and specialization of production" (Biggs and Levy, 381).

[18]Biggs and Levy note this transactional efficiency is a result of (1) the increased numbers of participants which lowers search costs (because of increased physical and social proximity); and (2) the expanded number and history of transactions which increases (Biggs and Levy).

Chinese cultural proclivities have also fostered the proliferation of SME and have enabled this vertical disintegration. Market expansion of Taiwan's family firms has been limited by the cultural norm of trust or "connections" (*guanxi*) limited to a close-knit circle of family members and friends and the absence of trust (Silin's "non-trust") beyond this circle (Silin; Hamilton and Kao). This "small kingdom" (*xiao diguo*) mentality often limits the size of the firm to a scale that core members of the family can personally control.

This bounded authority pattern has several consequences. As the basic building blocks of Taiwan's industrial division of labor, these small family firms are remarkably flexible in terms of labor, savings, and entrepreneurial capacities, and are nimble in their abilities to make swift management decisions and to shift product lines rapidly. The unwillingness to trust outsiders makes it virtually impossible, however, for non-family members in smaller firms to rise from the position of worker or "black hand" (*heishou*) on the shop floor to positions of management (Shieh, 1992).

This promotion ceiling combined with low entry barriers for new ventures leads to extremely high rates of defection in order to succeed on one's own.[19] This "spinning-off" of new bosses creates additional small links in Taiwan's subcontracting chains, transfers technology downward in the system (carried by the defecting personnel), and further narrows the level of specialization of each firm (Shieh, 1990, 260).

These factors have combined to create a system of production that "emphasizes a speed and agility that even the Japanese . . . cannot match" (*BW*, December 7, 1992). But as Taiwan's capacity to compete in labor-intensive industries declines, the very virtues of the system constrain its capacity to adapt. Those firms wishing to remain competitive (and remain in Taiwan) face very difficult obstacles as they seek to upgrade production and create not just flexible firms but flexible manufacturing systems based on constant, costly, and increasingly sophisticated technological innovation.

Spot market transactions and short-term contracting are adequate as long as components are simple and manufacturing processes are divisible (Smitka, 8). But the increasing technical complexity of design and manufacturing processes requires constant innovation, which in turn requires firms to cooperate in the sharing of resources and to trust in each other's willingness to commit for the long-term. The enabling factors discussed in this section work against such cooperation and trust on several counts.

Unlike the Korean *chaebol*, whose vertical integration allows economies of scale and resource capacities, Taiwan's SME have limited technical and financial resources for sustained quality improvements (Mody). Japanese subcontractors over-

---

[19]This is perhaps best expressed in the Chinese aphorism "It is better to be the head of a chicken than the tail of an ox" (*ningwei jikou, buwei niuhou*).

come these limitations through long-term cooperative linkages with contracting assemblers (Smitka). Taiwan's circumstances work against both hierarchy and long-term relational contracting as solutions.

Taiwan's familial cultural norms circumscribe the boundaries of trust, limiting both vertical integration and contractual fidelity. Whitley notes that Taiwan's subcontracting networks, while highly specialized, are "opportunistic and imitative" and are not usually integrated through an authority system. Connections in the system are "embedded in elaborate networks of personal obligation," but "are often not long term ones and commitments between contractors are unstable compared with those in Japan" (Whitley, 1990, 53). DeGlopper notes that SME entrepreneurs in Taiwan prefer a wide network of suppliers and partners because of the personal autonomy and freedom it gives them to "take advantage of opportunities" (*chen jihui*) that might arise, which they deem crucial to entrepreneurial success (DeGlopper, 209).

Taiwan's subcontracting networks are nimble precisely because they are fluid. While this enhances flexibility, it breeds cutthroat competition and opportunism and stifles cooperation. Under these conditions, multiple short-term linkages are more rational for both contractors and suppliers than favored or exclusive long-term ties. Long-term commitments obligate the contractors to provide work continuously under circumstances of wide fluctuations of demand and they make the contractor vulnerable to subcontractor defection. Subcontractors too fear the vulnerability of exclusive dependence (Shieh, 1990, 142).

Past behavior reinforces these suspicions. Contractors and large firms in general are notorious for squeezing the subcontractors by delaying payments, shortening the length of time between order-placing and delivery, or dumping the subcontractors during downturns or when a cheaper supplier can be found.[20] In response, subcontractors may collude in fixing prices or simply seek out new contractors (Shieh, 1992). Under these circumstances of mutual distrust, multiple ties are very rational, reducing risks by ensuring market discipline.

This combination of microfragmentation (impeding hierarchy) and mutual distrust (undermining contractual cooperation) has made innovation and the mastery of complex technology very difficult. Shieh notes that while the "circulation of innovations among the units of production, both upward and downward, is quick in the Japanese sub-contracting system," there is "no institutionalized accumulation of knowledge" in Taiwan's system (Shieh, 1990, 189). Technology transfer in Taiwan occurs most often through defection of skilled personnel or pirating, decidedly zero-sum enterprises.

---

[20]Shieh quotes one informant in a subcontracting firm: "The contractors eat the meat and leave the bones for the subcontractors, or (in less favorable economic situations), the contractors lick the bones and leave the soup for the subcontractors" (Shieh, 1990, 83).

Nor is there typically sufficient incentive to upgrade production technology. Like Taiwan's contractors, American auto manufacturers utilized large numbers of suppliers, playing them off of each other with competitive bids. Although the auto firms secured cheap parts, "without the assurance of future orders . . . , suppliers naturally limited their investment in modern machinery. Similarly, they were reluctant to innovate; proprietary design could hardly be put out for competitive bids" (Smitka, 3). The American solution was to integrate vertically. This is not a likely option on "Boss Island."[21]

Though much less common, Shieh notes that under certain circumstances, "soft" or even "hard" exclusive ties have emerged in Taiwan's subcontracting networks. These typically occur, however, only when the contractors are famous large factories and the subcontractors meet certain quality standards (Shieh, 1990, 189). These conditions are precisely the two attributes the government sought to promote and replicate in its center-satellite production system discussed in the final section. The government's difficulty in doing so points to the problems Taiwan faces as it seeks to fully realize the gains of flexible production systems.

V. THE STATE AS PROMOTER OF FLEXIBLE SPECIALIZATION

While pleased with the social and political benefits of Taiwan's penny capitalist industrial structure, government officials constantly fret about the economic dangers and technological vulnerabilities of an economy dependent on small firms. With few large private firms or integrated business groups capable of adequately handling internally the purchasing of inputs, international marketing, or the funding of research and development, the government has seen its role in building the technological competence of the SME as particularly crucial (Wade, 103). In essence, market failure has been managed by the state through the "nationalization of risk" (Mody; Whitley, 1991).

This final section discusses the state's efforts to promote flexible specialization in Taiwan through the provision of collective financial and technical services to private firms and the promotion of cooperation within the subcontracting networks. The former effort has met with significant success, while results of the efforts to rationalize the subcontracting network have been less notable.

Despite government rhetoric about the importance and benefits of small-scale industry, the government did little if anything to assist the SME prior to the 1980s. Significantly, however, the government did avoid the "large distortions in macroprices" that were adopted, for example, by South Korea in its promotion of large-scale private enterprise. High interest rates and other sound financial and fis-

---

[21]I borrow the term from Shieh, 1992.

cal policies "did not overly distort relative factor prices," which lowered entry costs for the SME (Park and Johnston, 195).

By the early 1980s, industry analysts both inside and outside the government recognized the need for Taiwan's firms to upgrade and the unlikelihood that market forces would motivate this move. Tracing the government's efforts to create and support institutions designed to provide technological upgrading, management training, and financial assistance to the SME becomes an exercise in acronyms. In 1981, the Ministry of Economic Affairs (MOEA) set up the Small and Medium Sized Business Administration (SMBA) with the goal of structurally upgrading the SME by dealing with their problems of finance, technology, management, and marketing. The SMBA holds management seminars, works with local banks to ease restrictions on loans to the SME, and sends three-person teams to individual firms to identify and analyze problems and offer solutions. (*EN,* various issues).

In addition, the government has set up numerous technical research centers and advisory task forces designed to assist firms in acquiring the appropriate technology and technical skills for upgrading their production. This includes the Industrial Technology Research Institute (ITRI) and its laboratory arm, the Electronics Research and Service Organization (ERSO). The latter is now at the center of Taiwan's $8 billion electronics industry, creating spin-offs of its own, including public-private, joint-venture fabrication firms such as Taiwan Semiconductor Manufacturing Corporation (TSMC) and United Microelectronics Corporation (UMC) (Mody; *FEER,* March 25, 1993).

In order to prevent it from becoming a rival to smaller, private firms, TSMC is forbidden to design products of its own. Instead, it relies on more than 40 specialized private firms (many started by defecting ERSO engineers) that contract their manufacturing to the larger fabrication firms, especially TSMC and UMC (*FEER,* March 25, 1993). Many of these firms, both public and private, have set up shop in the government-established Hsin Chu Science-based Industrial Park (HSIP). Here, foreign and domestic high technology firms operate in close proximity to ITRI and the government lures new ventures with its promise to invest up to 49% (Wade).

This pattern of public–private cooperation is being replicated in the Machine Institute Research Laboratory (MIRL), the Development Center for Biotechnology (DCB) and comparable institutional arrangements in other emerging high-technology industries (*AB,* April 1991). The government's role as risk socializer and agent of change for the private sector extends to managerial and productivity advice through the China Productivity Center (CPC) and a variety of state-controlled lending facilities offering low-interest loans for the purchase of CAD/CAM equipment, factory automation technology and the funding of management training courses (*FCJ,* June 18, 1993).

This combination of state research and development assistance and private initiative in high technology industries has had impressive results. A 1993 assessment of

Taiwan's computer component industry reads like a tribute to flexible specialization. The report notes that while Taiwan was once relegated "a bit part in the global division of labor," it is today an innovator, relying not on cheap labor, but on quick design, short turnaround times and remarkably low overheads." The key to this has been Taiwan's "leaner and meaner" SME that have "mastered speed and flexibility in the best possible way." Taiwan has become the "supplier of first resort" for many of world's biggest computer component companies and "manufacturing site of choice for everything from modems to motherboards to fully assembled computers." Boasting overhead costs a third of their giant foreign competitors, these manufacturers have pioneered a "lean, hungry design and manufacturing style" that can move ideas from the drawing board to mass production in just 90 days (*FEER*, December 16, 1993, 44–45).

The report concludes that with this quick design and turnaround time, Taiwan is doing with PCs what Japan did with automobiles: that is "purg[ing] the manufacturing process of high inventories, and the need for large amounts of working capital—while delivering the goods even faster than in the past." Their assessment of the sources of this success speak to the "embedded" nature of these flexible SME in government and social institutions: a plentiful supply of experienced and relatively inexpensive engineers and a business culture encouraging job-hopping and rewarding start-up companies (*FEER*, December 16, 1993, 45).

Although much heralded, state efforts to rationalize the subcontracting networks through its Center-Satellite Program (CSP) have been much less effective. Frustrated by the unwillingness of Taiwan's entrepreneurs to vertically integrate production through either merger or interfirm cooperation, the MOEA's Industrial Development Bureau (IDB) launched a program in 1984 encouraging the formation of long-term, industrial subcontracting networks with the Japanese auto and machine tools industries as explicit models.

The objectives of the program were severalfold. Its promoters hoped to eliminate the cutthroat competition and destructive price-cutting practices of the SME by encouraging closer, interdependent, and long-term ties between major plants and their subcontractors. The program was designed to encourage larger "center" firms (upstream suppliers, final assembly factories, large local trading companies) to assist their "satellites" (downstream manufacturers, parts and component suppliers) in management, production, technology, financing, quality control and the development of new product lines. The program, it was hoped, would also encourage the parent firms to further specialize, focusing on single industries and single processes (interviews; Bai; Guo; *EN,* January 10, 1983).

The government encouraged, but did not compel, both large and small firms that qualified to participate in the program. To qualify, centers were required (in 1984) to have minimum paid in capital of approximately $3.5 million, minimum annual revenue of approximately $20 million for the past 3 years, top grades in both plant classification and quality control performance, a sound accounting system and a minimum of 20 qualified satellite plants. Satellite plants were required to have paid-in-capital of less than $1.5 million, under $750,000 in average annual sales, passing grades in either plant classification or quality control performance, and roughly 30% of sales going to one major manufacturer (or 30% of raw materials coming from one supplier) (ROC, 1983, 1987; *EN*, January 10, 1983).

The government promoted the program by pointing out the potential benefits of participation. Benefits to the satellites from the center firms were to include investment capital and loan guarantees, stable markets, management and organizational assistance, machinery and raw materials purchasing, and overseas marketing. The parent companies could expect from the satellites parts and components at lower cost and higher quality (if a final assembler or trading company) or increased stable demand (if a supplier) (ROC, 1983, 1987; *EN*, January 10, 1983).

Participating firms, both centers and satellites, were eligible for government-subsidized, long-term, low-interest loans, accelerated machinery depreciation, tax reductions and exemptions, easier acquisition of industrial sites, government-provided technical assistance and management training. In addition, the government pledged to enforce the standardization of components and parts, assist in the formation of supporting factory associations, design and inspect products, and set up model plants and warehouses (ROC, 1983, 1987; *EN*, January 10, 1983; October 10, 1983).

Despite these incentives and a decade of promotion, firms have been slow to participate in the program. One of the touted "success" stories, Yue Loong Motors, in fact already had a relatively stable, Japanese-style subcontracting network (200 suppliers) before the program began because of its joint-venture status with Nissan (*EN*, January 10, 1983). Citing Taiwan's unfamiliarity with long-term subcontracting relations, Wade concludes the results of the CSP have "so far been meager," with only 42 central factories and 874 satellite factories participating in 1987 (Wade, 187).

Lorch and Biggs also conclude the government failed in its efforts to support the formation of integrated subcontracting systems modeled on the Japanese.[22] Analysts in Taiwan attribute the failure to the lack of adequate government incentives necessary to overcome the inherent Chinese unwillingness to trust and cooperate beyond family bounds (Bai; Guo).

By the end of 1991, the program could claim a total of 101 central plants with 1650 satellite plants, accounting for 40% of the total value of Taiwan's manufacturing industry. The IDB predicted this would rise to 150 networks by 1994, comprising 45% of total production (*EN*, January 20, 1992). While these figures are substantial, they are misleading in terms of the success of the government program. Of the 101 established systems, well over half are in high technology industries already characterized by relatively stable and cooperative relational contracting (Biggs).

Moreover, most of these center firms are established large manufacturers able to attract quality contractors, precisely those firms Shieh assessed as most likely to

---

[22]Lorch and Biggs as cited by Hamilton and Biggart, 1004.

have "hard" or "soft" exclusive ties (Shieh, 1990, 189). Most telling is the fact that
of the 45% of total production expected by center-satellite networks in 1994, less
than 20% of this will come from the satellites and these satellites will represent only
two percent of Taiwan's total SME (EN, January 20, 1992).

VI. CONCLUSION

Writing on subcontracting networks in developing countries, Mead concludes it may be feasible for the state "to use parent firms as a channel for assistance
which reaches beyond them to large numbers of their small suppliers" (Mead,
1103). In a recent study of SME in ASEAN, Hill disagrees, arguing that the conventional wisdom of the 1990s is that with the exception of specific instances of
market failure and externalities, market-oriented solutions are superior to direct
government intervention in assisting SME. He notes that in ASEAN, enforced subcontracting schemes "are conspicuous for their lack of success" when measured in
efficiency, not welfare, terms (Hill, 2, 26).

The limited success of Taiwan's government in attempting to rationalize Taiwan's subcontracting networks should not detract from the state's crucial role as
provider of collective goods to the private sector nor obscure the fact that many of
Taiwan's industries are already characterized by a significant degree of flexible specialization. There is remarkable flexibility and entrepreneurial vitality in Taiwan's
family-based subcontracting networks, as well as its individual small-scale firms. As
more of Taiwan's firms migrate or invest abroad in Southeast Asia and "Greater
China," these subcontracting networks are being reproduced and stretched across
Asia and beyond.

Moreover, Taiwan has a substantial pool of engineering talent, abundant capital, and a government that has demonstrated its ability to serve effectively as "fa-
cilitator, impartial broker, agent of change, and to some extent banker" (AB, April
1991). The government is bringing a variety of firms—foreign and domestic, public and private—together in "technology alliances" designed to realize the gains of
flexible production under the particular circumstances of dependent development
in Taiwan's political and sociocultural setting.

The social and political benefits of Taiwan's industrial structure and pattern of
industrial governance measured in terms of stability, relative equity, and emerging
democracy have also been substantial. While decades of authoritarian rule is certainly responsible for much of labor's quiescence in Taiwan, the subcontracting system has also contributed to labor peace and social stability.

Shieh argues that because the system allows virtually any worker to eventually "spin-off" as his or her own boss and provides upward economic mobility for
many, this option of "exit" reduces the need for frustrated workers to "voice"
grievances as wage workers on the shop floor or in the streets and increases their

"loyalty" to the system (Shieh, 1990, 3, 309). Moreover, the small size of firms militates against a radical labor movement and a relatively equitable distribution of wealth in Taiwan, as it has in Japan (Smitka, 2). The creation of a broad middle class has also facilitated the gradual emergence of democratic institutions and a remarkably peaceful transition to democracy.

Gates, however, is less sanguine, noting that the "flexibility" of Taiwan's (and other East Asian) production systems "comes from the capacity of large firms to exploit and lay off small ones, and of small firms to manipulate both hired and family labor, sometimes through the 'hirings' and 'firings' of marriage and adoption" (Gates, 224). But she too believes these SME have played a crucial role in Taiwan's democratization. She notes that this "petty capitalist majority now makes its voice heard through the newly free press and newly possible rallies and election campaigns. That voice is also heard in the conversations of ordinary people in shops and factories, during family evenings before the television set" (Gates, 237–238).

Taiwan's experience with flexible specialization has had significant impact beyond its borders as well. But despite the significant role of market factors in enabling Taiwan's flexible specialization, the replication of Taiwan's experience elsewhere is perhaps limited to those areas sharing Taiwan's Sinic ethnic and cultural attributes. With 1.2 billion Chinese across the Taiwan straits and ethnic Chinese communities scattered throughout Asia and across the globe, this remains a huge hinterland for enterprising Chinese bosses to exploit and a vast petri dish for social scientists to observe.[23]

REFERENCES

Amsden, A. (1977). The division of labor is limited by the type of the market: The case of the Taiwanese machine tool industry," *World Development* **5**, 217–233.

Amsden, A. (1985). The division of labour is limited by the rate of growth of the market: The Taiwan machine tool industry in the 1970s, *Cambridge Journal of Economics,* 271–284.

Amsden, A. H. (1991). Big business and urban congestion in Taiwan: The origins of small enterprise and regionally decentralized industry (Respectively), *World Development* **19**, 1121–1135.

Asian Business (*AB*) Hong Kong.

Asian Wall Street Journal (*AWSJ*) Hong Kong.

Automotive Engineering (*AE*).

Bai, K. (1986, September). *Zhongxinweixing gongchangzhidu yu zhongxiaoqiye jingying helihua* [The center-satellite manufacturing system and the rationalization of small- and medium-sized enterprise management], *Taiwan jingji yanjiu yuekan* [*Taiwan Economic Research Monthly*] **9**, 67–71.

[23]A recent editorial noted that in hyperdeveloping China, "the engines of this new juggernaut are the multitude of small enterprises called township companies. . . ." The article notes that in 1993, China had roughly 25 million of these essentially private SMEs, employing 20% of China's 600 million workers, and generating 60% of China's total industrial output (*AWSJ,* March 27, 1995, 16).

Biggs, T. (1991). Heterogeneous firms and efficient financial intermediation in Taiwan, *in* "Markets in Developing Countries: Parallel, Fragmented and Black" (M. Roemer and C. James, Eds.). San Francisco: ICS Press.

Biggs, T., and Levy, B. (1991). Strategic inverventions and the political economy of industrial policy in developing countries, *in* "Reforming Economic Systems in Developing Countries." (D. Perkins and M. Roemer, Eds.). Cambridge, MA: Harvard Institute for International Development.

Business Week (BW) New York.

Mingzhang, C. (1983, October). *Daqiye yu zhongxiaoqiye hezuojingying zhi dao* [Cooperative management of large enterprises and small- and medium-sized enterprises], *Qiye yinhang jikan* [*Enterprise Bank Quarterly*] **7**, 53–65.

Chou, T.-C. (1992). The experience of SMEs' development in Taiwan: High export contribution and export intensity. *Rivista Internazionale di Scienze Economiche e Commerciali* **39**, 1067–1084.

DeGlopper, D. R. (1995). "Lukang: Commerce and Community in a Chinese City."Albany: State University of New York Press.

Doner, R., Deyo, F., and Fields, K. (1993, September). "Industrial Governance in East and Southeast Asia." Paper presented at the Social Science Research Council Workshop on Industrial Governance, New York City.

Economic News (EN) Taipei.

Far Eastern Economic Review (FEER) Hong Kong.

Fields, K. J. (1995). "Enterprise and the State in Korea and Taiwan." Ithaca: Cornell University Press.

Free China Journal (FCJ) Taipei.

Gates, H. (1996). "China's Motor: A Thousand Years of Petty Capitalism." Ithaca: Cornell University Press.

Gereffi, G. (1993). The organization of buyer-driven commodity chains: How U.S. retailers shape overseas production networks, *in* "Commodity Chains and Global Capitalism" (G. Gereffi and M. Korzeniewicz, Eds.). Westport, CT: Greenwood Press.

Gold, T. B. (1986). "State and Society in the Taiwan Miracle." Armonk, NY: M.E. Sharpe.

Guo Pinhung. (1986, September). *Zhongwei tixi yu zhongxiaoqiye jingying helihua"* [Center-satellite structure and the rationalization of small- and medium-sized enterprise management]. *Taiwan jingji yanjiu yuekan* [*Taiwan Economic Research Monthly*], 34–44.

Hamilton, G. (ed.). (1989). "Business Networks and Economic Development in East and Southeast Asia." Hong Kong: University of Hong Kong Press.

Hamilton, G., and Biggart, N. W. (1991, January). The organization of business in Taiwan: Reply to Numazaki. *American Journal of Sociology* **96**, 999–1006.

Hamilton, G. and Kao Cheng-shu. (1987). "The Industrial Foundations of Chinese Business: The Family Firm in Taiwan." Program in East Asian Culture and Development, Working Paper Series, No. 8, University of California, Davis: Institute of Governmental Affairs.

Hill, H. (1995). Small-medium enterprise and rapid industrialization: the ASEAN experience. *Journal of Asian Business* **11**, 1–31.

Hirst, P. and Zeitlin, J. (1991, February). Flexible specialization versus post-Fordism: Theory, evidence and policy implications. *Economy and Society* **20**, 1–56.

Levy, B. (1988, Spring). Korean and Taiwanese firms as international competitors: The challenges ahead. *Columbia Journal of World Business,* 43–51.

Levy, B. (1991). Transactions costs, the size of firms and industrial policy: Lessons from a comparative case study of the footwear industry in Korea and Taiwan. *Journal of Development Economics* **34**, 151–178.

Levy, B. and Wen-Jeng Kuo. (1991). The strategic orientations of firms and the performance of Korea and Taiwan in frontier industries: Lessons from comparative case studies of keyboard and personal computer assembly. *World Development* **19**, 363–374.

Lorch, K., and Biggs, T. (1989). "Growing in the Interstices: The Limits of Government Promotion of Small Industries." Paper presented at the annual meeting of the Association for Asian Studies, Washington, D.C.

March, J. G., and Olsen, J. P. (1984, September). "The new institutionalism: Organizational factors in political life. *American Political Science Review* **78**, 734–749.

Mead, D. C. (1984). Of contracts and subcontracts: Small firm in vertically disintegrated production/distribution systems in LDCs. *World Development* **12**, 1095–1106.

Meyanathan, S. D., and Munter, R. (1994). Industrial structure and the development of small and medium enterprise linkages: An overview, *in Industrial Structures and the Development of Small and Medium Enterprise Linkages* (Meyanathan, Ed.). New York: World Bank, EDI Seminar Series.

Mody, A. (1990). Institutions and dynamic comparative advantage: The electronics industry in South Korea and Taiwan. *Cambridge Journal of Economics* **14**, 291–314.

Orru, M., Biggart, N. W., and Hamilton, G. G. (1991). Organizational isomorphism in East Asia: Broadening the new institutionalism, *in* "The New Institutionalism in Organizational Analysis" (W. W. Powell and P. DiMaggio, Eds). Chicago: University of Chicago Press.

Park, A. and Johnston, B. (1995). Rural development and dynamic externalities in Taiwan's structural transformation. *Economic Development and Cultural Change* 1995, 181–208.

Piore, M. J., and Sabel, C. F. (1984). "The Second Industrial Divide: Possibilities for Prosperity." New York: Basic Books.

Powell, W. W., and DiMaggio, P. J. (1991). Introduction, *in* "The New Institutionalism in Organizational Analysis" (W. W. Powell and P. J. DiMaggio, Eds.). Chicago: University of Chicago Press.

Regnier, P. (1993). The dynamics of small and medium-sized enterprises in Korea and other Asian NIEs. *Small Business Economics* **5**, 23–36.

Republic of China. Taiwan. Ministry of Economic Affairs. Industrial Development Bureau. (1983). "Guidelines for Establishing the Principal/Satellite Manufacturing System Under Governmental Assistance." Mimeo (internal English translation).

Republic of China. Taiwan. Ministry of Economic Affairs. Industrial Development Bureau. (1987). *Zhongxinweixing Gongchangzhidu Tuidongxiaozu* [Center-Satellite Production System Promotion Team]. Pamphlet.

Shea, J.-D. (1992, September). The welfare effects of economic liberalization under financial market segmentation: With special reference to Taiwan. *Academia Economic Papers* **20**, 697–716.

Shieh, G.-S. (1990). "Manufacturing 'Bosses': Subcontracting Networks under Dependent Capitalism in Taiwan," Ph.D. dissertation, University of California at Berkeley.

Shieh, G.-S. (1992). " 'Boss' Island: The Subcontracting Network and Micro-Entrepreneurship in Taiwan's Development." New York: Peter Lang.

Silin, R. H. (1976). "Leadership and Values". Cambridge, MA: Harvard University Press.

Smitka, M. (1991). "Competitive Ties." New York: Columbia University Press.

Stites, R. (1982, April). Small-scale industry in Yinge, Taiwan. *Modern China,* 247–279.

Tang, S.-y. (1995). Informal credit markets and economic development in Taiwan. *World Development* **23**, 845–855.

Tsay, C-L. (1993, January). Industrial restructuring and international competition in Taiwan. *Environment and Planning* **25**, 111–120.

Wade, R. (1990). "Governing the Market: Economic Theory and the Role of Government in East Asian Industrialization." Princeton: Princeton University Press.

Whitley, R. (1990). Eastern Asian enterprise structures and the comparative analysis of forms of business organization. *Organization Studies* **11**, 47–74.

Whitley, R. D. (1991). The social construction of business systems in East Asia. *Organization Studies* **12**, 1–28.

Williamson, O. E. (1985). "The Economic Institutions of Capitalism: Firms, Markets, Relational Contracting." New York: The Free Press.

Wu, H.-l. and Chou, T.-C. (1988, March). Small and medium enterprises and economic development in Taiwan. *Industry of Free China* **69,** 15–25.

Yen, G.L. (1985, April and August). Industrial policies as they relate to SMBs in Taiwan: A financial perspective. *The Asian Economic Review* **27,** 63–84.

Yen, G., and Yen, E. C. (1994). Government financing policies for small- and medium-sized business in Taiwan: A further analysis. *Advances in Financial Planning and Forecasting* **5,** 355–361.

CHAPTER 7

Industrial Flexibility, Economic Restructuring, and East Asian Labor[1]

Frederic C. Deyo
Institute for Development Studies
University of Auckland
Auckland, New Zealand

Continuing industrial growth across much of East Asia, especially among the Four East Asian Tigers (Hong Kong, South Korea, Taiwan, and Singapore), has been associated with a number of social transformations and external pressures that would seem to support the development and empowerment of trade unionism in these countries. These favorable contextual factors include rapid expansion of a waged, urbanized, and increasingly settled industrial proletariat, rising levels of literacy and education, democratic reforms, tightening labor markets, and growing international pressure for fuller observance of labor and human rights.

But with only a few exceptions, organized labor remains politically marginalized and ineffectual across the region, as seen in the general inability of workers and unions to substantially influence the economic strategies of states and firms, to contest the sometimes negative labor consequences of those strategies, or to seize new opportunities created by democratic reforms. This chapter seeks to explain this anomaly by reference to the adverse labor impact of the economic strategies of firms in this region in response to new conditions of global competition.

While it is clear that the Four Tigers differ substantially in industrial structure and in their socioeconomic trajectories of change, they also share a number of characteristics related to their highly successful experience of export-led industrial

[1]Sections of this chapter are drawn from Deyo (1997, February). Labor and post-Fordist industrial restructuring in East and Southeast Asia. *Work and Occupations* **24** (1), 97–118. Used by permission of Sage Publications, Inc., copyright © 1997.

growth. By confining discussion to the Four Tigers themselves, we are led to emphasize their differences. But in order to highlight the commonalities among these countries, as well as to place them in a broader comparative perspective, the following discussion includes reference as well to Thailand and Malaysia, industrializers whose experience throws that of the Tigers into sharper relief.

I. INDUSTRIAL TRANSFORMATION
AND LABOR RESPONSE

By global standards, several East Asian countries have achieved remarkable rates and levels of industrialization over the past two decades. This rapid economic transition is especially apparent in South Korea, Taiwan, Singapore, and Hong Kong, the most industrially advanced developing countries in the region. Table 1 shows high percentages of workers employed in industrial and manufacturing sectors, as well as high levels of literacy among these countries, all useful predictors of social awareness, political participation, and union density.

Further, in South Korea, Taiwan, Thailand, and arguably Hong Kong, democratization and political liberalization have provided new opportunities for organized labor. Democratic reforms have generally been associated with a liberalization of previously restrictive labor laws and regimes, thus providing new political space for labor organizing and collective action. These democratic reforms have been urged and reinforced by growing international pressure for fuller observance of labor and human rights. The United States in particular has linked preferential developing country trade status and other forms of economic cooperation to improved human rights in Asia. Similarly, international trade union organizations, the International Labour Organization, and a number of international nongovernmental organizations have continued to publicize and attack violations of labor rights in the region.

But despite these various favorable socioeconomic and political changes, organized labor remains politically marginalized and ineffectual across the region, even in these six rapidly industrializing countries. Trade union densities, ranging from a high of 18% in South Korea to a low of roughly 5% in Thailand, provide one indicator of such marginalization. In all cases, densities have actually declined over recent years, even in South Korea and Taiwan where industrial development and democratic reforms have progressed farthest. Following sharp increases between 1987 and 1990, South Korean unionization rates dropped from 23% to 18% during the 1990s (Song, 1993). Similarly, Taiwanese union membership increased by over 50% between 1986 and 1989, thereafter falling gradually (Frenkel, Hong, and Lee, 1993). Singapore's union density declined from 24.5% in 1979 to the current level of roughly 17% by 1988, while that in Malaysia dropped from 11.2% in 1985 to 9.4% in 1990 (Kuruvilla, 1995), or from 18% to about 14% of the nonagricultural workforce over the 1980s. Union density in Malaysia's private sector is

Table 1

Industrial and Social Indicators

	Industry as percentage of GDP[a] (1993)	Manufacturing as percentage of GDP[a] (1993)	Heavy industry* as percentage of total manufacturing value-added[a] (1992)	Percent industrial** employment[b] (1988–1993)	Percent urban population[a] (1993)	Percent literacy[c] (1994)	Wage employment as percentage nonagricultural total (1988–1993)
Republic of Korea	43	29	40	33	78	96	70
Taiwan	39[e]	30[e]	n.a.	39[c]	75[d]	90	
Hong Kong	21	13	23	30	95	88[e] (1990)	89
Singapore	37	28	63	34	100	87	86
Malaysia	n.a.	n.a.	45	28	52	80	80
Thailand	39	28	45	14	19	89	63

*Chemicals, machinery, and transport equipment.
**Mining, manufacturing, construction, utilities.
[a]World Bank, 1995 (except Taiwan).
[b]ILO, *WLR*, 1995.
[c]*World Almanac*, 1995 (except Hong Kong).
[d]Frenkel, 1993, p. 18.
[e]The *Europa World Yearbook*, 1995.

especially low, at only about 7% (Arudsothy and Littler, 1993). While during the 1980s unionization rates in Thailand's private sector grew slowly from a very low base (roughly 5% during the late 1980s), the forced dissolution of unions in the highly organized state enterprises following the 1991 military coup brought a sharp overall union decline and subsequent stagnation in the private sector extending into the post-coup restoration of democratic rule (see below). In Hong Kong, an over-all density of about 17% by the late 1980s was well below the 23% to 24% levels of a decade earlier (Chiu and Levin, 1994).

The marginal role of collective bargaining provides further evidence of the weakness of organized labor in the region. Collective bargaining is virtually nonexistent in major manufacturing industries in Hong Kong, and is confined largely to what Chiu and Levin (1993) term "defensive economism." Collective agreements, they note, cover only about 4% of the work force, and contain only very general regulative language. In Taiwan, about 9% of manufacturing employees work under collective agreements, which cover only 5% of all enterprises (Frenkel, Hong, and Lee, 1993). Similarly ineffectual and circumscribed is collective bargaining in South Korea (Kim, 1993), in Malaysia, where private sector bargaining declined in the mid-1980s (Arudsothy and Littler, 1993), and in Thailand (Brown and Frenkel, 1993).

Labor's participation in national-level economic governance presents a more mixed picture. In Singapore, a long-standing state commitment to coopted union participation in tripartite national decision making ensures labor representation in wage recommendations, in labor dispute arbitration, and in a broad range of social policy deliberation. In Hong Kong, recent democratic reforms have been associated with enhanced participation in public policy, especially through worker representation on the Labor Advisory Board and in a more socially inclusive Legislative Council. Such increased representation has eventuated in government legislative efforts to raise labor standards and to regulate and restrict local reliance on immigrant labor (Chiu and Lui, 1994). In South Korea, the growth of an increasingly assertive and independent labor movement has reinforced the existing government commitment to improved labor standards, including expanded pension and medical insurance plans and, most recently, a new unemployment insurance program (Lee and Park, 1995). In Thailand, democratic reforms and political liberalization beginning in the mid-1980s and resuming after the collapse of interim military rule in 1992, have been accompanied by increased labor influence in national policymaking, as seen in the success of a long-standing campaign by organized labor for enactment of important new social security legislation in 1990 and of a parallel drive to slow privatization programs.

But having said this, it is clear that the economic gains enjoyed by East Asian workers have generally flowed less from labor's political or organizational strengths than from labor market pressures associated with growing labor scarcities in critical skill areas. Hong Kong's colonial government, strongly committed to nonintervention in labor and economic affairs, has been strongly adverse to labor market regulation. In Taiwan, wage rates are determined largely by market forces (Lee and Park, 1995). In both Hong Kong and Taiwan, labor standards legislation is poorly enforced among the many small- to medium-sized firms that dominate both economies (Chiu and Lui, 1994). In South Korea, the dramatic political gains on the part of increasingly independent trade unions from 1987 until 1990 were halted and partially reversed following negative public reaction to labor and student activism after 1990. In Thailand and Malaysia, labor standards enforcement is uneven and ineffectual. In the case of Thailand, Labor Department inspectors are under strong pressure not to prosecute firms that violate minimum wage, safety, and other labor laws for fear that increased costs may undercut the competitive position of firms.[2]

It is primarily in Singapore that one finds a credible case of positive state intervention in labor markets and effective enforcement of labor standards, safety, and health, and other labor legislation. But there, as in South Korea and Taiwan until the late 1980s, the peak labor organization has been more an instrument of state policy than of labor representation. For this reason, Singapore's progressive record of labor safeguards is more realistically understood as a pillar of a larger system of developmental paternalism than as an outcome of labor pressure (Deyo, 1992).

II. THE POLITICAL SOURCES OF LABOR'S WEAKNESS

The discussion thus far would suggest the importance of political factors in undercutting Asian labor. Indeed, political explanations have received the lion's share of attention in efforts to understand the weak position of regional labor movements. In several countries, strict union registration procedures have provided an effective deterrent to oppositional unionism while bolstering officially sanctioned unions and union federations. This is especially true in Singapore and South Korea, where state supported labor federations, the National Trades Union Congress (NTUC), and the Federation of Korean Trade Unions (FKTU), respectively, enjoy political protection from emerging oppositional federations. Similarly, in Malaysia, the ruling coalitional party has sought to support a new labor federation, the Malaysian Labour Organization, in preference to an older, larger oppositional federation, the Malaysian Trades Union Congress. Such government-sponsored unionism, particularly in Singapore, compromises the capacity of unions effectively to represent rank-and-file membership at enterprise or political levels.

In Malaysia and Singapore, labor relations legislation strictly precludes from collective bargaining such issues as work assignment, recruitment, retrenchment, and

[2]Based on conversations with a Thai Labor Department factory inspector during factory site visits in 1993.

dismissal, all defined as within the purview of "management discretion," thus eliminating altogether a number of topics of considerable interest to workers (Begin, 1995). Similarly, governments across the region, even under democratic regimes, circumscribe labor activities by strictly proscribing union political activities other than those permitted within state-sponsored corporatist structures. Such depoliticization assures labor's continuing political marginalization under democratization and a corresponding inability to press for favorable economic or social policy. In South Korea, efforts to contain and destroy independent, "democratic" trade unions and their national level federation, the National Alliance of Trade Unions, created in 1990 to push for industrial unionism and an enhanced political role for labor, partially define the institutional boundaries of political liberalization (Song, 1993).

Malaysian workers in the strategic electronics sector were denied union rights for many years, and union leaders have been periodically harassed and even jailed for union-related activities (Kuruvilla, 1995). In Thailand, it was noted that a 1991 military coup was followed by a banning of unionism and collective bargaining in state enterprises. Given that Thai state enterprise unions have played a lead role in Thai unionism, elimination of these unions effectively decapitated the national labor movement (Brown and Frenkel, 1993). And in Taiwan, unions and union leadership selection processes have historically been monitored and controlled by the ruling Kuomintang Party.

As important as restrictive political controls is the lack of positive support and protection for workers and their trade unions, an historically critical prerequisite for effective trade unionism in the West. Even in the context of democratic reforms, labor regime liberalization has largely been confined to "deregulation," a process that, if unattended by corresponding measures to strengthen trade unionism, eventuates in increased employer domination at the enterprise level along with heightened union factionalism and conflict. The governments of Thailand, Singapore, Malaysia, and South Korea, for example, have yet to ratify ILO convention #87 guaranteeing the right of workers freely to organize (ILO, World Employment 1995). The Malaysian and Thai governments have ratified only 11 of the ILO's labor conventions, and South Korea only 4 (ILO *World Labour Report,* 1995). In Thailand, Malaysia, Hong Kong, and elsewhere, it was noted that government enforcement of existing labor standards legislation has been lax, thus effectively subjecting workers to capricious managerial domination, attacks on unions, and noncompliance with minimum wage, health, and safety legislation (Brown and Frenkel, 1993). In Thailand, union organizers receive no legal protection during organizational drives up until the date of official union registration, thus discouraging unionization drives. And in Hong Kong, collective agreements enjoy no legal standing, and are thus outside the purview of state regulation (Chiu and Levin, 1995).

Even in cases where workers have mounted effective political movements, often during democratic transitions, workers have generally played a largely subordinate role, mobilized by and allied to elite/middle class/student leadership. In Thailand, the relatively successful labor resistance to ongoing privatization during the

1980s was in part rooted in cross-class support from military and bureaucratic elites who benefited politically and economically from the continuance of important state enterprises. In Taiwan, recent efforts by independent political parties and factions to garner electoral support has provided a critical base for new organizing efforts there (Frenkel, Hong, and Lee, 1993). And in South Korea, labor insurgence and organizational gains were strongly supported by student and middle-class groups.

But if cross-class coalitional support sometimes benefits workers and unions, the resulting dependency of labor on such non-working class support creates attendent vulnerabilities. Loss of bureaucratic and military support for Thai state-enterprise unions encouraged the 1990 military coup following which these unions were banned. And growing middle-class apprehension about labor militancy in South Korea, it was noted, encouraged a harsher government response to strikes after 1990.

It is clearly impossible to account for the weakness of Asian labor movements without understanding the unfavorable political context within which these movements operate. But having said this, it is nonetheless important to note a critical problem with purely political explanations. During recent years, regional labor movements have, if anything, declined in membership and effectiveness. Yet this decline has, with a few exceptions, occurred in an absence of heightened political controls. Indeed, in many cases it has proceeded despite continuing democratic reforms and a progressive *liberalization* of labor regimes. In part this decline may be understood by reference to the form such liberalization has taken, with its greater emphasis on deregulation than protection. But the larger issue remains. In the context of rising levels of education, literacy, urbanization, and waged employment, democratic reforms might be expected to enhance labor movements, especially in expanding industrial sectors. Conversely, labor movements in several countries of Latin America and elsewhere have remained viable and effective during interludes of labor repression as severe as that obtaining anywhere in capitalist Asia.

Such anomalies suggest a need for greater attention to other, nonpolitical, factors in understanding the decline of Asian labor movements. Of particular importance are enterprise-level economic strategies and their associated structural consequences. Indeed, the importance of such economic factors has become ever more central to our understanding even of political controls themselves, as state labor regimes have become dissociated from earlier anti-Communist campaigns and ever more attentive to the imperatives of economic development.

III. THE ECONOMIC STRUCTURAL DEMOBILIZATION OF LABOR

Light, export-oriented industrialization (EOI) in South Korea, Hong Kong, Taiwan, and Singapore in the 1970s, and in Malaysia and Thailand in the 1980s, was associated with the emergence of a relatively transitory labor force comprising large numbers of young women in unstable low-skill jobs with little career opportunity.

The difficulty of organizing such an unstable work force into effective unions continues to undercut union organizing efforts in the large export-manufacturing sectors of Thailand, Malaysia, and other lower-tier East Asian industrializers. Compounding such difficulties were the efforts on the part of regional governments to hold labor costs down and to ensure labor peace in order to attract domestic and foreign investment into labor-intensive export manufacturing (Deyo, 1989).

Second, international pressures to further open domestic markets to foreign imports, often associated with ongoing regional and global trade agreements, have subjected firms to intensified competition in both domestic and international markets. In East Asian developing countries, with their relatively labor-intensive, export-oriented industrial structures, managers have sought to meet these new competitive pressures through cost-cutting measures directed in large part at reducing labor costs. Such measures have in turn both reflected and reinforced a weakened bargaining position on the part of labor. Competitive pressures in particular have created a credible threat of shutdowns, retrenchments, and relocation of production to cheaper labor sites in the absence of effective labor cost containment. The increasing international mobility of capital alongside a heightened global integration of the production strategies of multinational enterprises has had the further effect of adversely affecting the ability of governments to enact and enforce labor legislation. Globalization, notes the I.L.O., give "governments an incentive to dilute, or fail to enact, measures intended to protect the welfare of workers, or to turn a blind eye to infringements of legislation with this in mind" (I.L.O. World Employment, 1995, 72–73). This same report notes, as well, an increasing erosion of the quality of formal-sector employment through reduced job security, the declining significance of local or national-level collective bargaining, new policies of "firm-centric cooperation," union-avoidance strategies, promotion of company unions, and reduced union bargaining leverage at the local level.

In addition, some cost-cutting measures, including the increased use of temporary and contract labor and greater outsourcing of production, have directly undercut union power while at the same time addressing a second set of competitive requirements, discussed below, stemming from the globalization of post-Fordist flexible production systems.

IV. FLEXIBLE PRODUCTION
AND THE NEW COMPETITION

There has been growing recognition of the competitive impact on firms of accelerated changes in world markets and technology. While these changes are more marked in some product sectors than in others, and more critical in some production phases than in others even for particular products, they are increasingly pervasive across most industries. Markets in particular have become ever more volatile, as economic globalization has rendered both domestic and export markets more vulnerable to the uncertainties of currency realignments, shifting fashions, and cross-nationally interlinked business cycles. In addition, product cycles in many industries have become ever shorter as new product technologies have rendered older products quickly obsolete. Markets are more fragmented as firms increasingly compete in a variety of culturally differentiated export markets, and as firms have themselves learned to create and exploit niche markets. In addition, both end-use and downstream buyers have become ever more demanding from the standpoints of quality and on-time delivery. Finally, increasingly rapid change in process technologies has both enabled and required firms to continually identify and adopt new ways of making products.

By consequence of these new pressures, firms have been required, as a condition of survival, to become ever more attentive and responsive to change. In addition to escalating competitive pressures from lower cost production sites in the context of global trade liberalization, East Asian firms have been forced to become more flexible: more able that is to continually scan the economic horizon for new information and opportunities, to quickly integrate this new information into product development, manufacturing, and marketing, to produce efficiently in relatively small volume for niche markets, and to continually introduce improvements in production and other operations. Production flexibility, more generally defined as the ability quickly, efficiently, and continuously to introduce changes in product and process, has thus become a competitive requirement for firms operating in global markets and in increasingly open domestic markets.

Colclough and Tolbert's (1992) distinction between "static" and "dynamic" forms of flexibility provides a useful starting point for examining the impact of flexible production system for labor. Static flexibility emphasizes short-term adaptability to market volatility and fragmentation through quick adjustments in product volume and mix, while dynamic flexibility enhances long-term adaptability through basic organizational and technological changes that increase the capacity for continuing product and process innovation and improvement. This distinction between static and dynamic flexibility is closely related to two further dimensions of industrial adaptation and change, the first relating to long-term economic upgrading and development, the second to social outcomes for workers. It is clear that dynamic flexibility more adequately addresses the long-term requirements of economic advance insofar as it better positions firms and industries to move into higher-value market niches in which innovative market *leadership* comprises a critical competitive factor than does static flexibility, with its greater relative emphasis on adaptive market *followership*.

Similarly clear are the quite different labor outcomes associated with these two forms of flexibility. Static flexibility emphasizes employment and capacity adjustments through reliance on external labor markets to fill positions and to obtain necessary skills, increased use of temporary or casual labor, and extensive subcontracting to outside suppliers. Such flexibility may often undercut longer-term investment in employment skills, technological innovation, work reorganization, and supplier capacities insofar as relations with employees and other firms are predominantly cost-focused, and are defined as short-term and expedient, rather than developmental in nature. By contrast, the research literature on firms in the developed countries of Japan, Europe, and North America suggests that dynamic flexibility is associated with longer-term relations within and among firms, and with a corresponding stress on mutual gains through collaboration and joint learning. From the standpoint of employees, this implies more opportunity for training and job advancement, greater job security, the instituting of various measures to encourage job stability and organizational commitment, and fuller participation in problem solving and production decisions (see Friedman, 1988; Kenney and Florida, 1993; Womack, Jones, and Roos, 1990). Similarly, to the extent firms rely increasingly on external supplier networks to enhance dynamic flexibility, technological upgrading of those suppliers encourages relatively more satisfactory employment conditions and pay for the growing number of workers in small firms.

V. FLEXIBLE PRODUCTION STRATEGIES IN EAST ASIA

Static flexibility strategies predominate in many East Asian industrial sectors, particularly among second-tier countries. There is evidence, for example, of increasing use of subcontracting, casualization, and contract labor ("numerical flexibility") in the large export sectors of the Philippines (Ofreneo, 1994), and Thailand (Deyo, 1995). Standing (1989) similarly documents increasing outsourcing and employment casualization in electronics and other export sectors in Malaysia. More surprising is the prevalence of such strategies even in industrially advanced Hong Kong (Chin and Levin, 1993), as noted below.

A. HONG KONG

Manufacturing firms in Hong Kong have generally responded to the new conditions of global competition through static flexibility strategies similar to those described for Thailand. This is most evident in the colony's two most important industries: clothing and electronics.[3]

Facing rising labor costs and increasing competition from China and elsewhere, Hong Kong garment makers have relocated or subcontracted out part of

---

[3]The following discussion draws heavily on the writings of Chiu, Lui, and Levin (see Lui and Chiu, 1996; Chiu, Ho, and Lui, 1995, 98–122; Levin and Chiu, 1993).

their production to China, a strategy reflected in a steady decline in garment employment in Hong Kong since the late 1980s (Chiu, Ho, and Lui, 1995). Some firms have begun to shift into high-value fashion segments of the garment industry on the one hand, and to redirect Hong Kong activities toward design and marketing activities on the other. More commonly, firms have increasingly relied on subcontract networks of small firms, and on casual and contract labor not only to cut costs, but also to enhance flexibility in response to volatile and uncertain apparel markets.

Lacking the locational constraints imposed by rules of origin agreements in the garment industry, electronics firms have more freely relocated production to China. By consequence, electronics employment has declined even more sharply than in garments, with a corresponding increase in the percent of electronics employment in clerical, professional, technical, and administrative activities (Lui and Chiu, 1996). While this latter occupational upgrading has enhanced career opportunities and job conditions for a small percentage of the work force, lack of upgrading in manufacturing itself has resulted in a massive redeployment of largely female assembly workers into lower paid work in the informal sector.

B. TAIWAN

Taiwan shares with Hong Kong an industrial structure centered on networks of small firms: a product in part of the horizontal expansion strategies of many Chinese families. As transnational marketing and manufacturing companies have sought lower cost production sites, they have worked through local trading companies to locate and engage Taiwanese firms to manufacture products on an OEM (original equipment manufacturing) basis (Gereffi and Hamilton, 1996). Fortuitously, the dense networks of small firms linked by family and personal connection have provided the flexibility demanded in uncertain export markets.

There is stronger evidence in Taiwan than in Hong Kong of industrial upgrading into more technologically sophisticated production requiring higher-order skills on the part of workers. Such upgrading has occurred within sectors as well as through diversification into more other, more demanding product niches (Pan, 1996). The production networks of small- and medium-sized firms in such traditional products as garments are strongly rooted in local networks of family and personal relationships. In these lower-technology sectors, largely static flexibility strategies are pursued as kin-based networks of firms respond on a short-term basis to rapidly changing production orders channeled by international buyers through local trading companies. Electronics, computer, and automobile parts producers, on the other hand, are organized more vertically, with closer direct links to transnational companies for OEM production. In these higher-technology sectors, more stringent quality and reliability requirements force firms to focus on skill development and process engineering capability, important bases of dynamic flexibility.

Conversely, as transnational buyers seek to improve their own supplier base, they cultivate relatively more stable, supportive, and developmental relations with local firms (Pan, 1996). And as local firms themselves acquire increased competence in specialized production processes and machinery, their bargaining position in negotiating risk and profit improves over time. For this reason, the economic position of these firms and the wages of their workers have tended to improve more consistently than in lower-technology production networks where developmental resources are confined to localized community and kinship-based social networks (Wang, 1996). By implication, efforts on the part of larger firms to enhance flexibility through outsourcing to smaller suppliers does not have as negative a social impact for workers as one finds in Hong Kong and Thailand, or in lower technology industries in Taiwan itself.

C. SOUTH KOREA

South Korea's industrial structure differs fundamentally from that of Taiwan and Hong Kong in its degree of economic concentration centering on large, family-owned, and vertically integrated industrial and trading conglomerates (*chaebol*) (see Chap. 5, this volume). Based on their privileged corporate access to capital, technology, and export markets, *chaebol* group firms have prospered, but largely in mass production sectors (e.g., in heavy and basic industry, electronics assembly, consumer electronics, and durable consumer goods). By consequence of a continuing choice to compete in these standardized production niches through organizational strategies of vertical integration, the flexibility requirements facing South Korean firms have differed in degree and kind from those facing firms in Taiwan and Hong Kong. Here, flexibility centers not so much on the demands of market volatility or fragmentation as on the need for continuous, incremental improvement (*kaizen*) in order to enhance productivity and quality. As noted earlier, under the Japanese "customized" mass production system typified by Toyota, *kaizen* is associated with continuous multiskill training and worker participation in problem-solving and continuous improvement programs. These human resource practices, in turn, are accompanied by such commitment-enhancing policies as seniority-based advancement, reliance on internal labor markets, employment security, and enterprise unionism that function to stabilize the work force and to enlist the involvement of workers. While elements of the Japanese system have been documented for managerial and white-collar workers in South Korean *chaebol*, they have generally not been utilized on the shop floor, where job specialization, autocratic rather than participatory decision making, reliance on external labor markets and harsh disciplinary procedures are associated with confrontational, rather than cooperative, labor–management relations.

While intra-*chaebol* supplier relations may be characterized as long-term and developmental, those extending to firms outside these groups tend to be short-term, cost-focused, and exploitative rather than developmental. Further, given the dominant position of *chaebol* firms in gaining access to technology, capital, and export markets, small- and medium-sized firms tend to be either economically marginalized or, alternately, highly dependent on larger firms for their major resources and thus unable to negotiate favorable terms of exchange with their major customers. This resource scarcity and dependency in part explains the lack of profitability and expansion among non-*chaebol* industrial firms in South Korea, and the resultant stagnation in productivity, wages, and employment conditions in such firms.

D. SINGAPORE

The implications of industrial restructuring for workers and small firms in Singapore must be understood in the broader context of domination of this city–state's finance and industry by transnational companies (TNCs). Indeed, TNC domination extends as well to supplier networks on which the large corporations depend.

In response to growing labor shortages, rising labor and production costs, and growing competition from Indonesia, Sri Lanka, and other low-cost production sites, Singapore's industrial restructuring has entailed a sharp decline in labor-intensive industries like garments alongside rapid expansion in higher technology industries. Foremost among these new industries is electronics, which, by 1991, accounted for 34.4% of total manufacturing employment in Singapore (Chiu, Ho, and Lui, 1995) and which by 1995 comprised 52% of all manufacturing output (*The Wall Street Journal,* September 21, 1996, A10). As important, Singapore's electronics industry has itself moved out of labor-intensive assembly production into the relatively more technology- and skill-intensive manufacturing of personal computers, semiconductor chips, and PC components (e.g., disk drives).

The electronics industry in Singapore and elsewhere is subject to both severe cost competition and short product cycles. Shorter-term market volatility has been relatively less severe in this sector so that production runs have tended to be relatively long between new product launches. Since local TNC electronics subsidiaries conduct little basic product design in Singapore, concentrating instead on process engineering, production, and the regional coordination of production chains, their competitive strategies have largely been driven by the needs to reduce costs and to regularly retool for the production of new products (Chiu, Lui, and Ho, 1995, 102–105). The requirements of rapid retooling have in turn pushed TNC producers to cultivate close, supportive relations with their local precision-engineering suppliers (Wong, 1996).

What are the social consequences of such industrial restructuring? First, in order to respond flexibly to periodic interruptions in production during retooling for new products, electronics firms resort to frequent layoffs of production workers. Chiu, Lui, and Ho (1995) note that such employment volatility is further exacerbated by the highly cyclical nature of the electronics industry in general, with pronounced industrywide retrenchments every 4 to 5 years. Given the increasing skill-intensity of these firms, the resulting high levels of turnover might seem to undercut firm-level performance. In fact it may not, since state-sponsored technical and engineering programs provide a substantial skill infrastructure for the firms while electronics production in Singapore does not require many firm-specific shop-floor skills. Thus, firms have relied fairly successfully on external labor markets to meet their production staffing needs.

If employment insecurity characterizes electronics production work, other employment practices, especially relating to health and safety, working conditions, work hours, and benefits, are more favorable. This follows in large measure from strict enforcement of Singapore's relatively progressive labor standards legislation, as noted earlier.

In contrast to their Taiwanese counterparts, Singapore's domestic small- and medium-sized manufacturing firms have been largely bypassed by foreign investment in electronics and other dynamic industrial sectors. It is true that transnational electronics firms have developed close ties with local suppliers, in part to foster rapid new product launches, just-in-time component delivery, and fast turn-around machining (cf. Rasiah, 1996), and in part because of encouragement under the government's Local Industries Upgrading Program (LIUP) (Wong, 1996). On the other hand, most of the first-tier suppliers have in fact themselves been foreign. Hill and Fujita (1996) report that only about 16% of all local electronics suppliers are domestic firms. Rather, domestic firms have largely remained in low-technology, more stagnant sectors serving domestic and regional markets.

VI. THE SOCIAL IMPACT OF RESTRUCTURING: ECONOMIC DUALISM

The foregoing discussion suggests a very mixed picture of the social outcomes of flexible industrial restructuring from the standpoint of production workers. The most obvious outcome is a growing dualism within and across sectors in the changing employment structures of these four countries. Industrial restructuring has sharply reduced employment opportunities for low-skilled and especially women workers in large, lead firms in garments and other low-technology industries. Where firms have continued to compete in these cost-focused niches, as in Hong Kong, they have casualized portions of their own workforce, while also subcontracting more production to small workshops. At the same time, they have created new, although limited employment, for higher skilled and technical workers in engineering, design, marketing, and other core functions. It has generally been male workers who have taken advantage of these latter opportunities, while women have figured more prominently in casualization and informalization strategies.

The resulting economic dualism has been especially apparent where firms have sought to pursue dynamic flexibility strategies This may be seen in the employment practices within lead firms, as well as in the evolving nature of interfirm and supplier relations. Given continued cost pressures even on firms competing in quality- and innovation-intensive market niches, the relatively expensive personnel practices associated with employee training, participation, and retention in core production processes are confined to critical employees, while part-time and short-term workers are employed in other operations. Similarly, first-tier and critical-component suppliers enjoy full access to the resources and support of lead firms, while other suppliers are mainly pushed to contain costs.

Two cases drawn from Thailand's auto industry illustrate this pattern of internal and interfirm dualism. At a Bangkok area Mitsubishi plant visited in 1993, it was found that while a small number of permanent workers and technicians enjoyed excellent pay, benefits, and job security, a larger proportion of workers were either contract workers, hired "on-loan" from suppliers, or casual hourly workers employed in low-skill, off-line duties. A parallel study of a Toyota plant, also in Bangkok, suggests a similar dualism in supplier networks. In recognition of the critical role of the suppliers of key components from the standpoints of just-in-time delivery, high quality, and participation in joint engineering and *kaizen* activities, Toyota cultivates close, long-term relations with its first-tier suppliers, mostly Japanese transplants, extending substantial technical assistance to them. Lower-tier, mostly Thai, suppliers, on the other hand, are pushed to reduce costs rather to enhance organizational capabilities. One consequence of these differences in the nature of the relations between Toyota and its various suppliers is to reproduce and deepen technological and other differences among supplier firms.

VII. DYNAMIC FLEXIBILITY, PARTICIPATION, AND AUTOCRACY

It was noted that dynamic flexibility in the industrially developed countries of Japan, Europe, and North America are typically associated with enhanced participation of workers in problem-solving, production planning, and *kaizen* activities. This does not appear to be the case in East Asia, where dynamically flexible firms have more often pursued top-down, autocratic systems of management.

In the higher-value-added market niches where technological and product quality requirements preclude continued reliance on low-skill temporary workers and static flexibility, Asian firms are pressed to make long-term investments in worker training, product development, organizational restructuring, and other programs supportive of enhanced dynamic flexibility. In addition, such firms may sometimes institute suggestion systems, quality circles, labor-management councils, and other means of mobilizing worker involvement in quality and productivity improvements (on Malaysia, see Rasiah, 1994). But even such instances of dynamic flexibility, typically accompanied by improved wages and benefits and other mea-sures to enhance the stability and commitment of workers, rarely permit the level of worker decision-making involvement found in Japan and elsewhere.

The suggestion that East Asian dynamic industrial flexibility is substantially more autocratic than its counterparts in more industrially advanced countries is supported by numerous case studies indicating that regional firms adopting flexible production systems do more fully tap their human resource base than do other firms, but that they are far more likely to employ systems of individual and infor-mal consultation than such collective forms of participation as labor-management councils or team-based decision making in eliciting worker ideas. Frenkel (1995) notes increased reliance on informal consultation but little encouragement of group-based worker participation in his study of a pharmaceutical firm in Taiwan. Kim (1995) reports the restriction of the activities of quality circles to narrowly de-fined duties and responsibilities in South Korean firms, a finding reflected in Deyo's (1995) study of automobile companies in Thailand. Kuruvilla (1995) notes the au-tocratic character of recent work reforms in Malaysian industry. Rodgers and Wong (1995), reviewing the evidence from an extensive survey of industrial firms in Sin-gapore, report only minimal development of quality circles, a finding confirmed by Begin (1995), who estimates that QCCs include only about 5% of Singapore's in-dustrial workers, and are severely limited in scope and influence.

VIII. ECONOMIC GOVERNANCE, LABOR, AND THE INSTITUTING OF FLEXIBLE PRODUCTION

Why are East and Southeast Asian patterns of flexible production predomi-nantly static in nature, and where dynamic, more autocratic than their counterparts in industrially more advanced countries?

As noted earlier, static forms of flexibility are encouraged in product niches characterized by volatile markets, stable technology, capital scarcity, and intense competition. In addition, they tend to be pursued in the absence of governance in-stitutions that encourage long-term investments in organizational reform, technol-ogy, human resources, and research and development. The following discussion focuses primarily on the way in which governance factors influence those aspects of enterprise-level competitive strategies that impinge most directly on labor.

Most important, perhaps, is the role of the state in providing requisite col-lective goods, in directly influencing competitive strategies, in creating a level play-ing field for firms, and in empowering labor to participate in enterprise strategies. Collective goods refer in this context to those elements of economic infrastructure that are both essential to dynamic flexibility strategies and unlikely to be provided by individual firms. These would include not only physical infrastructure (roads, ports, telecommunications) but, as important, technology support (research and development institutes, public funding for private sector R&D) and human resource development (education, vocational and technical training). That provision of this foundation infrastructure is unlikely to be provided by individual firms follows from the externalities associated with such investments, and the strong probability that competitors will benefit from them.

States also directly influence the nature of competitive strategies and related labor policies. Encouragement and financial support may be offered for long-term strategies of research and development, organizational and work reforms, and the acquisition of new technologies. Incentives may be extended for training programs and the instituting of quality circles and worker participation schemes. Firms may be encouraged to cooperate among themselves in the provision of collective goods, through joint training programs, cooperative R&D and marketing, and other forms of mutual assistance (Sabel, 1995).

States can also ensure a level playing field such that long-term, risky, firm-level investments in, say, R&D, employee training, and work reorganization, do not place firms at a severe cost disadvantage vis-à-vis other firms that do not incur such costs. Similarly, establishment of minimal labor standards, adequate wages and benefits, and fair labor practices discourages firms from competing through labor–cost containment and union avoidance; encouraging, instead, greater effort to enhance employee skills, productivity, and work involvement. And finally, states play an important role in empowering workers and labor organizations to participate more fully in the instituting of competitive strategies, and thus in ensuring that those strategies benefit workers as well as firms (Cole, 1989; Hollingsworth and Streeck, 1994).

It is clear that governments in Singapore, South Korea, and Taiwan have played a more forceful developmental role in these regards than in Hong Kong, Thailand, or Malaysia. In the industrially advanced Tigers, substantial public commitment to education in general, and to technical and vocational education in particular, provides a solid foundation for in-company employee training. Singapore, like Malaysia and now South Korea, has instituted a skills development payroll tax under which companies contribute to a government controlled training fund from which they can draw only for approved employee training programs (Begin, 1995). Such a levy strongly encourages company training as a way of realizing benefits from a collective good to which all firms contribute, thus effectively reversing the collective goods dilemma of "Who will pay for everyone's benefit?" to "Who will benefit from everyone's contribution?"

Similarly, Singapore, and to a lesser degree South Korea and Taiwan (Lee and Park, 1995), enforce basic labor standards so as to reduce the incentive for firms to view such standards as a competitive cost factor. Where such labor standards are less effective in moderating managerial practices, as in Thailand, Malaysia, and Hong Kong, and among smaller firms in South Korea and Taiwan, high rates of employee turnover and weak enterprise commitment undercut training and other human-resource programs necessary for dynamic flexibility.

If the static flexibility strategies of firms in the region, especially in Hong Kong, Thailand, and Malaysia, and among small firms in most countries, can be attributed in part to an absence of supportive state policy, they flow as well from failures of collective governance in the private sector. A burgeoning literature on flexible specialization and industrial districts (the "Italian" model) suggests the importance of interfirm cooperation for the provision of collective goods, and for the minimization and pooling of risk necessary for flexibility-enhancing investments and innovations (Sabel, 1989; Scott, 1992). A parallel literature on flexible production within firms and among hierarchically organized clusters of large firms and their suppliers (the "Japanese" model), demonstrates the importance of trust-based, enduring relations among firms for high quality, diversified production (Streeck, 1990; Doner, 1991). Both models suggest that stable associational bonds both within and among firms provide an essential foundation for long-term strategies of dynamic flexibility. It should also be noted in this regard that the state may play a critical, if indirect, role in encouraging such private sector cooperation. In Taiwan, for example, the state has instituted a "center-satellite" program under which larger firms or assemblers organize large numbers of suppliers among whom R&D, planning, procurement, and other functions are jointly carried out. This program points to the potential importance of the state in generalizing to local small and medium-sized firms the dynamic flexibility strategies of lead firms, a role played even more effectively in Singapore. There, it was noted, the government has established a Local Industries Upgrading Program through which local precision-engineering firms have been offered substantial R&D, financial, and other assistance as part of a broader effort to ensure a deepening and extension of technology upgrading in key industrial sectors (Wong, 1996).

Finally should be noted the important role of labor relations and institutions. At some risk of oversimplification, labor movements in the region may be characterized as weak and ineffectual (Hong Kong, Thailand, Malaysia), state-coopted (Singapore, pre-1987 South Korea), enterprise-coopted (Taiwan) and strong although vulnerable (post-1987 South Korea) (see Frenkel, 1993). In all but the latter case, organized labor was incapable of substantially influencing the direction of new managerial flexibility strategies during the 1980s and early 1990s. In the absence of labor pressure, firms instituted strategies of static flexibility without substantial labor opposition to increased reliance on contract labor, outsourcing, and use of temporary workers (Levin and Chiu, 1993).

Finally, it should be noted that strategies of static flexibility, prevalent in countries and sectors characterized by institutionally "thin" governance (especially Hong Kong and Thailand), present a long-term developmental cost through lack of encouragement of industrial restructuring into high-value-added production and a corresponding continuation of an ultimately self-defeating effort to compete in low-cost, low-value-added market niches. Whether autocratic forms of dynamic flexibility engender corresponding developmental costs is less certain. To this question we now turn.

IX. AUTOCRATIC FLEXIBILITY AND LEARNING-BASED INDUSTRIALIZATION

It has been noted that East Asian flexibility strategies are more autocratic, and less participatory, than those obtaining in the industrially advanced countries where in any event they are more prevalent. In part, the explanation for this difference is to be found in the incapacity of unions to discourage or resist the instituting of forms of flexibility that preclude effective collective voice on the part of workers. As elsewhere, Singapore provides an important exception to this pattern. There, local union affiliates of the PAP-backed National Trades Union Congress has effectively pushed for greater training and employee involvement in both local and foreign firms.

In some cases, too, autocratic flexibility is an outcome of political constraint: indirectly through the undercutting of union power, and directly, through an underwriting of managerial authority. As noted earlier, in both Singapore and Malaysia, autocratic flexibility is encouraged through legislative exclusion from collective bargaining of such matters as job assignment and work transfers, important elements of labor flexibility. Correspondingly, multinational corporations often insist on operating in a union-free environment (Rasiah, 1994; Kuruvilla, 1994), an insistence to which states may readily accede in their efforts to attract foreign investment.

Second, it may be that worker participation and empowerment are less critical to the success of programs of dynamic flexibility in Asia than in industrially mature economies. Following Amsden (1989), we may distinguish between innovative and learning-based industrialization. Innovative industrialization relies on development of a stream of new products and technologies for changing markets. Learning-based industrialization, by contrast, relies on local adoption of technologies and products developed elsewhere. It may be suggested that insofar as newly developing countries pursue technology-dependent, learning-based industrialization, employers may seek to institute forms of flexibility that minimize worker participation in favor of unchallenged managerial control over production. This is so because learning-based industrialization depends mainly on local adaptation and implementation of already debugged production processes and products, thus minimizing need for an extensive involvement of workers in solving shop-floor production problems. In such a context, engineers and production managers assume the primary role in reorganizing production around imported technologies. Thus, more autocratic forms of flexibility are adequate to the demands of industrialization. Given that multinational firms, whose investments provide a major conduit for technology transfer and diffusion to Asian firms, are reluctant to relocate major

R&D functions to foreign subsidiaries in developing countries, the perpetuation of learning-based industrialization into future years may imply a long-term stability of such autocratic forms of flexibility and a corresponding discouragement of union or worker empowerment at the workplace level. In such a context, human resource mobilization will continue to confine collective forms of shop-floor participation to cooptive, officially sanctioned, and closely circumscribed deliberative fora such as quality circles and labor-management councils, and to more generally eschew collective participation in favor of suggestion systems, informal consultation, merit-based incentives, job ladders, and other individualized modalities of worker participation and involvement in organizational development.

X. TRADE UNIONISM UNDER INDUSTRIAL RESTRUCTURING

To return full circle, how have new flexible production strategies influenced trade unionism in this region? It was noted that labor's existing weakness across the region has ensured the instituting of competitive strategies that generally disregarded labor or social agendas in favor of the more narrowly defined competitive strategies of owners and managers. A number of implications have followed from this. First, in the absence of market or institutional pressures or constraints, firms have often pursued static flexibility strategies that have undercut organized labor through casualization, outsourcing and corporate downsizing, and anti-union measures. These trends are especially evident in Hong Kong and in Thailand, where unions have fought strenuously to restrict the use of temporary workers in larger firms (Charoenloet, 1993; Ofreneo, 1994).

Alternately, where market/technology pressures or state and other institutional constraints or support have fostered more dynamic competitive strategies, these strategies have been confined to core workers and production processes. The resultant sharp dualism between core and peripheral employees has in itself undercut unionism by restricting growth in employment sectors characterized by job security and employment stability, wherein unionism is encouraged, and by creating a favored and well-off core of workers whose interests diverge from those of most other workers. Such interest divergence discourages many established unions from active involvement in organizing non-core workers while at the same time creating divisions among workers themselves. Further, states and firms have been successful in constructing systems of control among core employees that tend to preempt or discourage horizontal, collective worker organization in favor of elite-sponsored, hierarchically controlled modes of participation and interest articulation. In Singapore, the PAP-aligned trade union movement has largely preempted and bypassed more independent unions, organizationally fragmented industrywide unionism, and encouraged (with mixed results) formation of "house" or enterprise unions in local firms. In large Japanese firms in Thailand, enterprise unions have been created where labor activists have threatened to organize independent unions. And in Taiwan's networks of small firms, patriarchy and kinship have provided powerful bases for both control and interest articulation among family members, while at the same time marginalizing and excluding nonfamily production workers among whom high rates of job turnover undercut unionization efforts. Despite government restrictions, South Korea, with its continued adherence to Fordist principles of vertical integration and mass (if increasingly "customized") production, remains the locus of relatively effective independent industrial unionism among its core production workers in larger *chaebol*-affiliated firms.

Parallel to these the preemptory, vertically aligned systems of control among core workers are the relatively autocratic management systems that do not so much preclude upward communication of information and interests as confine these to individualized forms of participation. This combination of autocracy and individualized participation further undermines collective resistance among workers.

Finally, it is clear that outside of South Korea, flexibility strategies have been more generally associated with deepened reliance on networks of small companies, among which unionization efforts have been hampered by personal, if not always amicable, relations between employers and workers.

XI. CONCLUSION

In response to new imperatives of changing technology, more volatile and fragmented markets, and global economic liberalization, firms in the successfully industrializing countries of East Asia have instituted greater adaptability and flexibility in all phases of production. From the standpoint of human resources, such flexibility has taken both static and autocratic-dynamic forms. Static flexibility has entailed increased reliance on temporary and contract workers and on outsourcing to low-cost suppliers, while dynamic-autocratic flexibility has been based on increased internal "functional" flexibility, higher skill levels, circumscribed worker participation in production, and more adequate wages and worker benefits. It has been argued that these emergent patterns of flexible production have in part reflected labor's existing weakness at the enterprise level. But in addition, it is clear that such strategies have in turn further undermined local influence, thus perpetuating a vicious circle between labor weakness and labor-undercutting managerial strategies. Here we see most clearly the way in which the political resources and effectiveness of labor determine institutional outcomes that reinforce existing power inequalities.

Characteristics of economic governance and of the export niches occupied by firms in most countries and industrial sectors of developing East Asia would seem to structurally impede an early shift from static and autocratic to more participative, dynamic forms of flexibility, thus reducing the likelihood that continued industrial development will empower workers and unions in future years. Such nonconvergence on industrial organizational patterns obtaining in industrially more advanced countries will entail variable economic costs. Industries adopting static forms of flexibility will experience difficulty in moving into higher-value-added product niches requiring continuing process and product innovation. This transitional difficulty will prove particularly problematic in Thailand, Malaysia, Hong Kong, and other countries now attempting to shift to higher-value-added niches in world markets. Industries adopting dynamic-autocratic forms of flexibility will struggle to move into more innovation and technology-intensive market niches requiring more deeply penetrating human resource systems and correspondingly greater employee participation and involvement in shop-floor change. This second transitional difficulty will most affect South Korea, Taiwan, and Singapore, where continued industrial advance is increasingly impeded by the negative legacies of state and enterprise autocracy.

While the political implications of industrial restructuring are far more uncertain, a few speculative comments may be offered. To the extent East Asian economic strategies have generally undercut the capacity of organized labor to participate in shaping industrial restructuring at enterprise or national levels, national governments may enjoy somewhat greater scope in responding positively to growing domestic and international demands for political liberalization and labor market deregulation without precipitating increased labor militancy and thus threatening processes of capital accumulation. Such a pattern also provides a solution to the problem posed by the internal instability of authoritarian regimes under sustained economic development, in part by enhancing the prospects for democracy by reducing the likelihood that organized labor can exploit new political opportunities offered by political reforms. Alternatively stated, the structurally rooted exclusion of labor from democratic politics may enhance both the usefulness to business of parliamentary institutions and business support for further democratic reforms.

REFERENCES

Applebaum, R. and Smith, D. (1996, October 3–6). "Global Restructuring and Industrial Location: Some Lessons from East Asia." Paper presented at the International Conference on Economic Governance and Flexible Production in East Asia, National Tsing Hua University, hsingchu, Taiwan.

Arudsothy, P. and Littler, C. R. (1993). State regulation and union fragmentation in Malaysia, in "Organized Labor in the Asia-Pacific Region" (S. Frenkel, Ed.), pp. 107–130. Ithaca: ILR Press.

Amsden, A. (1989). "Asia's Next Giant: South Korea and Late Industrialization." New York: Oxford University Press.

Begin, J. P. (1995). Singapore's industrial relations system: Is it congruent with its second phase of industrialization?, in "Industrialization and Labor Relations" (S. Frenkel and J. Harrod, Eds.), pp. 64–87. Ithaca: ILR Press.

Brown, A. and Frenkel, S. (1993). Union unevenness and insecurity in Thailand, *in* "Organized Labor in the Asia-Pacific Region" (S. Frenkel, Ed.), pp. 82–106. Ithaca: ILR Press.

Charoenloet, V. (1993). Export-oriented industry in Thailand: Implications for employment and labour, *in* "NIC's in Asia: A Challenge to Trade Unions" (A. Wehmhorner, Ed.), Singapore: Friedrich-Ebert-Stiftung.

Chiu, S., Ho, K. C., and Lui, T. (1995). "A Tale of Two Cities Rekindled," *Journal of Developing Societies*, XI, 1: 98–122.

Chiu, S. and Levin, D. A. (1993). The world economy, state, and sectors in industrial change: Labor relations in Hong Kong's textile and garment-making industries, *in* "Organized Labor in the Asia-Pacific Region" (S. Frenkel, Ed.). Ithaca: ILR Press.

Chiu, S. and Levin, D. A. (1995, May 31–June 4). "Prosperity without Citizenship: Industrial Relations and Industrial Democracy in Hong Kong." Paper presented at the 10th World Congress of the International Industrial Relations Association Annual Meetings, Washington, D.C.

Chiu, S. and Lui, T. (1994). Horizontal expansion and spatial relocation: Production and employment restructuring of the electronics industry in Hong Kong. Unpublished manuscript, Department of Sociology, Chinese University of Hong Kong.

Cole, R. E. (1989). "Strategies for Learning: Small-Group Activities in American, Japanese, and Swedish Industry." Berkeley: University of California Press.

Colclough, G. and Tolbert, C. M. II. (1992). "Work in the Fast Lane: Flexibility, Divisions of Labor, and Inequality in High-Tech Industries." Albany: State University of New York Press.

Deyo, F. (1989). "Beneath the Miracle: Labor Subordination in the New Asian Industrialism." Berkeley: University of California Press.

Deyo, F. (1992). The political economy of social policy formation: East Asia's newly industrialized countries, *in* "States and Development in the Asian Pacific Rim" (R. Appelbaum and J. Henderson, Eds.), pp. 289–306. Newbury Park, CA: Sage Publications.

Deyo, F. (1995). Human resource strategies and industrial restructuring in Thailand, *in* "Industrialization and Labor Relations" (S. Frenkel and J. Harrod, Eds.), pp. 23–36. Ithaca: ILR Press.

Deyo, F. (Ed.). (1996). "Social Reconstructions of the World Automobile Industry." Basingstoke, England: Macmillan.

Deyo, F. (1997, February). Labor and post-Fordist industrial restructuring in East and Southeast Asia. *Work and Occupations* **24** (1), 97–118.

Doner, R. (1991). "Driving a Bargain: Automobile Industrialization and Japanese Firms in Southeast Asia." Berkeley: University of California Press.

Europa World Yearbook. (1995). London: Europa Publications Ltd.

Frenkel, S. (Ed.). (1993). "Organized Labor in the Asia–Pacific Region." Ithaca: ILR Press.

Frenkel, S. (1993). Variations in patterns of trade unionism: A synthesis, *in* "Organized Labor in the Asia–Pacific Region" (S. Frenkel, Ed.), pp. 309–346. Ithaca: ILR Press.

Frenkel, S. and Harrod, J. (Eds.). (1995). "Industrialization and Labor Relations." Ithaca: ILR Press.

Frenkel, S., Hong, H.-C. and Lee, B.-L. (1993). The resurgence and fragility of trade unions in Taiwan, *in* "Organized Labor in the Asia–Pacific Region" (S. Frenkel, Ed.). Ithaca: ILR Press.

Friedman, D. (1988). "The Misunderstood Miracle: Industrial Development and Political Change in Japan." Ithaca: Cornell University Press.

Gereffi, G. (1990). Paths of industrialization: An overview, *in* "Manufacturing Miracles" (G. Gereffi and D. Wyman, Eds.), pp. 3–31. Princeton: Princeton University Press.

Gereffi, G. and Hamilton, G. (1996, October 3–6). "Commodity Chains and Embedded Networks: The Economic Organization of Global Capitalism." Paper presented at The International Conference on Economic Governance and Flexible Production in East Asia, National Tsing Hua University, Hsingchu, Taiwan.

Hill, R. C. and Fujita, K. (1996, October 3–6). "Economic Governance and Flexible Production: matsushita in Southeast Asia." Paper presented at The International Conference on Econommic Governance and Flexible Production in East Asia, National Tsing Hua University, Hsingchu, Taiwan.

Herzenberg, S. (1996). Regulatory frameworks and development in the North American auto industry, *in* "Social Reconstructions of the World Automobile Industry" (F. Deyo, Ed.). Basingstoke, England: Macmillan.

Hollingsworth, J. R. and Streeck, W. (1994). Countries and sectors: Concluding remarks on performance, convergence, and competitiveness, *in* "Governing Capitalist Economies" (J. R. Hollingsworth, P. C. Schmitter and W. Streeck, Eds.). New York: Oxford University Press.

International Labour Organization. (1995). "World Labor Report 1995." Geneva: ILO.

International Labour Organization. (1995). "World Employment 1995." Geneva: ILO.

Kenney, M. and Florida, R. (1993). "Beyond Mass Production: The Japanese System and its Transfer to the U.S." New York: Oxford University Press.

Kim, H.-J. (1993). The Korean union movement in transition, *in* "Organized Labor in the Asia-Pacific Region" (S. Frenkel, Ed.), pp. 133–161. Ithaca: ILR Press.

Kim, T. (1995). Human resource management for production workers in large Korean manufacturing enterprises, *in* "Industrialization and Labor Relations" (Frenkel and Harrod, Eds.), pp. 216–235. Ithaca: ILR Press.

Koo, H. (1994, March 24–27). "Middle Classes and the Emerging Civil Society in South Korea." Paper presented at the Annual Meeting of the Association for Asian Studies, Boston.

Kuruvilla, S. (1994, January 3–5). "Industrialization Strategy and IR Policy in Malaysia and the Philippines: Implications for Comparative Industrial Relations," *in* Proceedings of the Forty-Sixth Annual Meeting, pp. 222–230. Industrial Relations Research Association, Boston.

Kuruvilla, S. (1995). Industrialization strategy and industrial relations policy in Malaysia, *in* "Industrialization and Labor Relations" (Frenkel and Harrod, Eds.), pp. 37–63. Ithaca: ILR Press.

Lee, J. and Park, Y.-B. (1995). Employment, labour standards and economic development in Taiwan and Korea. *Labour: Review of Labour Economics and Industrial Relations*. Special Issue, S223–S242.

Leggett, C. (1993). Corporatist trade unionism in Singapore, *in* "Organized Labor in the Asia-Pacific Region" (S. Frenkel, Ed.), pp. 223–246. Ithaca: ILR Press.

Levin, D. and Chiu, S. (1993). Dependent capitalism, a colonial state, and marginal unions: The case of Hong Kong, *in* "Organized Labor in the Asia-Pacific Region" (S. Frenkel, Ed.), pp. 187–222. Ithaca: ILR Press.

Lui, T. and Chiu, S. (1996, October 3–6). "Economic Restructuring Under Unorganized Industrialism." Paper presented at The International Conference on Economic Governance and Flexible Production in East Asia, National Tsing Hua University, Hsingchu, Taiwan.

Ofreneo, R. E. (1995). "The Changing Terrains for Trade Union Organizing." Unpublished manuscript, School of Labor and Industrial Relations, University of the Philippines.

Ofreneo, R. E. (1994). The labour market, protective labour institutions and economic growth in the Philippines, *in* "Workers, Institutions and Economic Growth in Asia" (G. Rodgers, Ed.), pp. 255–301. Geneva: International Institute for Labour Studies.

Pan, M. (1996, October 3–6). "Technology, Institutions, and Governance Structures: Sectoral Differences in Taiwan's Manufacturing production Networks." Paper presented at The International Conference on Economic Governance and Flexible Production in East Asia, National Tsing Hua University, Hsingchu, Taiwan.

Rajasekaran, G. (1993). Look East policy: Successful in which way?, *in* "Trade Unions in NIC's" (Wehmhorner, Ed.), pp. 24–28.

Rasiah, R. (1996, October 3–6). "Government-Business Coordination and Operative Flexibility: Electronics Transationals and Linkages in Malaysia." Paper presented at The International Conference on Economic Governance and Flexible Production in East Asia, National Tsing Hua University, Hsingchu, Taiwan.

Rasiah, R. (1994). Flexible production systems and local machine tool subcontracting: Case of electronics components transnationals in Malaysia. *Cambridge Journal of Economics* **18**.

Rodan, G. (1993). Preserving the one-party state in contemporary Singapore, *in* "Southeast Asia in the 1990's: Authoritarianism, Democracy, and Capitalism" (K. Hewison, R. Robison and G. Rodan, Eds.), pp. 77–108. London: Allen and Unwin.

Rodgers, R. A. and Yit-Yeng, J. W. (1995). "Transferring Japanese Manufacturing Methods to Singapore." Working Papers Series #95-10. Faculty of Business Administration, National University of Singapore.

Sabel, C. (1989). Flexible specialization and regional development, *in* "Reversing Industrial Decline" (P. Hirst and J. Zeitlin, Eds.). London: Berg.

Sabel, C. (1995, Winter). Bootstrapping reform: Rebuilding firms, the welfare state, and unions. *Politics and Society.*

Scott, A. J. (1992, July). The Roepke Lecture in Economic Geography: The collective order of flexible production agglomerations: Lessons for local economic development policy and strategic choice. *Economic Geography* **68**, 3, 219–233.

Siengthai, S. (1988). Thai-Hino Industry Co., Ltd., *in* International Labour Office, Case Studies in Labour-Management Cooperation for Productivity Improvement, pp. 265–308. Bangkok: ILO.

Song, H. K. (1993). After the struggle: Labor unions in the politics of liberalization in South Korea, *in* "Trade Unions in NIC's" (A. Wehmhorner, Ed.), pp. 60–73.

Standing, G. (1989). The growth of external labour flexibility in a nascent NIC: Malaysian labor flexibility survey (MLFS). World Employment Programme Research Working Paper #35. Geneva: ILO.

Streeck, W. (1990). "The Social Foundations for Diversified Quality Production." Mimeo, Department of Sociology, University of Wisconsin, Madison.

Wall Street Journal. (1996, August 21). "Singapore's Economy May Lose Its Juice," p. A10.

Wang, H. (1996, October 3–6). "Family or Business? Contradictions of Social Values and Market Principles." Paper presented at The International Conference on Economic Governance and Flexible Production in East Asia, National Tsing Hua University, Hsingchu, Taiwan.

Womack, J. P., Jones, D. T., and Roos, D. (1990). "The Machine That Changed the World." New York: Rawson Associates.

Wong, P.-K. (1996, October 3–6). "Supply Infrastructure for Flexible Production: The Case of Hard Disk Drive Industry in Singapore." Paper presented at The International Conference on Economic Governance and Flexible Production in East Asia, National Tsing Hua Universisty, Hsingchu, Taiwan.

World Almanac, 1995 (1994). Mahwah, NJ: Funk and Wagnalls Corporation.

World Bank. (1995). World Development Report. New York: Oxford University Press.

Zuesongtham, S. (1993). Trade union struggle in Thailand: A cycle of defeat, *in* "Trade Unions in NIC's" (A. Wehmhorner, Ed.), pp. 17–23.

CHAPTER 8

Crisis in Korea and the IMF Control

Su-Hoon Lee
Kyungnam University
Seoul, South Korea

As in a drama, the once highly lauded Korean "miracle" became a mirage when the Korean government announced its request for an International Monetary Fund (IMF) bailout on November 13, 1997. Like a contagion, financial crisis spread through the economies of Southeast Asia beginning in the summer 1997. Most thought that Korea[1] would be robust, but to the surprise of many, it also fell.

As early as the summer of 1996, the rather unexpectedly high trade deficit, a key macroeconomic index, sent a warning signal to key decision makers in Korea. Many warned of the seriousness of the impending economic crisis in Korea, but no one truly anticipated such a shocking scenario.

After agonizing negotiations with the IMF delegation, the Korean government had no choice but sign a tough economic adjustment agreement on December 3, 1997, in return for a $57 billion rescue fund. Before coming to Seoul to sign the agreement—demanding "maximum efforts" from the Korean government—Michel Camdessus said in Kuala Lumpur "things will never be the same again" (*The Korea Times,* 1997, Dec. 4) in Korea. His statement is threateningly insightful. Indeed, after the implementation of the IMF package things will never be the same in Korea. The application of the orthodox IMF program predicates a fundamental and far-reaching social change in Korea.

[1] By Korea, we are referring to South Korea.

The Four Asian Tigers: Economic Development and the Global Political Economy

This chapter presents a synopsis of the causes of the crisis in Korea and speculates about some of the major impacts of the IMF intervention. Analyses and commentaries of the Asian crisis by Western scholars and journalists already abound. Local scholars have already begun to discuss the IMF control of Korean economic policies. This paper is the first of its kind on the IMF control written in English by a local scholar.

Western observers tend to view the Korean crisis as a financial shakeup—a problem of temporary illiquidity. The prevailing view is that the "fundamentals" of the Korean economy are solid and thus if the current financial crisis is handled properly, the Korean economy will bounce back and resume its past growth trajectory (*The Economist,* 1997). They perceive it to be a currency crisis or a financial crisis brought about by financial market failure or governmental policy mismanagement. Of course, the Korean economy has experienced a currency crisis. The financial sector abnormalities were grave enough to make the entire economy vulnerable to external viccisitudes.

However, its causes are deeper and more complex. The Korean crisis has been a long time in the making. The true roots of the current crisis lie within the very development model that provided Korea with the miracle. What is happening now is the unravelling of the development model (Hart-Landsberg, 1998). In other words, the world-market dependent, state-led, *chaebol*-centered model of development has lost its steam. This chapter focuses on what went wrong with the development model. In doing so, it will include a discussion of anomalies in the financial sector that have been generated and deepened by the development model and the short-term mismanagement of policies or "human errors." Along these lines, it will argue that the Korean economy is in a transition toward a new development model.[2]

I. THE STRUCTURAL DIMENSION: THE MODEL

The condensed and unprecedented economic growth through high-speed industrialization in Korea was sustained by a particular model of development that in essence is world-market dependent, state-led and *chaebol*-centered. This model was extremely effective from its take-off until the late 1980s. The world-market—primarily the United States—was favorable to Korean products; state coordination and intervention were very effective; and large business groups received the benefits of markets of scale domestically and a competitive edge in the international market. Of course, there are various explanations for the miracle, (So and Chiu, 1995, part 1) but this is not the place to debate the validity of different explanations.

Instead, the task here is to explain why such a powerful model lost its steam in the late 1980s and resulted in the current crisis. Policymakers in Korea and the

---

[2]To some, this is precisely what the term crisis means.

Korean people had a great deal of confidence in their development model. They believed that it would continue in spite of the warnings of skeptics (Krugman, 1994) and critics (Hart-Landsberg, 1993; Bello and Rosenfeld, 1990; Deyo, 1989; Eder, 1996; Smith and Lee, 1990). Because of this shared belief, key economic actors in Korea neglected serious reform even when the model showed signs of fatigue and perhaps exhaustion.

Reform or structural adjustments were protracted because a short-term solution was provided from the outside. For instance, when serious difficulties arose in the 1970s, due to oil shocks, they were alleviated or solved by the construction boom in the Middle East and the inflow of the petrodollars. In the 1960s, the aid, military assistance, and loans arranged by the United States contributed substantially to the formative stage of capital accumulation in Korea (Cumings, 1987). In the mid-1980s, the strong yen was one of the key factors that buttressed the record-high trade surplus in the period from 1986 through 1989. Throughout this rising phase, the United States provided Korean producers with privileged access to its market, not to mention political and financial support for the growth model of South Korea. Japan willingly sold its technology, components, and machinery to South Korea's large manufacturers. Protective policies of the Korean government of its industries were benignly neglected by the United States. For example, the rapid development of the Korean automobile industry is inexplicable unless these factors are properly taken into consideration (Kim and Lee, 1994).

Generally, dependence on the international market represents a constraint or control on the national economy. It is more often than not an impediment to sustained growth, as was evidenced by many Latin American economies. Contrastingly, in the case of South Korea during this phase, dependence on the world-market provided a great opportunity. The geopolitical position of South Korea at the forefront of the "Free World" in the Cold War era was of great value to the United States and Japan. The geostrategic value of South Korea was instrumental to the containment policy of the United States. Under these circumstances, the Korean model of development worked (Palat, 1993).

However, the world scene changed greatly in the late 1980s. The Cold War rivalry melted away and eventually ended in 1989. As a consequence, the geopolitical value of South Korea decreased substantially. The United States had to divert its geostrategic concerns to other areas of the world such as the former socialist countries of Eastern Europe and the Middle East in order to consolidate the unified capitalist world market. U.S. intervention in internal warfares in Bosnia and in the Gulf War in the early 1990s are examples of this.

Coincidentally, during the same period, South Korea ran its first and only sizeable surpluses. The export success during the period between 1986 and 1989 forced the existing trade relationship between Korea and the United States to enter a new stage. The United States began to see Korea as a trade competitor, especially as it suffered chronic twin debt. It began to withdraw the privileged market access previously given to Korean exports and instead pressed Korea to open its markets to U.S. goods. Korea was forced to open its service and agricultural markets. The trade relationship turned into a truly bilateral one between the two countries. Trade disputes between the two "blood brothers" frequently surfaced. Anti-American sentiments by Korean students were expressed. The United States quickly became skeptical of its long-time beneficiary.

The export success of this period also threatened Japanese producers. They began to withdraw key inputs from Korean *chaebol*. Japanese firms stopped the transfer of industrial technology to Korean manufacturers. Export competition from Japanese firms located in the Southeast Asian countries severely undermined the competitive edge of Korean manufactured goods.

Because of these external and internal developments, we argue that the late 1980s were the turning point in which the opportunity structure of the world market became a "pressure structure" for which Korea was unprepared. Worse still, the latecomers in Southeast Asia and China began to compete with Korean products in the world market, eroding the conventional Korean share in the world commodity market (Hart-Landsberg, 1998). Korean products began to lose their competitive edge because of their higher costs of production. In the past, labor was effectively repressed by the state to keep wages under control. But after the mid-1980s, in part because of the export success and in part due to political liberalization, wages increased significantly. The price of land was notoriously high (Kang, 1996, 323). For world-market dependent Korea, the late 1980s meant the end of the rising phase and the beginning of the declining phase.

The state-led strategy also began to show its limitations. The once highly effective and powerful intervention of the state in the private sector gradually turned into high costs and inefficacy. The greatly enlarged size of the economy could no longer be managed efficiently by the state. State intervention meant a curb on fair competition and the control of financial institutions meant the distorted and arbitrary distribution of valuable resources. The government funneled money from banks to large firms. Institutions such as regulations and practices became barriers to the smooth operation of business. They were an impediment to the implementation of fair rules of the game in the market. The market discipline had no space to operate. Through the intermediary of the financial sector, a predatory symbiosis between the government and business was set into play and raised social costs (Kim, 1997). The developmental state became the predatory state.

Military regimes that lacked popular legitimacy relied upon economic growth as their source of legitimacy. They were caught in the growth trap. They had to sustain the high rate of growth to maintain their regime. However, during the 1980s, the populace started to become skeptical of their state. In the 1990s, they withdrew their belief in the state as the provider of protection and welfare. Something of a "legitimacy crisis" occurred. The key to success in the past years became something the people distrusted and even abhorred. It is an irony that the much heralded civilian government of Kim Young Sam laid an irrevocable blow to the general public's image of the state.

The *chaebol*-centered side of the development model displayed typical rent-seeking behavior regime involving the government and the financial sector in tripartite symbiotic alliances with the *chaebol*. In the regime, the government prevents competition and promotes monopoly through favorable loans to the *chaebol*. They believed that the government would never let them go out of business because they were one of the core composite agencies of the development model that the state tried to implement. If threatened with bankruptcy, they believed they would be rescued by "cooperation loans" arranged by the government. They learned the rule that if you are not going into bankruptcy, you should increase your size. "Too big to fail" was a given rule of the game (Chung, 1998, 76). Thus companies made every attempt to expand and enlarge their enterprises. With nearly unlimited financial assistance from banks, they were able to expand enormously. This is the very mechanism by which the *chaebol* was formed in the first place.

The low interest rate loans channeled to the *chaebol* under the tripartite alliance regime contributed to the creation of bubbles. Under this regime, the companies did not bother promoting the efficiency of production. Even without high value-added production activities, these conglomerates could cash in large rents through speculative activities. The *chaebol* was the major culprit for implanting the high inefficiency structure which over the years has eroded the competitive edge of Korean products in the international market. I will explain how this happened.

Once you grow to be a *chaebol,* you are free from bankruptcy because individual companies within the *chaebol* structure are knitted through cross repayment guarantees. A nonprofitable or marginal company can survive because of this institution within the *chaebol* structure. This replaces the principle of the survival of the fittest with "the survival of the largest," violating all the conventional rules of the market and normal business practices. Of course, this is precisely what monopoly capital means. Small and medium-size companies are at a great disadvantage. They simply cannot compete in the market.

Another institution that the *chaebol* succeeded in establishing was cross investment between member companies of a particular *chaebol*. This allows them to expand and penetrate into all kinds of business enterprises without the necessary capital. Within the *chaebol*, Company A's money can be used for Company B's new entry into a business and vice versa. This mechanism provides the *chaebol* with an unlimited opportunity to expand their business without adequate investment capital. In a way, the high-debt financial structure of Korean *chaebol* is an outcome of this mechanism. This also means that a handful of *chaebol* leaders can exercise monopolistic management on the basis of a relatively small size of ownership. This is an exclusive exercise of management power. The majority of shareholders are excluded from exercising their ownership.

Decision making is generally a one-man show, unchecked and unsupervised. Needless to say, authoritarian decision making can generate grave consequences. A case in point is the entry of Samsung into automobile manufacturing. It is often noted in Korea that the decision was influenced by Chairman Lee Kun-hee's personal interest in cars. The automobile manufacturing industry in Korea was already known for overinvestment, predicating business troubles in terms of both domestic and international demands. Samsung had to pour in money to build a local assembly line in Pusan at the jeopardy of the survival of the entire group. Overinvestment and overlapping investment by the *chaebol* in automobile, petrochemical, semiconductor, and shipbuilding industries were one of the main causes of today's crisis (Chung, 1998, 84)

Overinvestment led to oversupply. The stock of export items began to pile up. This caused a reduction in the prices of export items. An example of this was the sharp decline in the price of semiconductor chips in the international market in 1996. This was the main cause of that year's unexpectedly large trade deficit, which in turn signaled the current crisis.

Korea needed a sound and balanced industrial policy, but the powerful *chaebol* were in a position to make their own investment decisions. From a national industrial policy point of view, overlapping investment meant taking scarce resources away from investments in infrastructure development or research and development (R&D). Underdeveloped infrastructure became one of the high cost factors of the Korean economy in the 1990s. Today, Koreans belatedly deplore their neglect of technological advancement.

In this vein, we like to highlight the *chaebol's* and government's mismanagement of the aforementioned large trade gains in the period between 1986 and 1989 period. The *chaebol* used their profits for speculative rather than productive investments. The government failed to coordinate the *chaebol* to channel their profits into R&D. Infrastructure development was much needed, but both the government and business did not care to bother. Instead they poured their gains in real estate, pushing the prices of land and housing up, and causing a bubble. In retrospect, this period was the right time for the Korean government to revalue its currency and the right time for the business sector, especially the *chaebol*, to launch restructuring.

The third mechanism that the *chaebol* used to expand and protect their companies was the use of inside transactions. Companies within a *chaebol* sell and buy each other's products. The inside transaction mechanism can be used to rescue troubled individual companies in the group. It can also be used as a blockade against sales from a quality firm which produces the same item. It can put healthy and profitable small and medium-size firms into the subcontracting regime of a particular *chaebol*.

Through these institutions and mechanisms, the *chaebol* dominated the market and the entire economy of Korea. Although the *chaebol* played a key role in the high-speed industrialization during the rising phase, the long-term damages to the economic and industrial structures are too grave to overlook. Under the auspices of the government and by the assistance of the financial sector, they distorted and disarticulated the Korean economy. Market abnormalities have continued to widen and deepen.

For these reasons, the *chaebol* should have been restructured a long while ago. On the part of the *chaebol* themselves, there was no reason to launch a voluntary reform because the status quo served their interests. The pressure had to come from the government. However, the Korean government, once referred to as "the maker and breaker of the *chaebol*," lost its power vis-a-vis the *chaebol*. The reversal of the power relationship became obvious from the late 1980s, when the *chaebol* began to neglect what the government told them to do and began instead to demand the government take a hands-off approach. The balance of power between the government and the *chaebol* was totally shaken up during the Kim Young Sam government under the slogan of liberalization and globalization.

Now under IMF control, the much needed *chaebol* reform is being imposed. The IMF demands transparency of the corporate financial structure through the adoption of consolidated financial statements. Cuts in "policy loans" or "cooperation loans" and government subsidies are also being abandoned. Several measures are scheduled to take effect soon to reduce the *chaebol's* high debt/equity ratios (*The Korea Times,* 1997, Dec. 4, & 1998, Feb. 5).

Domestic pressures for *chaebol* reforms are coming from all sectors of society. Kim Dae Jung, the new President of Korea, appears to be determined to press forward with *chaebol* reform. Right before his inauguration on February 25, in an interview with the German magazine, *Der Spiegel,* he made his position very clear by saying that "the era of *chaebol* is over" (*The Korea Times,* 1998, Feb. 21). Civic associations also called for chaebol reforms. Kim Dae Jung said all the prerogatives will be taken away, hinting that bank loans will no longer be an instrument that the *chaebol* utilize in their business.

In sum, the world-market dependent, state-led and *chaebol*-centered development model of Korea brought a miraculous growth to the country within a very specific geopolitical and world-market context. The timing of the take-off was right. However, as geopolitics and the world-market situation changed drastically in the late 1980s, the dependence on the world commodity market began to become a "structural squeeze." Effective state intervention gradually changed to interferences with the smooth operation of the private sector, resulting in high social costs. The motor of exports, the *chaebol*, ended up a typical rent-seeking behavior regime characterized by speculation, predatory symbiosis between the government and business, and deepening market abnormalities.

II. THE INSTITUTIONAL DIMENSION: THE FINANCIAL SECTOR

The financial sector was the intermediary in the tripartite alliances discussed above. The effectiveness of state intervention results from its control of the central bank under whose guidance and umbrella major commercial banks operated. Thus, growth was sustained in large part by low-interest "policy loans" granted to the *chaebol*. But the tight control of the financial institutions by the government deprived them of any opportunity to autonomously develop themselves.

The government controlled financial sector lost its autonomy and could not fulfill its function adequately. Korean financial institutions failed to correct imbalances in the financial market in order to minimize barriers to growth and achieve the optimal distribution of financial resources. In essence, banks lent "policy loans" to companies and managed them. Quite naturally, the financial sector could not be developed or advance its techniques under such circumstances. Korea's financial sector was underdeveloped in view of Korea's economy and its standing in the world economy. Prudence was missing. Instead, "connectionism" flourished. Procedures such as loan reviews and audits were conveniently ignored. Personal networks and connections were more influential than prudential regulations in banks.

Banks made no efforts to develop advanced business techniques because there was no incentive to do so. As long as the government was behind them, they were free from bankruptcy. The appointment of executive officers were political decisions rather than decisions based on sound personnel management principles. An individual's political connections mattered, not his qualifications. There was competition between banks, but the real competition was about maintaining strong political connections. The bank's business also greatly depended on this network of influence. For instance, increasing deposits in your bank was determined by your personal network. There was no business in the true sense of the meaning.

The development model of Korea was a high-debt model from a financial point of view. Because of the government's growth strategy, a financial structure of high corporate debt/equity ratio emerged and was consolidated. The average debt/equity ratio of the *chaebol* in Korea was four to one (Bank of Korea, 1998). This is in a stark contrast to the situation in advanced economies. Some argue that the high-debt financial structure of Korean firms had a lot to do with high savings rates (Wade and Venerosa, 1998). The reasoning is as follows. Households somehow save. The deposits are held in banks because banks are believed to be safe. Banks have to lend. Firms that have to mobilize a large amount of resources borrow from banks. The interventive government intermediates between banks and firms, and this is the way in which the tripartite alliances work. Such a high-debt financial structure requires cooperation between banks and firms, and considerable government support. When the model was in high gear, the high-debt financial structure presented no severe problem.

But very high levels of corporate debt are not immune to risks and shocks. Political unstability or a sharp rise in interest rates can shake the structure. In other words, the Korean high-debt model could only work while close collaboration between banks, firms, and the state is maintained. It has worked over the years with only a few exceptional episodes of failure.

In the late 1980s things began to unfold differently. The rough trajectory is as follows. Large-size policy loans to bigger firms—at the request of the government—tended to become nonperforming loans. In recent years, nonperforming loans piled up as corporate gross profits were not large enough to serve debt repayment. The ratio of nonperforming loans to total loans was nearly 20% (Chung, 1998, 83). This figure is incomparable to any banking system in the world. For instance, the equivalent ratio in the case of the United States is 1 or 2%. Banks became nearly insolvent as their loans became nonperforming. But the government intervened to prevent the bankruptcy of banks. The banks had to continuously lend to their customer firms to stop them from going out of business. This process formed a vicious circle that drove both banks and firms to the worst possible situation.

In the case of merchant banks, the Korean government failed to strengthen bank supervision. It removed or loosened controls on merchant banks' foreign borrowing and abandoned any coordination of borrowing and investments (*Munwha Ilbo*, 1998, Feb. 13) For the majority of merchant banks, the game rule was "high risk, high return." In pursuit of high returns, these banks borrowed heavily on a short-term basis from foreign banks or funds and lent their borrowing not only to domestic commercial banks at a higher interest rate but also to Southeast Asia, Russia, and Latin America. All of these areas were risky. For an example, Korean merchant banks bought 15% of the total Russian state bonds, recording a heavy loss (*Munwha Ilbo*, 1998, Feb. 14). Southeast Asian investors poured money into speculative activities such as real estate development projects and these failed when the crisis hit these countries in the summer of 1997, incurring a heavy loss on the part of merchant banks.

Domestic commercial banks incurred heavy losses because their loans were channeled to companies that were already highly debted and running on a deficit. Many companies went bankrupt and defaulted on their loans. As a result, merchant banks' loans to commercial banks tended to become nonperforming. Loans thus could not be called in when they had to be. It was not tight regulation but rather loose government supervision of the financial sector that triggered the currency crisis in Korea (Wade and Venerosa, 1998). As a matter of fact, the first measure taken by the Korean government after the agreement with the IMF rescue plan on December 3 was the suspension of nine troubled merchant banks' operations.

The *modus operandi* of Korean commercial and merchant banks was extremely absurd in the eyes of Westerners. In particular, the full opening of the financial market was scheduled from 1998. The foreign prospective investors' assessment of the Korean financial market was that it was hopeless and business could not be done unless unreasonable practices were abandoned. They actually demanded the reform of the financial market but with no real outcome (Feldstein, 1998). This caused the precipitation of Korea's confidence in the international financial market in 1997, which was already brought into question by some cautious outside observers.

At the heart of Korea's current crisis lies the foreign debt problem. In large part, the weakened and troubled financial sector and financial market abnormalities are attributable to the currency crash of 1997. Internationally, "Korea, Inc." is highly indebted and in order to overcome the current crisis the problem of the foreign debt should be somehow dealt with. This issue will be discussed in more detail later in the chapter.

In sum, the state-controlled financial sector was an efficient mechanism for channeling valuable resources to where they were needed during the early decades of high-speed industrialization. The policy or cooperation loans given to large firms were instrumental in the export drive. However, persistent intervention and control of the financial sector by the state caused abnormalities in the financial market. There was no space for the development of financial techniques responsive to the much enlarged and diversified Korean economy. The lag between the advancement of Korea's economy and its underdeveloped financial sector was obvious. Since the late 1980s, global financial capital has wanted Korea to open its financial markets and reform its practices of the tripartite symbiosis. But the financial sector failed to restructure itself. This was perhaps due to the maintenance of Korea's high debt model of development.

III. THE SHORT-TERM POLICY DIMENSION: HUMAN ERRORS

The early signs of the current crisis emerged in the summer of 1996 when the trade deficit was unpredictably large. In 1996, the current account deficit amounted to $23.7 billion. In an economy that is export-oriented and operates on high debt, the deficit was severe enough to alarm economists and decision makers in Korea. Additional signs of danger included the bankruptcies of a number of the *chaebol*. The myth of "too big to fail" also collapsed.

In January 1997, the Hanbo loan scandal broke out, bankrupting the conglomerate. The Hanbo group went bankrupt because of its overambitious and unfeasible investment in a large steel mill project. The bankruptcies of other *chaebol* such as Jinro, Daenong, Kia, and New Core followed like a contagion. This meant that the high-debt model of development lost its vigor. Instead of reforming the economic structure, policymakers protracted the crisis and in essence enlarged the bubble. During this process, concern by foreign investors about the creditworthiness of Korean firms and banks was increased.

The prevailing diagnosis by economists during this period of protraction however was that the macroeconomic index was healthy and that the fundamentals of the Korean economy were solid. This view was shared by the key decision makers within the government, including the president. Many Western analysts added to the optimism by showing similar diagnoses. The prognosis thereby was that the Korean economy had hit the bottom of its business cycles and thus would soon enter a rising phase. Government-affiliated research institutions provided the government with the same diagnosis and prognosis. In other words, economists, state-run research institutes, and the government decision makers all failed to read the warning signs of disaster.

The fatal blow came from the way key decision makers within the government and top business leaders of the Korean economy handled the "Kia incident" of September 1997. Kia Motors, Inc., one of three major Korean automobile manufacturers, was about to become bankrupt because of serious financial troubles. The conventional government response had always been to prepare a large-size rescue loan from major banks through government intervention to avoid the grave and far-reaching shock of bankruptcy. To the surprise of many, the minister of finance and economy emphasized that government intervention would cease in business in order to let market principles come into play. The chairman of Kia rebutted by stating that it was unfair and that the minister's intent was to "kill" his company, and thereby enabling it to be sold to a third party. The third party then was widely believed to be Samsung, which entered the auto industry belatedly and was thus experiencing difficulties. The minister allegedly had personal interests in helping Samsung.

In any case, the tug-of-war continued for more than 2 months. During this period, the Korean economy suffered an enormous loss. Most secrets of the "Korea, Inc." operation were unveiled. The stock market plunged and both foreign and domestic investors experienced extreme grief and disillusionment. Confidence in Korea crashed. Nervous foreign investors began to call in their assets from Korean financial markets. Korean banks had difficulties in borrowing from abroad. Korean banks were hemorrhaging. The overseas branches of the *chaebol* also had difficulties in borrowing. The merchant banks' investments in Southeast Asia were nonperforming as the economies in the region already were in default. As is well-known now, about $27 billion worth of short-term foreign loans were due to mature in early 1998. All of these factors combined and contributed to the rapid depletion of foreign reserves.

After the unfolding of the Hanbo loan scandal, in which some of his trusted aides and his son were involved, Kim Young Sam lost his dignity and power as president—he lost his legitimacy and popular support. His leadership, already weak, totally disappeared. The mismanagement of the continually worsening economic and currency situation by his economic policy team was obvious. The lack of an adequate short-term financial policy, coupled with the misperception of his management team, was a direct cause of the currency crisis.

Like Mexico in 1994, the political instability in 1997 played no minor role in catalyzing the economic crisis. Korean politics has been chronically unstable in the sense that it negates even the most modest prediction. Prediction becomes an even more difficult and frustrating issue during the succession of power. Without exception, the succession of power in the past has caused great instability and curtailed economic activities. The anticipation of the 1997 December presidential election was uncertain and not qualitatively different from past elections. In that sense, political instability and unpredictability in the fall of 1997 were sources of disturbances that hampered local businessmen in their business operations and stopped foreign would-be investors from taking any action.

Disturbances in the foreign currency market appeared from the time of the Hanbo loan scandal. Foreign creditors began to call in their loans. During the more than 2 month-long tug-of-war between Kia's top managers and the government, foreign creditors speeded up their call-in. In order to stabilize the foreign currency market and to defend the won, the government released a large amount of dollars from the foreign reserves. The result was a failure in defending the won and the drastic depletion of foreign reserves. During 1997, the government wasted $26 billion in its vain attempt to stabilize the exchange rate (*Munwha Ilbo,* 1998, Feb. 16).

IV. IMPACTS OF IMF CONTROL

As a result of the drastic devaluation of the Korean won against the U.S. dollar, the per capita GDP plunged to $6,600 (*The Korea Times,* 1998, Feb. 21). Recall that in 1995, Koreans self-complacently saluted the surpassing of the per capita GNP of $10,000. Now almost everyone admits that the won has been overvalued. Like many other countries, Korea too stood on a bubble. The protracted currency devaluation enlarged the bubble. It only burst when the foreign reserves dried up and the IMF was called in as a cure. But the devaluation brought harsh realities to the Korean population in general. All of a sudden, the standard of living was lowered substantially. Furthermore, the combination of rising prices and falling income on the part of the majority of the population predicates a difficult life for some years to come.

Undoubtedly, IMF control of the economy will have long-lasting and deep economic, social, and political impact on Korean society. Recall Camdessus's discomforting prognosis that was quoted in the beginning of this chapter. The long-term consequences are unpredictable. Here we will discuss some of the short- to mid-term impacts and speculate about the long-term trajectory of the Korean economy and society.

Even such well-known IMF specialists as Sachs and Stiglitz (Sachs, 1997; Stiglitz, 1997) criticized the application of the IMF's harsh austerity program to Asian economies, including Korea. In their view, the IMF prescription is an overdose and may kill the patient instead of resuscitating him, implying that the package will push the Korean economy into severe recession. This position appears to be well-taken.

Tightened fiscal and monetary policies have seemed to bring more troubles than solutions in the Korean crisis (Feldstein, 1998). Cutting demand and liquidity in the Korean situation drives the value of most firms down if not driving them into bankruptcy. The IMF demands that the Korean government maintain the current high interest rate in order to stabilize the foreign currency market and defend its currency. In spite of the high interest rate, the Korean won is free-floating. There is no sign of the won's stabilization. Unbearably high interest rates, coupled with the tightening lending policies of commercial banks that are struggling to meet the Bank of International Settlements (BIS) criterion, puts a great strain on business firms, households, and individuals. If the crisis occurred because of illiquidity, the IMF prescription for the crisis would worsen the problem

Business bankruptcies are inevitable but alarmingly high and widespread. The industrial base of the Korean economy is crumbling as a consequence of the IMF's demand for high interest rates. If this continues, the once solid "fundamentals" will be substantially weakened. Restoration of confidence will then mean little because the Korean economy would have already lost its industrial base for the highly aspired "second take-off." It should be emphasized that the real strength of Korea's economy is to be found in its manufacturing base and nothing else. Now the manufacturing base is crumbling as a result of the IMF's strong austerity package. Concerns that the Korean economy is losing its foundation are not groundless.

The most common negative consequences of IMF control have appeared only 2 months after the implementation of the package. They include high unemployment, high inflation, dissolution of society, political instability, and the loss of hope.[3] None of these is an easy issue to deal with, but perhaps the most devastating issue seems to be high unemployment.

A surge in the number of jobless is an agonizing social issue in Korea today. The legalization of layoffs, in theory, provides employers with an easy way to cut costs. Restructuring business firms primarily means the downsizing of personnel. For years, employers have persistently argued that economic difficulties in Korea are a result of the high cost structure, in which high wages are frequently listed at the top.

Needless to say, flexibility in the labor market signals hard times for workers. Lower wages and worsened working and living conditions are ahead. More serious is the fact that the East Asian employment culture is not used to layoffs. Today, no one expects life-long employment in which the East Asian corporate culture once took pride. The society is not prepared to adequately deal with massive unemployment.

---

[3]The consensual tone of the Korean mass media and political elites tends to regard the case of the IMF package in Mexico in 1995 as a model to emulate as a way to "graduate" from IMF control. But some analysts of the Mexican case emphasize similar negative consequences in spite of the tepid recovery (Pastor, 1997).

Because it is far from a welfare state, the government is totally unprepared for this emerging social issue.

The trilateral agreement[4] among labor, business, and the government highlights the establishment of a 5 trillion won "unemployment fund" in return for the trade unions' concession to the legalization of layoffs and worker dispatch systems (*The Korea Times*, 1998, Feb. 7). However, one of the three fundamental principles of the IMF program is fiscal austerity. In addition, the base for taxation is rapidly shrinking. The issue is how to realistically mobilize revenue for such a fund from an eroding tax base and a deficit fiscal structure. Furthermore, the more radical and militant wing of the trade union organization is negating the agreement. When they withdrew the scheduled general strike on February 7 to demonstrate their discontent, they demanded a 10 trillion won unemployment fund instead of the 5 trillion won fund initially agreed upon.

The problem of unemployment is even more serious when we take into account the projected zero or minus growth in 1998. Mass unemployment is easily foreseeable. The impact of chilled economic activity is already showing. According to official data recently released by the Office of Statistics, the unemployment rate in January 1998 rose to 4.5%, the highest rate in 11 years (*The Korea Times*, 1998, Feb. 28). As of the end of February 1998, the number of the jobless officially neared one million. The exact statistics on the unemployment are unknown. But many predict about two million people will be unemployed this year. It may also be noted that flexibility of the labor market is not acquired through social consensus and thus represents a main source of social disintegration and future social conflicts.

Korean society is now rapidly deteriorating. Economic troubles are shaking its foundations. The present rampage of global and local capital escalates social decay. Traditionally strong social bonds among people of Korea were already severely damaged during the course of the high-speed industrialization and urbanization. The social safety net that should replace the traditional communal solidarity is yet to be constructed. Under such circumstances, the neoliberal assault on society will result in widespread pain and disillusionment. In this regard, a fundamental task that would confront the Korean people during or after the implementation of IMF program should be the maintenance and/or restoration of society.

Symptoms of social disintegration are beginning to appear. One of the classical tenets of social psychology is that stress and frustration lead to violence. Distraught Koreans increasingly show behaviors that support this tenet. Crimes

[4]By the initiative of Kim Dae Jung, then the president-elect, the "Committee of Labor-Business-Government" was formed on January 14, 1998. The IMF stressed that layoffs were a key to winning rollovers of Korea's short-term foreign debt obligations. Kim agreed with the IMF position, but legalizing layoffs was a very sensitive social and political issue. He wanted it to be done through a socially justified mechanism. Labor union representatives together with entrepreneurial and major political party representatives all participated in the Committee. The main objective of the Committee was to reach an agreement on legalizing layoffs. After a chain of panel meetings lasting more than 20 days, the tripartite Committee announced its package agreement, in which labor unions consented to layoffs (*The Korea Times*, 1998, Jan. 15 and Feb 7).

allegedly related to the IMF "squeeze" are frequently reported on the news. Petty theft, murder, suicide, arson, bank robbery, and embezzlement appear to be increasing. Empirically, one can not prove these crimes are attributable to the IMF control, but it is safe to argue that increasing social pathology in Korea today is directly or indirectly related to difficulties imposed on the population caused by the IMF's tightening program.

Korea has been praised for its comparatively equal social structure. Its growth with equity has been frequently envied by Latin Americans; however, in the 1990s the distribution of income began to be skewed in favor of the wealthy. Even before the IMF control, Korea tended to ride on the worldwide trend of polarization because of the neoliberal assault on the society. Now the IMF control will surely accelerate the worsening of the income distribution. This is easy to understand. The high interest rates, reduced taxes, deregulation of foreign currency, and so on will all work to the benefit of the wealthy. In contrast, skyrocketing prices, growing household debt servicing due to high interest rates, and decreasing incomes will impose a harsh life on the majority of the population. The white collar workers' life will rapidly deteriorate. The lower strata will have to struggle to survive. So troubles that rise from the IMF control are unequally distributed.

There is a strong notion in Korean culture that troubles and pain should be equally shared by the entire populace. Labor, business, and the government should bear equally the burden of the socioeconomic impacts of IMF control. The "grand accord" agreed on February 6, 1998, by the tripartite commission—of labor, business, and the government—in theory ensures an even distribution of pain. But the reality unfolds very differently.

Pain-sharing is likely to become mere rhetoric. The consent to legalize layoffs by labor union representatives in the tripartite commission is irrevocable. The National Assembly hurriedly passed the new labor bill that legalized layoffs. Labor made its share of concessions; however, the government is unlikely to restructure itself in spite of the strong intent of the president. The bureaucracy has an inertia that is structurally difficult to reform and the *chaebol* pretend to seek reform but actually resist the demands of the government. This can only add to the anxiety of the people who are already distraught.

As mentioned earlier, Korea's foreign debt is a national and international issue of enormous importance. Statistics on the size of the debt vary, depending on the source. A conservative estimate as of the end of February 1998 indicates that the total amount of Korea's foreign debt surpassed $200 billion. This figure is alarmingly high in terms of the estimated 1998 GDP of $312.1 billion. (*The Korea Times,* 1998, Feb. 21). The size of the foreign debt is more than threatening to the Korean economy and to the Korean people. Financing the debt becomes a major task. For instance, according to the February 17 renegotiation between the Korean government and the IMF, the current account surplus is projected to be $8 billion in 1998 (*Munwha Ilbo,* 1998, Feb. 18). There is simply no way to pay the interest charges, let alone the principle.

The focus of Korea's foreign debt policy today is not aimed at solving the problem but instead at renewing or extending the payment of debts. Since the renewal or extensions are negotiated through interest rate hikes, this policy simply increases the size of the debt. This is precisely what took place in New York in January 1998 during the rescheduling negotiations between the Korean government delegation and foreign creditors. The matured $27 billion short-term loans were transformed into mid- to long-term with increased interest rates. Similar rescheduling negotiations will follow in the future, resulting in an increase in the debt.

The policy also desperately seeks additional sources for borrowing, leaving the conditions of the borrowing a tertiary issue. In a high debt/equity system such as Korea, firms have to use much of their gross profits to pay interest charges. A significant rise in interest rates may not be able to be met out of profits, in which case it will have to be recapitalized into debt. Indeed, this has been what has happened to the majority of Korean firms. In a high debt/equity system, the high interest rate policy demanded by the IMF will snowball in terms of debt. It will accelerate the indebtedness of the corporate sector and the aggregate debt of the government. The IMF rescue fund will be of no use, for it not only adds to the existing foreign debt, it also increases indebtedness. The IMF charges more than 7% interest on its rescue fund. As a result of the aforementioned conditions, the foreign debt sits at the heart of the Korean problem. It will be a major factor hindering the stabilization of the macroeconomic index, contrary to the expectation of the IMF.

The "debt trap" scenario cannot be ruled out in the case of Korea. The scenario is as follows. A debt mountain, that is, more than $200 billion, is already present. Gross surpluses in coming years are projected to fall short of interest charges. Korea will have to borrow more, and this will add to the existing debt. The country will be caught in the debt trap.

The prescribed solution to the debt crisis is very classical: increase exports, reduce imports, and induce foreign investment. This is the policy position of the new government. The validity of this policy is dubious at best and may be catastrophic at worst. If it works, it means deepening of the dependence of the Korean economy on the world market, one of the underlying causes of the current crisis. This may also lead to a catastrophe in terms of national wealth, as explained below.

The national wealth of Korea will be rapidly transferred to foreign interests. This represents the reversal of the earlier rising phase during which wealth in other countries was transferred under the name of Korea. One can think of several mechanisms in which this will occur. One is the simple transformation of private sector foreign debt to state-guaranteed debt. The government is indebted through guaranteeing private banks' short-term debt to foreign creditors in the rescheduling negotiations. This already happened in New York in January 1998. Government debt guarantees will soar as other short-term foreign debts mature and private borrowers are unable to repay. A surge in the issuance of public and state bonds for sale abroad is also a mechanism by which national wealth will come under foreign control. The Korean government will have to sell its enterprises to repay its debt. Foreign interests are pressing for the privatization of highly profitable state enterprises like Pohang Steel, Inc., and Korea Cummunications, Inc., in pursuit of their mergers and acquisitions (M&A) of privatized companies.

Another mechanism is the acquisition of Korean private enterprises, assets, and real estate by foreign investors. The Korean government is eager to attract foreign direct investments, lifting all regulating measures and providing numerous privileges such as tax breaks. The bubble has burst and the value of banks, firms, and real estate have been reduced nearly by half; foreign interests can acquire these with a modest amount of dollars and take over the right to control. Debt-laden Korea has no option but to allow and even encourage these movements. Key economic policymakers in the Kim Dae Jung government also believe that the inflow of foreign direct investment is the only solution to the current crisis.[5] Putting the actual long-term consequences of foreign direct investment aside (*The Korea Times,* 1998, Feb. 12), this policy posture will increase the take-over of Korean enterprises by foreign interests.

From a different angle, the liberalization of capital flows will doubly allow the transfer of Korean national wealth overseas. The financial market is open and liberalized, and barriers to foreign investors in the stock market have been lifted. For instance, one can list relaxation of the daily fluctuation band for stock prices, elimination of the delimiting size of stock purchase by foreign investors, and deregulation of the maximum ownership of a particular company. These are incentives that short-term foreign capital can enter and exit more easily than before. Indeed, "hedge" funds seem to enter and exit. Reportedly, the composite stock price index is now very sensitive to the operation of foreign investors (*The Korea Times,* 1998, Feb. 19).

Conversely, the relaxation of capital movements at the border means an open door policy for Koreans to take dollars overseas. In the past, this has been tightly monitored and controlled by "the foreign currency management law," which is currently being reformulated to guarantee maximal cross-border flow. Presumably, this measure too will escalate the process of transfer of Korean wealth to overseas.

V. AN ALTERNATIVE MODEL?

Unlike the prevailing or mainstream optimistic prognosis—predicting the rejuvenation of the Korean economy, this chapter presents a skeptical view of the mid- to long-term course of the Korean economy. Our view is straightforward.

---

[5]We should be reminded of the bulky empirical literature that highlights the negative long-term consequences of the increase of foreign direct investment in a dependent economy.

Most importantly, IMF structural adjustment policies will solve nothing to advance Korean economic development. Because they are "wrong" prescriptions for the Korean economy, they will do more harm than good. On the basis of our discussion in this chapter, we argue that Korea, after the IMF control, will resemble a typical Latin American country, that is, a chronically indebted and foreign capital-dependent structure in which political instability and social conflicts are juxtaposed in an escalating manner.

In Korea today, both intellectuals and lay people insist upon taking the current crisis as an opportunity, although what they mean by an "opportunity" is unclear and often confusing. Presumably, they are implying that the present time is a historical moment at which Korea collectively should be transformed and reborn. The questions then become transformed into and reborn into what? It appears that they have an alternative model of national development in mind.

Let us conclude this chapter by reflecting on the past and contemplating the future in terms of the development model of Korea. In the introduction, we argued that this is a time of transition from the existing model to an alternative model of development. We analyzed how the world-market dependent, state-led and *chaebol*-centered model lost its steam, wanting an alternative model of development. But let our position be clear. There cannot be "an" alternative model at this time of transition. There can only be "multiple" alternatives from which we may choose. Whichever alternative we will ultimately choose depends on our present collective struggles.

The conventional level of thinking to which many analysts tend to adhere is important in this vein. Suppose that this is a decisive historical moment at which we must push forward with bold and brave thinking. More than anything else, bold and brave thinking should go beyond the nation-state level. Koreans are no exception. Even if they succeeded in "inventing" an alternative model of national development, they should realize that it could work only within the larger context of regional and global economies. Capitalism is a global system. The current crises in Asia, including that in Korea, have a great deal to do with globalization and the financialization of global capital. They are not isolated episodes. Crises in Thailand, Indonesia, and Malaysia were caused by the regionalization strategy of Japanese manufacturing capital (Hart-Landsberg, 1998). Consequently, they will have grave impacts on Japanese economy because they are integral to the dynamics of the Asian regional economic system. Similarly, crises in the region will have grave impacts on other regions of the world economy precisely because they are integral to the dynamics of global capitalist system.

So, the troubled economies of Asia are not alone. Tides of globalization and financialization will generate many similar situations. We are witnessing worldwide frustration, discomfort, anxiety, social chaos, and violence. These phenomena are not exclusive to the South. They are widespread in the North. They will inevitably lead to widespread pain and disillusionment. Struggles will take shape and will be intensified. Although we are unsure that this is a decisive historical moment, a global strategy on the basis of a global perspective is required to present a feasible alternative. Of course, such a global strategy should also be sensitive to regional dynamics. The lesson the current crisis teaches us is that an export-oriented, state-driven, and monopolistic growth strategy has structural limitations. It cannot deliver sustainable development, regardless of how well it is orchestrated. We must therefore push our thinking beyond "exportism," state-centrism, and monopolism. Exportism precludes domestic popular needs, while state-centrism embraces corruption and the abuse of power. Monopolism excludes fair competition. It follows then that an alternative model of "national development"—we are dubious about the relevancy of this notion—must overcome limitations posed by exportism, state-centrism, and monopolism. The formulation of a feasible alternative model is an enormous task and represents a major challenge to the people of Korea.

Some call for an outright shift to a domestically oriented and free market economy. A national economic system must be responsive to domestic popular needs. However, the call for a domestically-oriented economy sounds unrealistic under the current circumstances characterized by a deep dependence on trade. While the call is justifiable in formulating an alternative model, the Korean economy simply cannot be shifted to a domestically oriented economy. A strategy to reestablish the economy in connection with other economies through negotiated trade agreements would be more feasible. Monopoly capital should be broken through the introduction of some degree of market discipline. However, the kind of market principles that the IMF and liberal economics emphasize must be approached very cautiously. Despite the failure of the state, some degree of state regulation of the private sector should be maintained.

The IMF formula applied to Korea is extremely controversial. The fiscal and credit policies of the IMF are doing more harm than good, as discussed earlier. The situation in Korea is unlike Mexico in 1994 or Russia in the early 1990s. Korea is also very different from the troubled economies of Southeast Asia. There is no denying that Korea had serious problems. Koreans are primarily responsible for those problems and thereby they are primarily responsible for curing them. The IMF's role must be limited to providing technical assistance to Korea, not determining the nation's economic structure. The provision of the rescue fund and technical advice are what Koreans need. The IMF should adhere to its defined function. The IMF has no right to interfere with the sovereignty of the Republic of Korea in return for a bailout. Koreans are dubious about the real intent of the IMF because "several features of the IMF plan are relays of the policies that Japan and the U.S. have long been trying to get Korea to adopt." As Feldstein aptly points out, "it should resist the pressure from the U.S., Japan, and other major countries to make their trade and investment agenda part of the IMF funding conditions" (Feldstein, 1998, 8).

Undoubtedly, Korea is in dire need of fundamental social reform. Reform should not be limited to the economic or financial structure alone. Rationality, transparency, predictability and so forth are important. However, the IMF cannot carry out Korea's reform. Historically, reforms imposed from outside rarely succeed. With this in mind, the IMF should restrict its role in providing technical and financial assistance.

REFERENCES

Bank of Korea. (1998). *Monthly Survey Statistics*. various months. Seoul: Bank of Korea.

Bello, W., and Rosenfeld, S. (1990). *Dragons in Distress: Asia's Miracle Economies in Crisis*. San Francisco: Food First.

Chung, W. C. (1998). "Korean Economy: Burst of Bubble and Institutional Reform" (in Korean). *Creation and Criticism* 99.

Cumings, B. (1987). "The Origins and Development of the Northeast Asian Political Economy," In F. Deyo (ed.) *The Political Economy of the New Asian Industrialism*, pp. 44–83. Ithaca: Cornell University Press.

Deyo, F. (1989). *Beneath the Miracle*. Berkeley: University of California Press.

The Economist. (1997). "Is It Over?" *The Economist* Home page.

Eder, N. (1996). *Poisoned Prosperity*. New York: M. E. Sharpe.

Feldstein, M. (1998). "Refocusing the IMF," *Foreign Affairs* 1998 March/April issue. *Foreign Affairs* Home page.

Hart-Landsberg, M. (1993). *Rush to Development*. New York: Monthly Review Press.

Hart-Landsberg, M. (1998). "The Asian Crisis: Causes and Consequences." Unpublished paper on the internet.

Kang, C. K. (1996). "Substance of Economic Crisis Debate and the Economic Structure of Crisis" (in Korean). *Creation and Criticism* 94.

Kim, E. M. (1997). *Big Business, Strong State: Collusion and Conflict in South Korean Development, 1960–1990*. New York: SUNY Press.

Kim, H. K., and S. H. Lee. (1994). "Commodity Chains and the Korean Automobile Industry." In Gary Gereffi and M. Korzeniewicz (eds.), *Commodity Chains and Global Capitalism*. Westport: Praeger.

The Korea Times. (1997). Various dates.

The Korea Times. (1998). Various dates.

Krugman, P. (1994). "The Myth of Asia's Miracle." *Foreign Affairs* 73, 6.

Munwha Ilbo. (1998). Various dates.

Palat, R. (1993). "Introduction: The Making and Unmaking of Pacific-Asia." In R. Palat (ed.), *Pacific-Asia and the Future of the World-System*, pp. 3–20. Westport: Greenwood Press.

Pastor, M. (1997). "Pesos, Policies, and Predictions: The Mexican Crisis and International Constraints on Policy Making." Paper presented at the State and Sovereignty in the World-Economy Symposium, University of California, Irvine, February 21–23, 1997.

Sachs, J. (1997). "The Wrong Medicine for Asia." *New York Times,* Nov. 3, 1997.

Smith, D., and Su-Hoon Lee. (1990). "Limits on a Semiperipheral Success Story? State Dependent Development and the Prospects for South Korean Democratization," pp. 79–95. In William Martin (ed.), *Semiperipheral States in the World-Economy*, pp. 79–95. New York: Greenwood Press.

So, A., and Chiu, S. (1995). *East Asia and the World Economy*. Thousand Oaks: Sage.

Stiglitz, J. (1997). "How to Fix the Asian Economies." *New York Times,* October 31, 1997.

Wade, R., and Venerosa, F. (1998). "The Asian Financial Crisis: The Unrecognized Risk of the IMF's Asia Package." Unpublished paper on the internet.

INDEX